THE WAR ON DRUGS: WINNING, LOSING OR TREADING WATER

THE WAR ON DRUGS: WINNING, LOSING OR TREADING WATER

NELSON V. ARCOS
EDITOR

Nova Science Publishers, Inc.
New York

For permission to use material from this book please contact us:
Telephone 631-231-7269; Fax 631-231-8175
Web Site: http://www.novapublishers.com

LIBRARY OF CONGRESS CATALOGING-IN-PUBLICATION DATA

Available Upon Request

ISBN 978-1-59454-235-0

Published by Nova Science Publishers, Inc. ✢ New York

CONTENTS

PREFACE

The war on drugs is a kind of declared war against a set of often invisible foes which is often fought with toothless policies, uncoordinated campaigns, and resisted by criminal organizations determined to punch two new holes in the dam for every one which is closed. This new book presents current issues relevant to an important but far from successful effort to thwart drug flow.

Chapter 1 - Located in the Executive Office of the President, the ONDCP Director, known also as the ``drug czar," is responsible for overseeing and coordinating the federal War on Drugs, preparing the National Drug Control Strategy, and running certain drug control programs, such as the High Intensity Drug Trafficking Areas (HIDTA) Program, the National Youth Anti-Drug Media Campaign, and the Drug-Free Communities Program. The office was created in 1988 and has now been reauthorized three times since then.

ONDCP's second reauthorization expired on September 30, 2003, and reauthorization bills were introduced in the 108th Congress but were not enacted.

Reauthorization efforts resumed in the 109th Congress with the introduction of H.R. 2829 and S. 2560. With action on these two reauthorization bills stalled, a compromise bill was drafted by House and Senate negotiators near the close of the 109th Congress. The Office of National Drug Control Policy Reauthorization Act of 2006 (H.R. 6344) passed both chambers in the final days of the 109th Congress and was signed into law (P.L. 109-469) on December 29, 2006, reauthorizing ONDCP through FY2010.

The new reauthorization act contains extensive amendments to current law. For example, it requires ONDCP's annual drug control budget to include all federal drug control activities, including demand reduction, supply reduction, and federally funded state, local, and tribal drug law enforcement. ONDCP revised its method for compiling the federal drug control budget in 2002, narrowing its scope. The new law forces a return to more inclusive budget numbers for the federal drug control budget. It statutorily creates the position of U.S. Interdiction Coordinator (USIC) and the Interdiction Committee (TIC) within ONDCP. It contains numerous new reporting requirements, including South American and Afghan heroin strategies, a report on iatrogenic addiction caused by doctor-prescribed opioid analgesic pharmaceuticals, a national drug interdiction plan, a report on intelligence sharing within HIDTAs, and a study on the results of an awards program newly created by the act to fund demonstration programs on coerced abstinence. It allows the media campaign to focus on marijuana prevention. Mycoherbicides will be studied and tested on U.S. soil as a means of eliminating illicit drug crops.

The Domestic Policy Subcommittee of the House Oversight and Government Reform Committee held an ONDCP oversight hearing on March 12, 2008. ONDCP Director John P. Walters presented testimony on the 2008 National Drug Control Strategy and the 2009 National Drug Control Budget. Two private sector drug researchers offered criticisms of the Bush Administration's continuing emphasis on supply reduction and law enforcement and urged increased funding for treatment programs directed at hardcore drug users.

Chapter 2 - Authorization of the National Youth Anti-Drug Media Campaign, a multi-media federal program to persuade America's youth not to use drugs, expired at the end of FY2002. H.R. 2829 (passed by the House on March 13, 2006) and S. 2560 (reported by the Senate Judiciary Committee on May 25, 2006) would reauthorize the media campaign, along with the other programs run by the Office of National Drug Control Policy (ONDCP). H.R. 5576, the House-passed appropriations bill that funds ONDCP, proposes \$100 million for the campaign for FY2007. The media campaign's effectiveness has been questioned, and the program has engendered its share of controversy. Nevertheless, ONDCP, the office of the "drug czar," is optimistic that recent changes in campaign strategy will help to reduce illegal drug use by young people.

Chapter 3 - The Safe and Drug-Free Schools and Communities Act (SDFSCA), Title IV-A of the Elementary and Secondary Education Act (ESEA), is the federal government's major initiative to prevent drug abuse and violence in and around schools. It was most recently reauthorized by the ESEA, as amended by the No Child Left Behind Act (P.L. 107-110), in January of 2002. Like all No Child Left Behind Act programs, it is being considered for reauthorization in the 110th Congress.

The SDFSCA supports two major grant programs — one for states and one for National Activities. State Grants are distributed to the states, the District of Columbia, and Puerto Rico, by a formula that allocates 50% of the funds on the basis of school-aged population, and 50% in proportion to ESEA Title I, Part A, concentration grants for the preceding fiscal year. State governors are permitted to use up to 20% of their state's grant for comprehensive activities that deter youth from using drugs and committing violent acts in schools. National Activities grants are awarded by the Secretary for a variety of National Activities to prevent substance abuse and support violence prevention. States award grants to local educational agencies (LEAs) using a formula that allocates 40% of an LEA's grant on the basis of school enrollment and 60% on the basis of an LEA's relative share of total Title I-A grants for the preceding fiscal year. The statute permits LEAs to use funds for a wide variety of activities intended to enhance violence prevention efforts and reduce drug and alcohol abuse.

For FY2008, \$513 million was appropriated for the SDFSCA. The majority of these funds are provided for State Grants (\$295 million), with the remaining funds (\$219 million) supporting National Activities. For FY2009, the Administration has requested \$282 million for the SDFSCA. Under this proposal, appropriations for State Grants would be reduced to \$100 million, and appropriations for National Activities would be decreased to \$182 million. In justifying the requested reduction in State Grant appropriations, the Administration has argued that the structure of the State Grants program is flawed and spreads funding too broadly to support quality interventions.

Many issues are likely to be considered during reauthorization of the SDFSCA program. Issues discussed in this report include the Administration's proposal, recommendations of the

Safe and Drug-Free Schools and Communities Act Advisory Board, recommendations of the Secretaries of the U.S. Department of Education (ED) and the U.S. Department of Health and Human Services (HHS), and the U.S. Department of Justice (DOJ), following the Virginia Tech tragedy, and issues of potential concern to Members of Congress.

Chapter 4 - There is no medical necessity defense against prosecution for the federal crimes of cultivating or distributing marijuana, even in places where state law recognizes such a defense. So said the Supreme Court in *United States v. Oakland Cannabis Buyers' Cooperative*, 532 U.S. 483, 486 (2001). Although there may be some question as to their vitality, the Court left undecided issues involving a necessity defense for possession and possible commerce clause, enactment clause, and due process clause challenges. In *Gonzales v. Raich*, 125 S.Ct. 2195 (2005), the Court held that Congress's' power under the commerce clause enabled it to enact a regulatory scheme that extended to the purely local cultivation and possession of marijuana for medical purposes. There are proposals in this Congress to reverse the impact of the Court's decisions.

Chapter 5 - Efforts to significantly reduce the flow of illicit drugs from abroad into the United States have so far not succeeded. Moreover, over the past decade, worldwide production of illicit drugs has risen dramatically: opium and marijuana production has roughly doubled and coca production tripled. Street prices of cocaine and heroin have fallen significantly in the past 20 years, reflecting increased avail-ability. The effectiveness of international narcotics control programs in reducing consumption is a matter of ongoing concern. Despite apparent national political resolve to deal with the drug problem, inherent contra-dictions regularly appear between U.S. anti-drug policy and other national policy goals and concerns. Pursuit of drug control policies can sometimes affect foreign policy interests and bring political instability and economic dislocation to countries where narcotics production has become entrenched economically and socially. Drug supply interdiction programs and U.S. systems to facilitate the international movement of goods, people, and wealth are often at odds. U.S. international narcotics policy requires cooperative efforts by many nations which may have domestic and foreign policy goals that compete with the requirements of drug control. The mix of competing domestic and international pressures and priorities has produced an ongoing series of disputes within and between the legislative and executive branches concerning U.S. international drug policy. One contentious issue has been the Congressionally-mandated certification process, an instrument designed to induce specified drug-exporting countries to prioritize or pay more attention to the fight against narcotics businesses. Current law requires the President, with certain exceptions, to designate and withhold assistance from countries that have failed demonstrably to meet their counter narcotics obligations. P.L. 106-246, "Plan Colombia," a $1.3 billion military assistance-focused initiative to provide emergency supplemental narcotics assistance to Colombia, was signed into law July 13, 2000. Recently, U.S. policy toward Colombia has focused increasingly on containing the terrorist threat to that country's security. The Bush Administration's FY2005 budget request continues a policy, begun in FY2002, to request authority for the State and Defense Departments to supply assistance to Colombia for counterterrorism purposes. For instance, U.S.-supplied helicopters and intelligence could be used to support military operations against guerrillas financed by drugs as well as against drug traffickers themselves. See CRS Report RL32337, *Andean Counter Drug Initiative (ACI) and Related Funding Programs: FY2005 Assistance.*

An issue likely to achieve increased attention in the 109th Congress is that of sky-rocketing opium poppy cultivation in Afghanistan and whether to press for aerial crop eradication against the wishes of the local Afghan leadership. See CRS Report RL32686, *Afghanistan: Narcotics and U.S. Policy.*

Drug control approaches addressed in this issue brief include:

- Expansion of efforts to reduce foreign production at the source.
- Expansion of interdiction and enforcement activities to disrupt supply lines.
- Expansion of efforts to reduce worldwide demand.
- Expansion of economic disincentives for international drug trafficking.

Chapter 6 - The international traffic in illicit drugs contributes to terrorist risk through at least five mechanisms: supplying cash, creating chaos and instability, supporting corruption, providing "cover" and sustaining common infrastructures for illicit activity, and competing for law enforcement and intelligence attention. Of these, cash and chaos are likely to be the two most important.

Different drugs, different trafficking routes, and different organizations have different relationships to terrorist threats. Therefore it might be possible to improve domestic security by targeting drug law enforcement on those drugs, routes, and organizations with the strongest known or potential links to terror. However, doing so would require new analytic capacities and decision-making strategies for all the agencies involved in drug law enforcement and there is no assurance that the policies that best implement the mission of protecting Americans from drug abuse will also perform best in protecting the country from terrorism. Indeed, the interests of ideology-driven terrorists and money-driven drug traders can sometimes diverge, as when increased resources deployed against terrorists adversely affect the activities of drug traders with no ties to terrorists.

Any terrorist threats exacerbated by the illicit drug markets might be reduced by shrinking the markets themselves, both in physical volume and financial revenue. It is not clear that increased drug law enforcement alone can succeed in that respect; the cocaine and heroin markets have proven stubbornly resistant to vigorous enforcement efforts.

Reducing demand for illicit drugs can also shrink the markets. The total number of users is much less important in determining drug volumes and revenues than the behavior of a relatively small number of chronic, high-dose drug-takers. Most of that "hard core" group consists of people who are repeatedly arrested, not only for drug offenses but for a wide range of property, violent, and public-order offenses. Acting to reduce the population of hard-core user-offenders, through treatment, drug courts, or testing-and-sanctions programs, may offer a better prospect for reducing the size of the drug markets, and thus potentially the contribution of drug trafficking to the terrorist threat.

Chapter 7 - At least 50 documented incidents in more than 20 countries around the world, many involving arrest or detention of North Korean diplomats, link North Korea to drug trafficking. Such events, in the context of credible, but unproven, allegations of large scale state sponsorship of drug production and trafficking, raise important issues for the United States and its allies in combating international drug trafficking. The challenge to policy makers is how to pursue an effective counter drug policy and comply with U.S. law which may require cutting off aid to North Korea while pursuing other high-priority U.S. foreign policy objectives including (1) limiting possession and production of weapons of mass destruction; (2) limiting ballistic missile production and export; (3) curbing terrorism, counterfeiting, and international crime; and (4) addressing humanitarian needs.

Reports that the Democratic People's Republic of North Korea (DPRK) maybe limiting some of its food crop production in favor of drug crop production are particularly disturbing given the country's chronic food shortages, though the acreage in question is comparatively small. Another issue of rising concern is the degree to which profits from any North Korean drug trafficking, counterfeiting, and other crime-for-profit enterprises may be used to underwrite the costs of maintaining or expanding North Korean nuclear and missile programs. As the Dark's drug trade becomes increasingly entrenched, and arguably decentralized, analysts question whether the Pyongyang regime (or any subsequent government) would have the ability to effectively restrain such activity, should it so desire.

Since 2003, overall seizures of North Korean-linked methamphetamine and heroin are generally down, arguably in response to enhanced international attention paid to such activity in the wake of the April 2003 seizure of heroin carried on the North Korean Vessel the "Pong Su." Some suggest that this decline in seizures being identified as DPRK origin is because North Korean source methamphetamine is now regularly being mistakenly identified as "Chinese source" given growing links of Chinese criminal elements to North Korea's drug production/trafficking activities. In line with such a conclusion are press reports in late 2006 of the arrests in differing locations in China of North Korean nationals involved with Chinese criminals in the trafficking of methamphetamine. However, it is not clear from the reports whether the drugs were of DPRK origin or whether the North Koreans arrested had links with DPRK officials. Reduction of illicit drug seizures linked to the DPRK has also given rise to speculation that North Korea has cut back on, if not dramatically curbed, its drug trafficking activity, and is compensating from the loss of income in this arena by beefing up its production and trafficking of counterfeit brand cigarettes.

It remains clear, however, that regardless of the mix of DPRK criminal activities at any particular given point in time, income from DPRK criminal activity continues to play a pivotal role in overall DPRK finances.

Chapter 8- In the last decade, Colombia — a key U.S. ally in South America — has made significant progress in reasserting government control over much of its territory, combating drug trafficking and terrorist activities by illegally armed groups, and reducing poverty. Since the development of Plan Colombia in 1999, the Colombian government, with substantial U.S. support, has stepped up its counter narcotics and security efforts. Congress has provided more than $6 billion to support Plan Colombia from FY2000 through FY2008. Since 2002, Congress has granted the State Department expanded authority to use counter narcotics funds for a unified campaign to fight both drug trafficking and terrorist organizations in Colombia. Proponents of the current U.S. policy towards Colombia point to the inroads that have been made in improving security conditions in Colombia and in weakening the Revolutionary Armed Forces of Colombia (FARC) guerrillas. Critics argue that, despite these security improvements, U.S. policy has not rigorously promoted human rights, provided for sustainable economic alternatives for drug crop farmers, or reduced the amount of drugs available in the United States.

President Alvaro Uribe, re-elected in May 2006, has made headway in addressing Colombia's 40-year plus conflict with the country's leftist guerrillas, as well as the rightist paramilitary groups that have been active since the 1980s. Uribe enjoys strong popular support, which has not been significantly affected by an ongoing scandal concerning past government ties to illegal paramilitary groups. Uribe's popularity soared after Colombia's March 2008 raid of a FARC camp in Ecuador resulted in the killing of a top guerrilla commander and the seizure of his computer files. It spiked again following the Colombian military's successful July 2, 2008 rescue of 15 hostages long held by the FARC. Those hostages included three

U.S. defense contractors and a former Colombian presidential candidate. Many Colombians are calling for President Uribe to seek a third presidential term, a move that would require a constitutional amendment.

Concerns in the 110th Congress regarding Colombia have focused on funding levels and U.S. policy regarding Plan Colombia, U.S. hostages, trade, and human rights. The FY2008 Consolidated Appropriations Act (P.L. 110-161) attempted to raise the level of U.S. funding provided for economic and social aid closer to that provided for security-related programs. In 2007, the Senate passed a resolution. (S.Con.Res. 53) demanding that the FARC release the 3 U.S. contractors that were being held in Colombia. In July 2008, both the House and Senate passed resolutions expressing gratitude to the Colombian government for successfully rescuing the U.S. hostages (H.Con.Res. 389/S.Res. 627). The House also passed an amendment (H.Amdt. 112 to H.R. 5959) expressing the importance of continuing to provide U.S. assistance to Colombia. While acknowledging the progress that the Uribe government has made in improving security conditions in Colombia, some Members of Congress have expressed concerns about labor activist killings and the Para political scandal. These issues came to the fore during consideration of the U.S.Colombia Free Trade Agreement (CFTA). For more information on CFTA, see CRS Report RL34470, *The U.S.-Colombia Free Trade Agreement: Economic and Political Implications*, by M. Angeles Villarreal. This report will be updated.

Chapter 9 - This report summarizes the congressionally mandated presidential designation procedures on major illicit narcotics producing and transit countries in Section 706 of the Foreign Relations Authorization Act for FY2003 (H.R. 1646/P.L. 107-228) enacted in September 2002. To put the new procedures in perspective, the report also provides information on the past procedures, the congressional modifications, and recent presidential designations under the revised procedures.

From the mid-1980s to 2001, Congress required the President to certify in early March that specified drug producing and drug transit countries were ``cooperating fully" with the United States in counter narcotics efforts in order to avoid a series of sanctions, including suspension of U.S. foreign assistance, and opposition to loans in the multilateral development banks. The sanctions would also apply if the Congress, within 30 calendar days, passed a joint resolution of disapproval to overturn the presidential certification. Spokesmen from many countries complained about the unilateral and non-cooperative nature of the drug certification requirements, and a movement to modify the process developed in Congress in 2000-2002.

In 2001 (on a temporary, one year basis) and in 2002 (on a permanent but initially transitional basis), a law with new procedures was enacted. This law requires the President to make a report in mid-September of each year that identifies the major drug producing or transit countries. At the same time, the President is required to designate and to withhold assistance from any of the named countries that has ``failed demonstrably," during the previous 12 months, to adhere to international counter narcotics agreements. Under the legislation, the President may waive the withholding of assistance if he determines this to be in the national interest.

Acting under this legislation, President Bush made designations on a transitional basis for FY2002 and FY2003 and then made determinations on the designated date for FY2004, FY2005, and FY2006.

- On February23, 2002, the President designated Afghanistan, Burma and Haiti as having "failed demonstrably'" but granted national interest waivers to Haiti and Afghanistan under the new government.
- On January 31, 2003, the President designated Burma, Guatemala, and Haiti, but granted national interest waivers to Guatemala and Haiti.
- On September 15, 2003, the President designated Burma and Haiti, but granted a national interest waiver to Haiti.
- On September 15, 2004, the President designated Burma as having "failed demonstrably" in counter narcotics efforts.
- On September 15, 2005, the President designated Burma and Venezuela but granted a national interest waiver to Venezuela to permit a continuation of U.S. assistance.

In: The War on Drugs: Winning, Losing or Treading Water ISBN 978-1-59454-235-0
Editor: Nelson V. Arcos

Chapter 1

WAR ON DRUGS: REAUTHORIZATION AND OVERSIGHT OF THE OFFICE OF NATIONAL DRUG CONTROL POLICY *

Mark Eddy

SUMMARY

Located in the Executive Office of the President, the ONDCP Director, known also as the "drug czar," is responsible for overseeing and coordinating the federal War on Drugs, preparing the National Drug Control Strategy, and running certain drug control programs, such as the High Intensity Drug Trafficking Areas (HIDTA) Program, the National Youth Anti Drug Media Campaign, and the Drug Free Communities Program. The office was created in 1988 and has now been reauthorized three times since then.

ONDCP's second reauthorization expired on September 30, 2003, and reauthorization bills were introduced in the 108th Congress but were not enacted.

Reauthorization efforts resumed in the 109th Congress with the introduction of H.R. 2829 and S. 2560. With action on these two reauthorization bills stalled, a compromise bill was drafted by House and Senate negotiators near the close of the 109th Congress. The Office of National Drug Control Policy Reauthorization Act of 2006 (H.R. 6344) passed both chambers in the final days of the 109th Congress and was signed into law (P.L. 109-469) on December 29, 2006, reauthorizing ONDCP through FY2010.

The new reauthorization act contains extensive amendments to current law. For example, it requires ONDCP's annual drug control budget to include all federal drug control activities, including demand reduction, supply reduction, and federally funded state, local, and tribal drug law enforcement. ONDCP revised its method for compiling the federal drug control budget in 2002, narrowing its scope. The new law forces a return to more inclusive budget numbers for the federal drug control budget. It statutorily creates the position of U.S.

* Excerpted from CRS Report RL 32352, dated April 23, 2008

Interdiction Coordinator (USIC) and the Interdiction Committee (TIC) within ONDCP. It contains numerous new reporting requirements, including South American and Afghan heroin strategies, a report on iatrogenic addiction caused by doctor prescribed opioid analgesic pharmaceuticals, a national drug interdiction plan, a report on intelligence sharing within HIDTAs, and a study on the results of an awards program newly created by the act to fund demonstration programs on coerced abstinence. It allows the media campaign to focus on marijuana prevention. Mycoherbicides will be studied and tested on U.S. soil as a means of eliminating illicit drug crops.

The Domestic Policy Subcommittee of the House Oversight and Government Reform Committee held an ONDCP oversight hearing on March 12, 2008. ONDCP Director John P. Walters presented testimony on the 2008 National Drug Control Strategy and the 2009 National Drug Control Budget. Two private sector drug researchers offered criticisms of the Bush Administration's continuing emphasis on supply reduction and law enforcement and urged increased funding for treatment programs directed at hardcore drug users.

Introduction and Background

Located in the Executive Office of the President, the Office of National Drug Control Policy (ONDCP) was created by the Anti Drug Abuse Act of 1988[1] 1 to coordinate the federal government's War on Drugs. The principal responsibilities of the Director of ONDCP, who is often referred to as the ``drug czar,'' include

- establishing policies, objectives, and priorities for the National Drug Control program;
- annually promulgating the National Drug Control Strategy and coordinating and overseeing the strategy's implementation by the respective drug control agencies of the federal government;
- making recommendations to the President regarding changes in the organization, management, budgets, and allocation of federal personnel engaged in drug enforcement;
- consulting with and assisting state and local governments with respect to their relations with federal drug control agencies and programs;
- appearing before committees and subcommittees of Congress to represent the drug policies of the executive branch; and
- notifying any federal drug control agency if its policies are not in compliance with the National Drug Control Strategy and transmitting a copy of the notification to the President.

ONDCP's first reauthorizing act, in 1994,[2] produced limited amendments to the agency's original enacting legislation. It strengthened the Director's powers to influence the allocation of funds and personnel within and between federal drug control departments and agencies. It

[1] P.L. 100-690, Title I, Subtitle A, National Narcotics Leadership Act of 1988, November 18, 1988, 102 Stat. 4181.

prohibited presidentially appointed ONDCP officials from participating in federal election campaign activities, except for making contributions to individual candidates. It required the Director to include, in every National Drug Control Strategy, an evaluation of the effectiveness of federal drug control efforts during the preceding year, and it mandated specific measures of effectiveness that the evaluation would include. It required the Director to assess periodically the accuracy of drug use statistics and the factors that restrict the availability of treatment services, and to propose corrective remedies.

ONDCP was reauthorized again in 1998 when Congress rewrote the agency's statutory mandate.[3] This time, Congress took advantage of the opportunity, through staff studies and several hearings, to assess the progress of the antidrug effort and to develop specific, measurable goals for reducing drug consumption and drug related crime in the United States. Annual reports to Congress containing specified measures of progress in implementing the National Drug Control Strategy were again required of ONDCP. This second ONDCP reauthorization act expired during the first session of the 108th Congress on September 30, 2003. Despite the act's sunset provision, however, Congress continued to appropriate funds to keep the agency alive.

In the 108th Congress, an ONDCP reauthorization measure (H.R. 2086/Souder) passed the House but was not acted on in the Senate. The Senate's own reauthorization bill (S. 1860/Hatch) also saw no Senate action beyond introduction and committee referral. These bills, many provisions of which reappeared in House and Senate reauthorization bills in the 109th Congress are discussed briefly in the final section of this report. Both bills died at the close of the 108th Congress, leaving the matter of extending ONDCP to the 109th Congress.

REAUTHORIZATION OF ONDCP BY THE 109TH CONGRESS

In the 109th Congress, a bill (H.R. 2829/Souder) was introduced to reauthorize ONDCP indefinitely and authorize funding in specific annual amounts through FY2011 for the HIDTA Program, the media campaign, a Southwest Border violence study, and a methamphetamine information clearinghouse. The bill passed the House, amended, on March13, 2006. A Senate reauthorization bill (S. 2560/Specter) was reported, amended, by the Senate Judiciary Committee on May 25, 2006. S. 2560 would have extended ONDCP through FY2010 and authorized appropriations for the HIDTA Program, the media campaign, the Drug Free Communities Act, and the methamphetamine information clearinghouse.

Toward the end of the 109th Congress, with action on these two reauthorization bills stalled, a compromise bill was drafted by House and Senate negotiators. H.R. 6344, the Office of National Drug Control Policy Reauthorization Act of 2006, was introduced by Representative Souder on December 5, 2006. It passed both chambers in the final days of the 109th Congress and was signed into law (P.L. 109-469) on December 29, 2006, reauthorizing ONDCP through FY2010. More detail on the making of ONDCP's third reauthorizing statute

---

[2] P.L. 103-322, Violent Crime Control and Law Enforcement Act of 1994, Title IX, Subtitle B, National Narcotics Leadership Act Amendments, September 13, 1994, 108 Stat. 1990.

[3] P.L. 105-277, Omnibus Consolidated and Emergency Supplemental Appropriations Act, 1999, Division C, Title VII, Office of National Drug Control Policy Reauthorization Act of 1998, October 21, 1998, 112 Stat. 2681-670, 21 U.S.C. § 1701 et seq.

can be found below. The new reauthorization act contains extensive amendments to current law. For example, it requires ONDCP's annual drug control budget to include all federal drug control activities, including demand reduction, supply reduction, and federally funded state, local, and tribal drug law enforcement. ONDCP revised its method for compiling the federal drug control budget in 2002, narrowing its scope. The new law forces a return to more inclusive budget numbers for the federal drug control budget. It statutorily creates the position of U.S. Interdiction Coordinator (USIC) and the Interdiction Committee (TIC) within ONDCP. It contains numerous new reporting requirements, including South American and Afghan heroin strategies, a report on iatrogenic addiction caused by doctor prescribed opioid analgesic pharmaceuticals, a national drug interdiction plan, a report on intelligence sharing within HIDTAs, and a study on the results of an awards program newly created by the act to fund demonstration programs on coerced abstinence. It allows the media campaign to focus on marijuana prevention. It provides for mycoherbicides to be studied and tested on U.S. soil as a means of eliminating illicit drug crops. A more complete description and analysis of the provisions of the new reauthorization act appear below.

Given the declining salience of drug abuse as a public policy issue and the shift in emphasis within federal law enforcement and the U.S. armed services from drug control to counterterrorism since the events of September 11, 2001,[4] it is noteworthy that the question of whether illicit drug control still warrants a special agency within the Executive Office of the President went unexamined during congressional consideration of ONDCP's reauthorization. Extended for an additional five years, the agency will continue to play a leading role in America's global War on Drugs.

OVERSIGHT OF ONDCP IN THE 110TH CONGRESS

In the House, both authorization and oversight of ONDCP lie within the jurisdiction of the Oversight and Government Reform Committee. Accordingly, that committee's Domestic Policy Subcommittee, chaired by Representative Kucinich, held an oversight hearing on March 12, 2008, entitled ``The National Drug Control Strategy for 2008, the Fiscal Year 2009 Drug Control Budget, and Compliance with the ONDCP Reauthorization Act of 2006: Priorities and Accountability at ONDCP." The stated purpose of the hearing was to examine (1) the priorities of the 2008 National Drug Control Strategy, (2) the priorities of the FY2009 national drug control budget, and (3) ONDCP's compliance with the reauthorization act, especially the revised budgetary reporting requirements and the mandated performance measurement system.

In his opening statement, [5] Chairman Kucinich set forth issues concerning "ONDCP's accountability and overall effectiveness" to be covered at the hearing, including

[4] See, for example, Josh Meyer, ``Burdened U.S. Military Cuts Role in Drug War," Los Angeles Times, January 22, 2007.

[5] This statement and the written testimony of the hearing witnesses are available on the subcommittee'swebsiteat [http://domesticpolicy.oversight.house.gov/story.asp?ID=1801]. A transcript of the hearing's proceedings is not yet available.

- the lack of transparency and accountability at ONDCP, which impairs ONDCP's and Congress's ability to determine which federal drug control programs are effective in combating drug abuse;
- the failure of ONDCP to include in the national drug control budget ``all funding requests for any drug control activity, including costs attributable to drug law enforcement activities such as prosecuting and incarcerating federal drug law offenders," as required by the new reauthorization act;
- ONDCP's unwillingness ``to comply with the standards of accountability Congress has imposed" in providing Congress with the reports mandated by the reauthorization act;
- the difficulty faced by Congress in determining whether progress is being made in combating drug abuse because ONDCP ``doesn't employ consistent or useful performance measures and frequently shifts its policy goals"; and
- the imbalance in the national drug control budget between supply- side programs (such as source country eradication and interdiction) and demand side initiatives (such as prevention and treatment), with the supply side receiving a growing share of the budget ``despite research that demonstrates that demand side approaches are generally more cost-effective than supply side approaches."

Chairman Kucinich also noted that the written testimony of the principal witness at the hearing, ONDCP Director John P. Walters, ``entirely omits discussion of ONDCP's compliance with the Reauthorization Act despite repeated clear requests that these issues be addressed." The prepared testimony of the other two hearing witnesses, however, did cover the concerns of the subcommittee.

Former ONDCP official John Carnevale expressed his disagreement with the current Bush Administration's emphasis on supply reduction:

> By the 1990's we had learned that interdiction was a relatively ineffective way of reducing drug use – and expensive besides. So we focused our efforts on demand reduction. Now, at the beginning of the new millennium we have – inexplicably – come to believe again that source and transit zone interdiction is an effective way to reduce drug use in America. There is no evidence to support this belief.... In short, what we now know is that so long as there is a demand for illicit drugs, supply will follow.

He pointed out ``significant shortcomings" in ONDCP's meeting of its statutory obligations and said, ``As a result of these failures, ONDCP is no longer seen as a serious player in the drug issue." He outlined some ways to restructure the agency so that it might regain ``a meaningful role in shaping drug policy in the next Administration," such as moving some of its programs to other drug control agencies so that ONDCP could return to being a policy office. According to Dr. Carnevale:

> ONDCP must rediscover its roots. By this statement, I mean that ONDCP should again focus on becoming a leader in policy formulation on behalf of the President to

allow the Administration to develop a drug policy that is evidence based and includes performance measurement to hold it accountable for results.

The final hearing witness, Economist Rosalie Liccardo Pacula, co Director of the Drug Policy Research Center at the RAND Corporation, testified on what research says about the reasonableness of the current priorities of national drug control. In her view, the 2008 National Drug Control Strategy supports programs in several areas that ``have already been shown to be completely ineffective" or that have ``never been scientifically proven to be effective and which on analytic grounds seem unlikely to be successful." These include efforts in Colombia and Afghanistan intended to decrease the supplies in the United States of cocaine and heroin, respectively; random student drug testing; and the National Youth Anti Drug Media Campaign.

According to Dr. Pacula, research conducted at RAND and elsewhere shows that source country crop eradication and interdiction efforts along with prevention and education programs work best in emerging drug markets at the early stages of a drug epidemic. Later in the cycle, after the size of the market for a particular has grown, the epidemic reaches its mature phase and the number of new users declines. At this point, research shows that treatment programs directed at heavy and dependent users become a more cost effective way of addressing the problem and reducing use. ``Given that drug markets for our three primary drugs of abuse (marijuana, cocaine and heroin) are all in mature stages," her written testimony states, ``the continued emphasis on supply side strategies is inappropriate." She concludes:

> The Strategy in its current form is neither balanced nor cost effective, and as such, suggests a need for Congress to carefully scrutinize the structure of the budget request. By cutting the budget for programs lacking scientific support or strong analytic arguments and reallocating those funds to program areas that are known to be effective, the nation will have a much better chance of successfully reducing substance abuse and its many costs on society. This would produce a Strategy that more closely addresses the drug situation that exists here in the United States.

The first oversight hearing since enactment of the new reauthorization act in 2006 thus provided criticisms and insights regarding ONDCP's leadership of the federal War on Drugs that might influence the appropriations process for FY2009 and beyond, inform future congressional oversight, and even provide the next Administration with ideas for restructuring ONDCP and rethinking the goals and strategies of the federal government's approach to the problem of drug addiction in American society.

ONDCP Reauthorization Bills in the 109th Congress

Enactment of H.R. 6344 (P.L. 109-469)

H.R. 6344, the Office of National Drug Control Policy Reauthorization Act of 2006, a compromise bill negotiated between the House and Senate during the waning days of the 109th Congress, was introduced by Representative Souder on December 5, 2006. Two days later, it passed the House by voice vote, under suspension of the rules, and was sent to the Senate, where it was approved by unanimous consent the following day, the final day of the 109th Congress. H.R. 6344 was signed into law (P.L. 109-469) on December 29, 2006, reauthorizing ONDCP through FY2010.

ONDCP's new reauthorization act was based on provisions contained in H.R. 2829, which had passed the House during the first session of the 109th , and on S. 2560, which had been reported in the Senate. Hurriedly drafted by Senate and House negotiators during the final weeks of the 109th Congress, and not without its drafting errors (some of which are mentioned below), the legislative history of H.R. 6344 is largely that of H.R. 2829 and S. 2560.

Introduction of H.R. 2829

The Office of National Drug Control Policy Reauthorization Act of 2005 (H.R. 2829) was introduced by Representative Souder on June 9, 2005. The language of H.R. 2829 was largely based on the House and Senate reauthorization bills from the preceding Congress,[6] making H.R. 2829 a blend of those two bills from the 108th with new provisions added at drafting and by subsequent amendments adopted in committee and on the floor of the House.

Actions Taken on H.R. 2829

The House reauthorization bill was referred to the Committee on Government Reform and to the Committees on the Judiciary, Energy and Commerce, and Intelligence (Permanent Select) for consideration of provisions that fall within the jurisdiction of the committee concerned.

The Government Reform Subcommittee on Criminal Justice, Drug Policy and Human Resources held a hearing to consider H.R. 2829 on June 15, 2005. [7] ONDCP Director Walters testified at this hearing, along with officials from the National HIDTA Directors Association and the Partnership for a Drug Free America.

The following day, at markup, the full Government Reform Committee approved an amendment in the nature of a substitute, offered by Representative Souder, that incorporated the provisions of the Clean Sports Act of 2005 (H.R. 2565, discussed below), which had been approved earlier by the committee. H.R. 2829was ordered to be reported favorably, as amended, with a recommendation that it pass.[8] (The committee also approved at markup a

---

[6] These bills from the 108th Congress are discussed briefly in the final section of this report.

[7] U.S. Congress, House Committee on Government Reform, Subcommittee on Criminal Justice, Drug Policy, and Human Resources, H.R. 2829, The Office of National Drug Control Policy Reauthorization Act of 2005, hearing on H.R. 2829, 109th Cong., 1st sess, June 15, 2005 (Washington: GPO, 2005).

[8] U.S. Congress, House Committee on Government Reform, Office of National Drug Control Policy Reauthorization Act of 2005, report to accompany H.R. 2829, 109th Cong., 1st sess., H.Rept. 109-315, part I (Washington: GPO, 2005). Hereinafter referred to as House Government Reform Committee Report.

report that critically analyzed the National Drug Control Strategy for 2005 and the proposed federal drug control budget for FY2006.) [9]

The House Energy and Commerce Committee marked up H.R. 2829 on February 16, 2006. The committee removed the Clean Sports Act from the bill on the grounds that it --- not the Government Reform Committee --- had jurisdiction over the issue of steroid use in professional sports and that it had already approved its own bill on the subject (H.R. 3084/Stearns). The Energy and Commerce Committee reported the bill, as amended, without recommendation. [10]

The House Judiciary Committee considered H.R. 2829 on March 2, 2006. [11] Five amendments were adopted, including one by Chairman Sensenbrenner to remove the Clean Sports Act provisions from the bill. The committee reported the measure favorably, as amended, with a recommendation that it pass.

The House Judiciary Committee's version of the bill was considered by the House on March 9, 2006. [12] The rule governing floor consideration (H. Res. 713) made 15 amendments in order, of which 14 were approved. Four of the adopted amendments dealt specifically with the control of methamphetamine. [13] The bill passed the House, as amended, by a vote of 399 to 5. On March 13, 2006, the bill was received in the Senate and referred to the Committee on the Judiciary, where it saw no action.

Introduction of S. 2560

The Senate's ONDCP Reauthorization Act (S. 2560) was introduced by Senator Specter on April 6, 2006. [14] The bill as introduced contained many provisions similar to the House and Senate reauthorization bills that were considered in the 108th Congress. It was also similar, in many of its provisions, to H.R. 2829.

Actions Taken on S. 2560

Referred to the Committee on the Judiciary, S. 2560 was considered by the full committee on May 25, 2006. The committee adopted, by voice vote, an amendment in the nature of a substitute offered by Chairman Specter. The substitute amendment contained the

---

[9] U.S. Congress, House Committee on Government Reform, The National Drug Control Strategy for 2005 and the National Drug Control Budget for Fiscal Year 2006, 109th Cong., 1st sess., H.Rept. 109-172 (Washington: GPO, 2005).

[10] U.S. Congress, House Committee on Energy and Commerce, Office of National Drug Control Policy Reauthorization Act of 2005, report to accompany H.R. 2829, 109th Cong., 2nd sess., H.Rept. 109-315, part II (Washington: GPO, 2006).

[11] U.S. Congress, House Committee on the Judiciary, Office of National Drug Control Policy Reauthorization Act of 2005, report to accompany H.R. 2829, 109th Cong., 2nd sess., H.Rept. 109-315, part III (Washington: GPO, 2006).

[12] Congressional Record, daily edition, vol. 152 (March 9, 2006), pp. H795-H847.

[13] On the same day, Pres. Bush signed into law the USA PATRIOT Improvement and Reauthorization Act of 2005 (P.L. 109-177), which contained extensive provisions to control methamphetamine and its precursor chemicals.

language of the original measure, with a few added provisions drawn from the House passed version of H.R. 2829, including studies of prescription drug abuse to be conducted by ONDCP and the creation of a National Methamphetamine Clearing House. The committee favorably reported the bill, as amended and without written report, to the full Senate by voice vote, but no further action was taken on S. 2560.

Introduction of H.R. 2565

Representative Tom Davis introduced an ONDCP reauthorization bill on May 24, 2005. H.R. 2565 would have extended ONDCP indefinitely by repealing the sunset provision of the agency's 1998 reauthorization act. [15] The bill also would have authorized the appropriation of such sums as necessary for ONDCP and its programs for FY2006 through FY2010.

The main purpose of H.R. 2565, however, was to amend ONDCP's 1998 Reauthorization Act by adding to it the Clean Sports Act of 2005, which would have established minimum drug testing standards for the major professional sports leagues. The Federal Trade Commission would promulgate regulations and levy fines in implementation of these standards. (The Clean Sports Act was also introduced in the Senate (S. 1114/McCain), but the Senate bill would not have amended ONDCP's 1998 reauthorization act, nor would it have reauthorized ONDCP.)

Actions Taken on H.R. 2565

H.R. 2565 was considered by the House Committee on Government Reform on May 26, 2005, and approved by voice vote. The provisions of the Clean Sports Act were added to H.R. 2829 at the Government Reform Committee markup on June 16, 2005. The House Energy and Commerce Committee, at its markup of H.R. 2829 on February 16, 2006, however, removed the Clean Sports Act from the ONDCP reauthorization bill on the grounds that it, not the Government Reform Committee, had jurisdiction over the issue and that it had already approved its own bill (H.R. 3084) to mandate drug testing of professional athletes.

Description and Analysis of H.R. 6344 (P.L. 109-469)

The discussion that follows describes and analyzes the provisions of H.R. 6344, as enacted, in the order that they appear in the new reauthorization act. The discussion deals primarily with amendments or changes made by H.R. 6344 to the expired act --- the Office of National Drug Control Policy Reauthorization Act of 1998. [16] Provisions of the prior law that

[14] Sen. Arlen Specter, ``Introductory Statement --- `Office of National Drug Control Policy Reauthorization Act of 2006'," Congressional Record, daily edition, vol. 152 (April 6, 2006), pp. S3217-S3218.

[15] P.L. 105-277, sec. 715, 21 U.S.C. § 1712.

[16] P.L. 105-277, Omnibus Consolidated and Emergency Supplemental Appropriations Act, 1999, Division C, Title VII, Office of National Drug Control Policy Reauthorization Act of 1998, October 21, 1998, 112 Stat. 2681-670, 21 U.S.C. § 1701 et seq.

remain unchanged are mentioned only where necessary to provide context for understanding the revisions made by H.R. 6344.

Short Title and Law Being Amended (Sec. 1)[17]

Unless otherwise stated, the Office of National Drug Control Policy Reauthorization Act of 2006 amends or repeals provisions contained in the Office of National Drug Control Policy Reauthorization Act of 1998 (P.L. 105-277) (21 U.S.C. 1701 et seq.). Since H.R. 6344 was written to amend the expired ONDCP reauthorization act, many of the provisions of this prior law remain untouched by the new reauthorization act. These provisions that are carried over from the expired act, along with the amendments provided in H.R. 6344, constitute ``current law" and are so designated in the remainder of this report.

Amendments to Definitions (Sec. 101)

The new reauthorization act changes the definition of certain terms as they were defined in the expired law (sec. 702) (21 U.S.C. §1701). Perhaps the most important changes are in the definitions of ``state and local affairs" and ``supply reduction." Domestic law enforcement directed against drug users has been dropped from the definition of ``supply reduction" and placed under the definition of ``state and local affairs." This change serves statutorily to move responsibility for handling domestic law enforcement matters from ONDCP's Office of Supply Reduction to its Office of State and Local Affairs. These changes are intended to make current law reflect what ONDCP is already doing, in practice, and would make it clear that domestic law enforcement activities serve a wider purpose than supply reduction.

The new act also expands the definition of demand reduction to include demand reduction efforts abroad, and it newly defines ``appropriate congressional committees" to mean the appropriations and judiciary committees of both chambers along with the Senate Caucus on International Narcotics Control and the House Government Reform Committee. [18]

Designation and Duties of ONDCP Officers (Sec. 102)

Responsibilities

Current law (sec. 703(a)) (21 U.S.C. § 1702(a)) requires that ONDCP evaluate the effectiveness of the national drug control policy and agency programs. The new reauthorization act has added language requiring that the evaluation be done "by developing and applying specific goals and performance measurements."

---

[17] The section numbers that appear in the subtitles of this report refer to H.R. 6344 (P.L. 109-469).

[18] The Committee on Government Reform has been renamed the Committee on Oversight and Government Reform in the 110th Congress.

Rank of Director

Current law (sec. 703(b)) (21 U.S.C. § 1702(b)) has been amended by H.R. 6344 to give the ONDCP Director the same ``rank and status" as the heads of the executive departments. (Current law already assigns the Director to the same pay scale as the executive department heads.)

Deputy Directors

As in the expired law, the new reauthorization act provides for deputy directors for demand reduction, supply reduction, and state, local, and tribal affairs. The new act specifies that these three deputy directors report to the Deputy Director of National Drug Control Policy, who reports to the Director. The new law further states that the Deputy Director for Supply Reduction must ``have substantial experience and expertise in drug interdiction and other supply reduction activities." The Deputy Director for State, Local, and Tribal Affairs is made responsible for the High Intensity Drug Trafficking Areas Program and the Counter Drug Technology Assessment Center.

Responsibilities of the Director (Sec. 103)

The new reauthorization act retains the current structure of ONDCP and makes limited changes to strengthen the authority of the Director. In addition to the Director's responsibilities contained in current law (sec. 704(b)) (21 U.S.C. § 1703(b)), the new act has added the following:

- supporting the substance abuse information clearinghouse administered by the Substance Abuse and Mental Health Services Administration;
- coordinating with the private sector to promote private research and development of medications to treat addiction; [19]
- seeking the support and commitment of state and local officials in the formulation and implementation of the National Drug Control Strategy;
- monitoring and evaluating the allocation of resources among federal law enforcement agencies in response to significant local and regional drug trafficking and production threats;
- submitting an annual report to Congress detailing how ONDCP has consulted with and assisted state and local governments with respect to the formulation and implementation of the National Drug Control Strategy and other relevant issues; and
- reporting to Congress, within one year after the date of enactment of the new reauthorization act, on the impact each federal drug reduction strategy has had upon the availability, addiction rate, use rate, and other harms of illegal drugs. [20]

---

[19] This and the following three provisions were taken from S. 1860 (sec. 103(b)(6)) in the 108th Congress.

[20] This provision was added to H.R. 2829 by an amendment offered by Rep. Robert Scott at the House Judiciary markup.

Country Certification

Both H.R. 2829 (sec. 6(g)(4)) and S. 2560 (sec. 105(d)(4)) would have added to the powers of the Director (sec. 704 (d)) (21 U.S.C. § 1703(d)) a requirement that the Director submit to the President, no later than August 1 of each year, a report that (1) identifies countries that are major drug transit countries or major drug producing countries; (2) assesses those countries' efforts to reduce the supply of illicit drugs to the United States; and (3) assesses whether application of the procedures set forth in the Foreign Assistance Act of 1961, as amended (22 U.S.C. § 2291j-1), should be applied against those countries that ``have not cooperated fully" with the United States. The standard by which the Secretary of State evaluates the cooperation of foreign nations in drug control efforts was reduced in 2003 from ``not fully cooperating" to ``failed demonstrably." The House Government Reform Committee wanted the President to receive a second, independent assessment from the ONDCP Director that would have been conducted under the older, more rigorous standard. [21] This requirement, however, was not included in H.R. 6344. Under the new reauthorization act, therefore, the Director will continue to participate in the State Department's country certification process, but will not be required statutorily to submit independent findings based on the pre- 2003 standard.

Fund Control Notices

The Director has the power to issue to the head of a National Drug Control Program agency a fund control notice to ensure that agency's compliance with the National Drug Control Strategy (sec. 704(d)(9)) (21 U.S.C. § 1703(d)(9)). A fund control notice may direct that all or part of an amount appropriated to the National Drug Control Program agency account be obligated by specific periods of time (monthly, quarterly, etc.) and by specific activities, functions, projects, or object classes. National Drug Control Program agencies are not permitted to expend funds contrary to a control notice issued by the ONDCP Director.

H.R. 6344 has amended the fund control notice provisions of current law (sec. 704(f)) (21 U.S.C. §1703(f)) to require that a copy of each fund control notice be transmitted to the appropriate congressional committees. It also has restricted the Director from issuing a fund control notice to direct that all or part of an amount appropriated to a National Drug Control Program agency account be obligated, modified, or altered in any manner contrary, in whole or in part, to a specific appropriation or statute. (Due to a drafting error, this provision is repeated later in H.R. 6344 (sec. 105(f)) with slightly different wording.)

Drug Interdiction (Sec. 103(f)) [22]

U.S. Interdiction Coordinator. In 2002, Congress legislatively created the position of U.S. Interdiction Coordinator (USIC) within the Department of Homeland Security. [23] The position had existed previously within ONDCP, but without statutory authority.

[21] House Government Reform Committee Report, p. 45.

[22] This section of H.R. 6344 appears to contain a drafting error. The language relating to drug interdiction is written as if it were replacing sec. 711 of the expired act, but the bill says the new language is to be added at the end of sec. 711. The old sec. 711 actually contains reporting and budget planning requirements relating to interdiction that are outdated and should be replaced, not added to. These and other drafting errors undoubtedly occurred because of the hurried manner in which the bill was prepared near the close of the 109th Congress.

[23] Homeland Security Act of 2002, sec. 878, P.L. 107-296, November 25, 2002, 116 Stat. 2245, 6 U.S.C. § 458.

S. 2560 (sec. 103(f)) would have amended the Homeland Security Act of 2002 to restore the position to ONDCP. H.R. 2829 (secs. 5(c) and 13) would have given the Deputy Director for Supply Reduction the additional title and responsibilities of U.S. Interdiction Coordinator but would not have amended the Homeland Security Act, presumably leaving the federal government with two interdiction coordinators. (Under the Senate bill, the interdiction coordinator would have been designated by the Director and would not necessarily have been the Deputy Director for Supply Reduction, as would have been required by H.R. 2829.)

The new reauthorization act has restored the position of USIC to ONDCP through amendment of the Homeland Security Act but is oddly silent as to certain details of the position, such as who appoints the USIC and where the position is to be located within the agency.

H.R. 6344 incorporated language that appeared in both H.R. 2829 and S. 2560 regarding the duties of the USIC. The USIC is responsible to the Director for

- coordinating the interdiction activities of the National Drug Control Program agencies to ensure consistency with the National Drug Control Strategy;
- developing and issuing, by March 1 of each year, a National Interdiction Command and Control Plan to ensure consistency with the National Drug Control Strategy;
- assessing the sufficiency of assets committed to illicit drug interdiction by the relevant National Drug Control Program agencies; and
- advising the Director on the efforts of each National Drug Control Program agency to implement the National Interdiction Command and Control Plan.

The new reauthorization act further specifies that the Director will assign permanent ONDCP staff, as appropriate, to help the USIC carry out the responsibilities of the position and may also request that appropriate National Drug Control Program agencies detail or assign staff to the Office of Supply Reduction for that purpose.

National Interdiction Command and Control Plan

The new reauthorization act provides that the National Interdiction Command and Control Plan (NICCP) prepared by the USIC will

- set forth the federal government's strategy for drug interdiction,
- state the specific roles and responsibilities of the relevant National Drug Control Program agencies for implementing the strategy,
- identify the specific resources required to enable the relevant National Drug Control Program agencies to implement the strategy, and
- be issued in consultation with the other members of the Interdiction Committee.

The NICCP cannot change existing agency authorities or the laws governing interagency relationships, but it may include recommendations about making such changes.

Report to Congress

The new reauthorization act further requires that, on or before March 1 of each year, the USIC will provide a report to Congress, [24] on behalf of the Director, that will include

- a copy of that year's National Interdiction Command and Control Plan;
- information for the previous 10 years on the number and type of seizures of drugs by each National Drug Control Program agency conducting drug interdiction activities, as well as statistical information on the geographic areas of such seizures; and
- information for the previous 10 years regarding the number of air and maritime patrol hours undertaken by each National Drug Control Program agency conducting drug interdiction activities, as well as statistical information on the geographic areas in which such patrol hours took place.

Any classified or sensitive information will be presented to Congress separately from the rest of the report.

Interdiction Committee

The Interdiction Committee (TIC) has existed for many years, and the new reauthorization act creates it statutorily for the first time. The purpose of the TIC, as stated in the new reauthorization act, is to

- discuss and resolve issues related to the coordination, oversight, and integration of international, border, and domestic drug interdiction efforts in support of the National Drug Control Strategy;
- review the annual National Interdiction Command and Control Plan and provide advice to the Director and the United States Interdiction Coordinator concerning that plan; and
- provide other advice to the Director concerning drug interdiction strategy and policies, as deemed appropriate by the committee.

Membership of the Interdiction Committee

The new reauthorization act is silent on the membership of the TIC. H.R. 2829, from which provisions relating to the TIC were drawn, however, specified that the TIC would consist of the following, one of whom would be designated Chairman by the Director:

- the Commissioner of the bureau of Customs and Border Protection at the Department of Homeland Security (DHS);
- the Assistant Secretary of the bureau of Immigration and Customs Enforcement at the DHS;
- the Commandant of the United States Coast Guard;

---

[24] This report will be provided, in the Senate, to the Committee on the Judiciary, the Committee on Appropriations, the Caucus on International Narcotics Control, the Committee on Homeland Security and Governmental Affairs, and the Committee on Armed Services and, in the House, to the Committee on Government Reform, the Committee on the Judiciary, the Committee on Appropriations, the Committee on Armed Services, and the Committee on Homeland Security.

- the Director of the Office of Counter narcotics Enforcement at the DHS;
- the Administrator of the Drug Enforcement Administration;
- the Assistant Secretary of State for International Narcotics and Law Enforcement Affairs;
- the Assistant Secretary of Defense for Special Operations and Low Intensity Conflict;
- the Deputy Director for Supply Reduction of the Office of National Drug Control Policy, acting in his role as the United States Interdiction Coordinator;
- the Director of the Crime and Narcotics Center of the Central Intelligence Agency;
- the Deputy Director for State and Local Affairs of the Office of National Drug Control Policy;
- the Chief of the National Guard Bureau's Counter Drug Program; and additional persons, as determined by the Director.

It is possible that this provision establishing the membership of the TIC was intended for inclusion in H.R. 6344 but was omitted due to a drafting error.

Meetings of the Interdiction Committee

The members of the The Interdiction Committee will meet, in person and not through any delegate or representative, at least once per calendar year, prior to March 1. At the call of either the Director or the current chairman, the TIC can hold additional meetings, which will be attended by the members either in person or through their chosen delegates or representatives.

Report of the Interdiction Committee

Not later than September 30 of each year, the TIC chairman will submit a report to the Director and to the appropriate congressional committees describing the results of the meetings and any other significant findings of the TIC during the previous twelve months. Any classified or sensitive information will be presented to Congress separately from the rest of the report.

Coordination with Other Agencies (Sec. 104)

The new reauthorization act amends current law (sec. 705(a)(3)) (21 U.S.C. § 1704(a)(3)) to mandate that the Secretaries of the Interior, Agriculture, Homeland Security, and Defense prepare annual reports for the Director and specified committees of Congress detailing specific aspects of their departments' drug control activities. The new act also requires a report from the Attorney General on drug violation arrests and prosecutions and drug seizures. These new reporting requirements are designed to help the agencies allocate resources and to aid the committees in their oversight function, especially as it relates to assessing the impact of diverting drug control assets to unrelated missions.

Budgetary Matters (Sec. 105)

The ONDCP Director develops a consolidated National Drug Control Program budget based on the budget request proposals received from the National Drug Control Program agencies. ONDCP revised its method for compiling the national drug control budget summary in 2002. As a result, total funding included in the FY2003 drug budget request was revised downward from $19.2 billion to $11.4 billion. Under the new method, activities were included only if they were deemed to have a ``primary" drug control purpose and if they had a separate line item account in the President's annual budget request. These changes resulted in lower budget numbers for many drug control agencies and the elimination of some agencies from the drug control budget altogether.

ONDCP said the new drug budget would better serve Congress and the public and bring greater accountability to federal drug control efforts. Others, however, including some Members of Congress, said the new drug budget distorted the true costs of the War on Drugs by, among other things, excluding the costs of incarcerating drug offenders and the costs of other drug law enforcement activities. This served to exaggerate the proportion of the budget slated for drug treatment expenditures, thereby making the budget appear more evenly balanced between enforcement and prevention than in previous years, even though little if any change had actually taken place.

The new reauthorization act contains provisions designed to force ONDCP to return to the older, more inclusive way of calculating the federal drug control budget summary. 25 26

Submission of Drug Control Budget Requests

Under current law (sec. 704(c)(1)) (21 U.S.C. §1703(c)(1)), the head of each National Drug Control Program agency must submit annually to the ONDCP Director a copy of the agency's proposed drug control budget request before it is submitted to the Office of Management and Budget. The new reauthorization act adds the requirement that drug control budgets submitted by departments, agencies, or programs must include all funds being requested for any drug control activity undertaken by that entity, including demand reduction, supply reduction, and state, local, and tribal affairs, and also including any drug law enforcement activities.

Furthermore, if an activity has both drug control and nondrug control purposes or applications, the department, agency, or program must estimate, by a documented calculation, the total funds requested for that activity that would be used for drug control, and must set forth in its budget request the basis and method used in making the estimate. (Both H.R. 2829 (sec. 6(c)) and S. 2560 (sec. 105(a)) contained these requirements, and they were carried over into H.R. 6344.)

National Drug Control Budget Proposal

In addition to consulting with the head of each drug control agency, as required by current law (sec. 704(c)(2)) (21 U.S.C. §1703(c)(2)), the new reauthorization act requires that the Director, in drawing up the national drug control budget proposal, also consult with ``the head of each major national organization that represents law enforcement officers, agencies, or associations." [25]

---

[25] This provision was added to H.R. 2829 by a floor amendment offered by Rep. Terry.

Certification of the National Drug Control Budget

The responsibility of the Director to review and certify the budget requests of national drug control program agencies is considered a vital tool of the Director in planning and implementing an effective national antidrug strategy. H.R. 6344 adds new requirements to the budget certification process. The Director is now prevented from approving any agency's proposed budget that requests funding for

- federal law enforcement activities that do not adequately compensate for transfers of drug enforcement resources and personnel to unrelated activities such as counterterrorism;
- law enforcement activities along U.S. borders that do not adequately direct resources to drug interdiction and enforcement;
- drug treatment activities that do not provide adequate results and accountability measures;
- any activities of the Safe and Drug Free Schools Program that do not include a clear antidrug message or purpose intended to reduce drug use;
- drug treatment activities that do not adequately support and enhance federal drug treatment programs and capacity; [26]
- activities of the Department of Education for FY2007, unless the request is accompanied by a report setting forth a plan for providing expedited consideration of student loan applications for all individuals whose applications were denied because of a conviction for a drug related offense that occurred when the individual was not receiving federal assistance; and
- the operations and management of the Department of Homeland Security that does not include a specific request for funds for the Office of Counter Narcotics Enforcement.

Reprogramming and Transfer Requests

The expired act contained a requirement (sec. 704(c)(4)(A)) (21 U.S.C. § 1703(c)(4)(A)) that no national drug control agency shall submit to Congress a request to reprogram or transfer any amount of appropriated funds over $5 million that is included in the federal drug control budget unless the request has first been approved by the Director. The new reauthorization act has reduced that amount to $1 million. The new act also provides that if the Director has not responded to an agency request for reprogramming within 30 days, the request shall be considered approved by the Director and forwarded to Congress.

Fund Control Notices

In an apparent drafting error, the provisions concerning fund control notices that appear in sec. 103of the new reauthorization act, and which are discussed earlier in this report, are repeated here with slightly different wording.

---

[26] This language, inspired by two amendments proposed by Rep. Cummings and adopted by voice vote at the House Government Reform subcommittee markup of H.R. 2565 in the 108th Congress, is intended to apply to the Substance AbusePrevention and Treatment block grant program and the Targeted Capacity Expansion grant program of the Substance Abuse and Mental Health Services Administration, Department of Health and Human Services.

Annual National Drug Control Strategies (Sec. 201)

Under the new reauthorization act, the preparation, submission, implementation, and assessment of the National Drug Control Strategy remain one of the most important responsibilities of ONDCP. The emphasis in the expired act (sec. 706(a)) (21 U.S.C. § 1705(a)) on a five year strategy supplemented by annual updates is shifted to the preparation of annual strategies. The new act does, however, keep the provision in current law that requires the strategies to include five-year projections for program and budget priorities. The annual strategies continue to be due from the President to Congress no later than February 1 of each year.

Strategy Contents

The contents that must be included in the annual strategies under the new reauthorization act are largely the same as those that were required under the expired law. A new requirement is a summary of the efforts made to coordinate with private sector entities to conduct private research and development of medications to treat addiction by screening chemicals for their potential therapeutic value, developing promising compounds, conducting clinical trials, seeking Food and Drug Administration approval for drugs to treat addiction, marketing drugs for the treatment of addiction, urging physicians to use such drugs in the treatment of addiction, and encouraging insurance companies to reimburse the cost of drugs used in the treatment of addiction.

Also newly required is a supplement to the strategy that reviews the activities of each individual National Drug Control Program agency during the preceding year with respect to the National Drug Control Strategy and that contains the Director's assessment of the progress of each agency in meeting its responsibilities under the strategy.

The new reauthorization act drops the specific numerical targets for reducing drug use contained in the expired law (sec. 706(a)(4)) (21 U.S.C. § 1705(a)(4)). These targets covered the period 1999 to 2003 and were largely unmet. The new act lets stand, however, the requirement for comprehensive, long-range, and quantifiable goals for reducing drug abuse and its consequences, backed by annual objectives and targets that are designed to move the country toward the strategy's goals and objectives.

Not included in the new reauthorization act was a provision in H.R. 2829 (sec. 8) that would have required the strategy to include data on current drug use trends that can be compared with previously compiled data to permit long-term assessment of the strategy's effectiveness and data that would permit a standardized and uniform assessment of the effectiveness of drug treatment programs in the United States.

Process for Development and Submission

Current law (sec. 706(a)(3)(A)(i)) (21 U.S.C. § 1705(a)(3)(A)(i)) requires the Director, in developing and effectively implementing the National Drug Control Strategy, to consult with

- the heads of the National Drug Control Program agencies;
- Congress;
- state, local, and tribal officials;

- private citizens and organizations, including community and faith- based organizations, with expertise in demand reduction;
- private citizens and organizations with experience and expertise in supply reduction; and
- appropriate representatives of foreign governments.

Tribal officials and community and faith based organizations were newly added to this list by the new reauthorization act. The new act also requires the Director to ensure, to the maximum extent possible, that state, local and tribal officials and relevant private organizations commit to support and take steps to achieve the goals and objectives of the National Drug Control Strategy.

Current law (sec. 706(a)(3)(A)(ii)) (21 U.S.C. § 1705(a)(3)(A)(ii)) permits the Director, with the concurrence of the Attorney General, to require the El Paso Intelligence Center to undertake specific tasks and projects to implement the National Drug Control Strategy and, with the concurrence of the Director of National Intelligence and the Attorney General, to request that the National Drug Intelligence Center undertake specific tasks or projects to implement the strategy. The new reauthorization act does not include a provision in H.R. 2829 (sec. 8) that would have allowed the Director to make recommendations to the Secretary of Health and Human Services (HHS) concerning research by the National Institute on Drug Abuse or other HHS agencies that would support or advance the National Drug Control Strategy.

Performance Measurement System

The expired act (sec. 706(c)) (21 U.S.C. §1705(c)) required that a performance measurement system be designed in consultation with affected National Drug Control Program agencies and be submitted to Congress no later than February 1, 1999, with modifications to be included in subsequent annual strategy reports. The new reauthorization act retains this requirement with certain changes. The performance measurement system is to be submitted annually as part of the strategy and will contain two- and five-year performance measures and targets for each National Drug Control Strategy goal and objective established for reducing drug use, drug availability, and the consequences of drug use. It will describe the sources of information and data to be used for each performance measure. It will also assess the adequacy of existing national treatment outcome monitoring systems to measure the effectiveness of drug abuse treatment in reducing illicit drug use and criminal behavior during and after the completion of substance abuse treatment.

Dropped is the provision in the expired act that required the drug control performance measurement system's performance objectives, measures, and targets to be revised to conform with National Drug Control Program agency budgets. Also dropped is the requirement that the performance measurement system be designed in consultation with affected National Drug Control Program agencies. Other aspects of the drug control performance measurement system remain largely unchanged.

Annual Report Requirements (Sec. 203) [27]

Media Campaign. [28] H.R. 6344 requires the Director to submit annually, by February 1 of each year, a report to Congress on the National Youth Anti-Drug Media Campaign that describes

- the strategy of the media campaign and whether specific objectives of the campaign were accomplished;
- steps taken to ensure that the media campaign operates in an effective and efficient manner consistent with its overall strategy and focus;
- plans to purchase advertising time and space;
- policies and practices implemented to ensure that federal funds are used responsibly to purchase advertising time and space and eliminate the potential for waste, fraud, and abuse;
- all contracts entered into with a corporation, partnership, or individual working on behalf of the media campaign;
- specific policies and steps implemented to ensure compliance with the media campaign provisions of this act; 29
- steps taken to ensure that the media campaign will secure, to the maximum extent possible, no cost matches of advertising time and space or in-kind contributions that are directly related to the statutory purposes of the campaign; and
- a review and evaluation of the effectiveness of the media campaign strategy for the past year.

Audit

The new reauthorization act requires the Government Accountability Office (GAO) to conduct, at least annually, an audit and investigation of the operations of ONDCP, including the High Intensity Drug Trafficking Areas program, the Counterdrug Technology Assessment Center, and the National Youth Anti-Drug Media Campaign. The GAO report, which will be provided to the Director and the appropriate congressional committees, must contain an evaluation of, and recommendations on, the policies and activities of ONDCP and its programs, their economy, efficiency and effectiveness, and any policy or management changes needed to prevent and detect fraud and abuse in the operation of the programs.

High Intensity Drug Trafficking Areas Program (Sec. 301)

The expired act (sec. 707) contained only four brief sub-sections relating to the High Intensity Drug Trafficking Areas (HIDTA) Program. The new reauthorization act greatly expands the statutory requirements that ONDCP must follow in conducting the program and reflects the high level of congressional interest in how the program should be run.

---

[27] Due to a drafting error, the new reauthorization act contains no sec. 202.

[28] Due to a drafting error, this reporting requirement is repeated in sec. 501 of the new reauthorization act minus the final three report elements shown here. The date of February 1 is also absent from the later iteration of this reporting requirement.

Program Purpose

The expired law did not explicitly state the purpose of the HIDTA Program. In the 108th Congress, the House bill (H.R. 2086) and the Senate bill (S. 1860) attempted to correct this omission, albeit with differing results. In their statements of purpose, both bills emphasized the importance of facilitating cooperation, intelligence sharing, and coordination of strategies and drug enforcement activities between federal, state, and local law enforcement agencies in the [29] groupings of U.S. counties now designated as HIDTAs. It was never clear, however, whether individual HIDTAs were created to deal with local and/or regional problems or if their activities must address drug problems of national scope. The Senate bill (sec. 301(2)) stated that these efforts were ``to reduce the supply of illegal drugs in HIDTA designated areas." The House bill (sec. 6(a)), along with the Government Reform Committee's report, [30] stressed that the purpose of HIDTA's is to deal with ``drug trafficking problems that harmfully impact other parts of the Nation."

In the 109th Congress, both H.R. 2829 (sec. 9) and S. 2560 (sec. 707) adopted the language from the previous Senate bill verbatim, except that the phrase ``to reduce the supply of illegal drugs in HIDTA designated areas" was modified to read ``to reduce the supply of illegal drugs in designated areas and in the United States as a whole" [emphasis added]. This dual purpose was carried over into H.R. 6344 and is now law.

Petitions for Designation

Previously, there were no statutory or even regulatory requirements concerning how HIDTAs are designated beyond the directive in the expired act that the Director may designate such areas in consultation with the Attorney General, the Secretary of the Treasury, heads of the National Drug Control Program agencies, and the governors of the applicable states. Most HIDTAs have been designated through this consultative process, although a few have been created by Congress in appropriations acts.

The new reauthorization act retains the consultative process for designating HIDTAs and, in addition, requires the Director to establish regulations under which a coalition of interested law enforcement agencies from an area may petition for designation as a HIDTA. These regulations must provide for a regular review by the Director of the petition, including a recommendation regarding the merit of the petition to the Director by a panel of qualified, independent experts.

Organization of HIDTAs

The expired act did not address how HIDTAs should be organized and operated. The new reauthorization act goes into considerable detail on this subject and would bring the law into alignment with current practice. Each HIDTA, as is now the case, is to be governed by an

---

29 In another apparent drafting error, this and the following reporting requirements refer textually to Title IV of the act, which covers the Counterdrug Technology Assessment Center, instead of Title V, which reauthorizes the media campaign. The incorrect reference to title IV probably comes from the Senate bill, S. 2560. The descriptions of the two reporting requirements that appear here are adjusted to reflect the intent of the law rather than its actual wording.

30 U.S. Congress, House Committee on Government Reform, Office of National Drug Control Policy Reauthorization Act of 2003, report to accompany H.R. 2086, 108th Cong., 1 st sess., H.Rept. 108-167, part 1, June 19, 2003 (Washington: GPO, 2003), pp. 21-25.

Executive Board. The Executive Board, composed of an equal number of votes between representatives of federal agencies and state and local agencies, [31] would be responsible for

- providing direction and oversight in establishing and achieving the goals of the HIDTA,
- managing the HIDTA's funds,
- reviewing and approving all funding proposals consistent with the overall objective of the HIDTA, and
- reviewing and approving all reports to the Director on HIDTA activities.

Treatment Prohibition

The new reauthorization act retains the provision in the expired act that no HIDTA funds may be used to establish or expand drug treatment programs. [32] It adds the requirement that up to 5% of federal funds appropriated for the program can be expended to establish drug prevention programs. [33] (The treatment prohibition provision caused consternation among some Members of the House Judiciary Committee during its markup of H.R 2086 in the 108th Congress. [34] It is helpful to remember that the HIDTA Program is a law enforcement program and that treatment and prevention funds are found elsewhere in the federal drug control budget, principally within the Department of Health and Human Services.)

Counterterrorism Activities

The new reauthorization act allows the Director to authorize the use of available HIDTA resources to assist federal, state, local, and tribal law enforcement agencies in investigations and activities related to terrorism and terrorism prevention, especially when such investigations and activities are also related to drug trafficking. The Director, however, is required to ensure that assistance provided for counterterrorism remains incidental to the HIDTA Program's purpose of reducing drug availability and carrying out drug related law enforcement activities, and that significant program resources are not redirected to activities exclusively related to terrorism, except on a temporary basis under extraordinary circumstances, as determined by the Director.

---

[31] This balance is mandated, in part, to help ensure that the HIDTAs maintain their focus, at least in part, on drug investigations of national importance.

[32] TheHouseONDCP reauthorization bill in the 108th Congress (H.R. 2086, sec. 6(a)) would have created an exception for the Baltimore/Washington HIDTA, which has historically and uniquely been a combined law enforcement and drug treatment program. No such exception exists in the new reauthorization act. Even so, although treatment programs cannot be established or expanded, existing HIDTA-funded treatment programs, such as those in the Baltimore/Washington HIDTA, can be continued.

[33] This 5% provision was added to H.R. 2829 at the House Judiciary markup by adoption of an amendment proposed by Rep. Linda Sánchez. The underlying bill would have prevented any HIDTA funds from being used for prevention.

[34] U.S. Congress, House Committee on the Judiciary, Office of National Drug Control Policy Reauthorization Act of 2003, report to accompany H.R. 2086, 108th Cong., 1st sess., H.Rept. 108-167, part 2, July 14, 2003 (Washington: GPO, 2003), pp. 114-119, 152-156, and passim.

Role of the Drug Enforcement Administration

The Director, in consultation with the Attorney General, is now required to ensure that a representative of the Drug Enforcement Administration is included in the Intelligence Support Center of each HIDTA.

Annual HIDTA Program Budget Submissions

Previously, the amount of funding received by each HIDTA was determined by the Director after the annual appropriations bill was enacted, thereby bypassing congressional scrutiny. The new reauthorization act requires the Director to include in ONDCP's annual budget justification to Congress a breakdown showing the amount being requested for each HIDTA, with a supporting narrative describing the rationale for each request. The narrative must include a detailed justification for each funding request that explains the reasons for the requested funding level, how the funding level was determined based on current assessments of the drug trafficking threat in each HIDTA, how such funding will ensure that the goals and objectives of each HIDTA will be achieved, how the requested funding supports the National Drug Control Strategy, and the amount of HIDTA funds that was used to investigate and prosecute organizations and individuals trafficking in methamphetamine in the prior calendar year along with a description of how those funds were used.

HIDTA Funding Formula

The House reauthorization bill in the 108th Congress (sec. 6(a)) would have codified a funding formula for the allocation of HIDTA funds. It would have required that 30% of program funds be expended in the seven HIDTAs determined to have the greatest impact on reducing overall drug trafficking in the country, 25% to the nine next most significant HIDTAs, and 10% to the remaining HIDTAs. No less than 20% of program funds would have gone to the Southwest Border HIDTA. The remaining 15% would have been expended by the Director on a discretionary basis. Instead of limiting the Director's discretion, this allocation formula was intended to reverse provisions in appropriations acts that have mandated that no HIDTA may be funded at a level below the previous year, thereby allowing the Director discretion to allocate only funding increases, if any, in any given year. The funding formula proved controversial, however, and it did not reappear in any of the 109th Congress's reauthorization bills.

Removal of Areas

The expired act said nothing about removing an area from designation as a HIDTA, and no HIDTAs or parts of HIDTAs have ever been removed from the program. The House reauthorization bill in the 108th Congress (sec. 6(a)) would have authorized the Director to remove all or part of a HIDTA from the program if it no longer met the required criteria --- or, presumably, if it had accomplished its mission. No such provision existed in any of the reauthorization bills in the 109th Congress. The Director can, however, under the new reauthorization act, achieve the same effect by requesting no funding for an area under the more detailed HIDTA budget submission process required by the new act, as described above.

Review of Current Areas

Likewise, the House reauthorization bill in the 108th Congress would have required the Director to conduct a review of each HIDTA, within one year of the bill's date of enactment, to determine if the area still warranted designation as a HIDTA. Any area or portion of an area that no longer warranted designation would be removed from the program. No such provision existed in any of the 109th Congress's reauthorization bills. The new reauthorization act, therefore, does not require such a review.

Emerging Threat Response Fund

Subject to the availability of appropriations, the new reauthorization act permits the Director to expend up to 10% of appropriated HIDTA funds to respond to any emerging drug trafficking threat in an existing HIDTA, establish a new HIDTA, or expand an existing HIDTA. In doing so, the Director must consider the impact of the funded activities on reducing overall drug traffic in the United States or on minimizing the probability that an emerging drug trafficking threat would spread to other areas of the country.

Evaluation of HIDTA Performance

Within 90 days of enactment and after consulting with each of the HIDTA Executive Boards, the new reauthorization act requires the Director to submit to Congress a preliminary report that describes, for every HIDTA,

- the specific purposes of the HIDTA;
- the specific long- and short-term goals and objectives for the
- HIDTA; and
- the measurements that will be used, and the reporting requirements needed, to evaluate the performance of the HIDTA in achieving its long- and short-term goals.

After the preliminary report, the Director must submit, as part of the annual National Drug Control Strategy, a report on the HIDTA Program that describes the specific purposes and long- and short-term goals and objectives of each HIDTA, and that includes an evaluation of the performance of each HIDTA in accomplishing its specific goals and objectives.

This provision responds to the Office of Management and Budget's (OMB's) finding, under its Program Assessment Rating Tool (PART) review of the HIDTA Program, that the program failed to demonstrate results. The Government Reform Committee believes that ONDCP did not provide OMB with sufficient data on HIDTA accomplishments and that this annual report will do so. [35]

Assessment of Drug Enforcement Task Forces. [36]

Within one year of enactment, and as part of each subsequent annual National Drug Control Strategy report, the new reauthorization act requires the Director to submit to Congress a report that assesses the number and operation of all federally funded drug enforcement task forces within each HIDTA. The report must describe

---

[35] House Government Reform Committee Report, p. 58.

[36] This provision was added to H.R. 2829 as the result of an amendment offered by Chairman Sensenbrenner at the House Judiciary markup.

- each federal, state, local, and tribal drug enforcement task force operating in the HIDTA;
- how the task forces coordinate with each other, with any HIDTA task force, and with investigations funded by the Organized Crime and Drug Enforcement Task Force Program (OCDETF);
- what steps, if any, each task force takes to share information regarding drug trafficking and drug production with other federally funded drug enforcement task forces in the HIDTA;
- the HIDTA's role in coordinating the sharing of such information among task forces;
- the nature and extent of cooperation by each federal, state, local, and tribal participant in ensuring that such information is shared among law enforcement agencies and with the HIDTA;
- the nature and extent to which information sharing and enforcement activities are coordinated with joint terrorism task forces in the HIDTA; and
- any recommendations for ways to ensure that task force resources are used efficiently and effectively to reduce the availability of illegal drugs in the HIDTA.

Assessment of Intelligence Sharing in HIDTAs

Within 180 days of enactment, and as part of each subsequent annual National Drug Control Strategy, the new reauthorization act requires the Director, in consultation with the Director of National Intelligence, to submit to Congress a report that evaluates existing and planned law enforcement intelligence systems that are supported by each HIDTA or used by task forces receiving any funding under the program, including the extent to which such systems ensure access and availability of intelligence to federal, state, local, and tribal law enforcement agencies within and outside the HIDTA. The report must also describe the extent to which federal, state, local, and tribal law enforcement agencies participating in each HIDTA are sharing law enforcement intelligence information to assess current drug trafficking threats and design appropriate enforcement strategies, and the measures needed to improve effective sharing of information and intelligence regarding drug trafficking and drug production among federal, state, local, and tribal law enforcement agencies that are participating in the HIDTA and between such agencies and similar agencies outside the HIDTA.

Coordination of Intelligence Sharing With OCDETF

The new reauthorization act requires the Director, in consultation with the Attorney General, to ensure that any drug enforcement intelligence obtained by a HIDTA Intelligence Support Center is shared, on a timely basis, with the OCDETF's new drug intelligence fusion center.

Use of Funds to Combat Methamphetamine Trafficking. [37]

The new reauthorization act requires the Director to submit to Congress, as part of the annual budget justification for ONDCP, a report on the use of HIDTA funds in the prior

[37] This subsection was added at the House Judiciary markup of H.R. 2829 by adoption of an amendment offered by Chairman Sensenbrenner. Some provisions of the original amendment were modified or dropped before inclusion in H.R. 6344.

calendar year to investigate and prosecute organizations and individuals trafficking in methamphetamine. The report must include

- the number of methamphetamine manufacturing facilities discovered in the previous fiscal year through HIDTA-funded activities;
- the amounts of methamphetamine or listed chemicals seized by HIDTA-funded initiatives during the previous year; and
- law enforcement intelligence and predictive data from the Drug Enforcement Administration showing patterns and trends in abuse, trafficking, and transportation in methamphetamine and listed chemicals.

Before awarding any funds to a HIDTA, the Director must certify that the law enforcement entities participating in that HIDTA are providing laboratory seizure data to the national clandestine laboratory database at the El Paso Intelligence Center.

Authorization of Appropriations

To fund the HIDTA Program, the new reauthorization act authorizes appropriations to ONDCP in the amounts of $240 million for FY2007, $250 million for FY2008, $260 million for FY2009, $270 million for FY2010, and $280 million for FY2011. (In FY2006, the HIDTA Program was appropriated $227 million, down from $228.4 million in FY2005.)

Funding for Certain HIDTA's (Sec. 302)

The Dawson Family Community Protection Act

This section of the new reauthorization act incorporates the Dawson Family Community Protection Act (H.R. 812), introduced in the 109th Congress by Representative Cummings. [38] The Director is required to use at least $7 million of HIDTA funds each fiscal year in HIDTAs with severe neighborhood safety and illegal drug distribution problems. (This amount represents a $2 million increase over the $5 million amount specified in H.R. 812.) [39] The funds must be used to ensure the safety of neighborhoods and the protection of communities, including the prevention of witness intimidation in drug cases, and to combat illegal drug trafficking through methods such as establishing and operating toll free telephone hotlines for the public to provide information about illegal drug related activities.

---

[38] The Dawson Family Community Protection Act was first introduced by Rep. Cummings in the 108th Congress (H.R. 1599) in response to the October 2002 firebombing of the Baltimore home of the Dawson family, in which the Dawsons and their five children all died. This crime, called in the bill's findings ``a stark example of domestic narco-terrorism," was committed in apparent retaliation for Mrs. Dawson's efforts to help the police end persistent drug dealing in her neighborhood. H.R. 1599 would have required that at least $1 million be used in HIDTAs for the purposes of the bill. The amount was increased to $5 million in H.R. 812 and to $7 million in the 109th Congress's reauthorization bills.

[39] The increase came about as the result of an amendment offered by Chairman Sensenbrenner at the House Judiciary markup of H.R. 2829.

Assessment of the ``Balloon Effect'' (Sec. 303)

The spread of urban drug traffickers into rural, suburban, and smaller urban areas to escape intensive law enforcement efforts against them is known as the ``balloon effect." The new reauthorization act requires the Director to assess the ability of the HIDTA Program to respond to the balloon effect by conducting a demonstration project in the New York/New Jersey HIDTA. The New York counties of Albany, Onondaga, Monroe, and Erie will be added to the New York/New Jersey HIDTA, and the ability of the HIDTA to deal with the movement of drug traffickers into these more rural areas will be assessed.

Counterdrug Technology Assessment Center (Sec. 401)

The head of the Counterdrug Technology Assessment Center (CTAC) has held the title of ``Director of Technology." The new reauthorization act changes this title to ``Chief Scientist."

The new reauthorization act requires the Secretary of Homeland Security to render assistance and support, to the maximum extent practicable, to ONDCP in the conduct of counterdrug technology assessment. (Existing law already requires the Secretary of Defense and the Secretary of Health and Human Services to do so.)

Technology Transfer Program

The new reauthorization act grants statutory authority to CTAC's counterdrug technology transfer program for the first time. The Chief Scientist, with the advice and counsel of experts from state, local, and tribal law enforcement agencies, is responsible to the Director for coordinating and implementing CTAC's technology transfer program. The purpose of the program is to transfer technology and associated training directly to state, local and tribal law enforcement agencies.

Technology transfers will be made in priority order based on

- the need of potential recipients for such technology,
- the effectiveness of the technology to enhance current counterdrug activities of potential recipients, and
- the ability and willingness of potential recipients to evaluate transferred technology.

Agreement Authority

The new act provides that the Director may enter into an agreement with the Secretary of Homeland Security to transfer technology with both counterdrug and homeland security applications to state, local, and tribal law enforcement agencies on a reimbursable basis.

Reporting Requirement

Before July 1 of each year, the Director is required by the new reauthorization act to submit to the appropriate congressional committees a report that contains

- the number of technology transfer requests received during the previous 12 months, including the identity of each requesting agency and the type of technology requested;
- the number of requests fulfilled during the previous 12 months, including the identity of each requesting agency and the type of technology requested;
- a summary of the criteria used to determine which requests were funded and which were not;
- a general assessment of the future needs of the program, based on expected changes in threats, expected technologies, and the likely needs of potential recipients; and
- an assessment of the effectiveness of the technologies transferred, based in part on the evaluations provided by the recipients, with a recommendation of whether the technology should continue to be offered through the program.

Despite these provisions contained in the reauthorization act, the administration's FY2008 budget request proposed ending CTAC's technology transfer program and devoting all CTAC funding to its research and development program. Subsequently, CTAC was appropriated $1 million for research activities in FY2008, a significant reduction from the agency's $20 million allotment in FY2007. CTAC no longer accepts technology transfer applications from law enforcement agencies.

National Youth Anti-Drug Media Campaign (Sec. 501)

The Drug-Free Media Campaign Act of 1998, [40] less than two pages in length, is the law that has governed the media campaign since its inception. It instructed the ONDCP Director to ``conduct a national media campaign ... for the purpose of reducing and preventing drug abuse among young people in the United States." It specified uses of campaign funds that were permitted and prohibited, established the matching requirement, and required the Director to report annually to Congress on the campaign's activities. It is repealed by the new reauthorization act, which greatly expands upon the language of the old act, and adds many new program requirements, to become sec. 709 (21 U.S.C. 1708) of current law. [41]

Purpose of the Campaign

The new reauthorization act restates somewhat the campaign's purpose --- from ``reducing and preventing drug abuse among young people" to ``preventing drug abuse among young people." Dropping the goal of reducing youth drug abuse seems to emphasize the preventive nature of the media campaign --- ``stopping drug use before it starts" as the National Drug Control Strategy puts it. The new act also adds two additional purposes: ``increasing awareness of adults of the impact of drug abuse on young people" and ``encouraging parents and other interested adults to discuss with young people the dangers of illegal drug use." The addition of adults as a key target audience of the campaign brings the

[40] P.L. 105-277, Division D, Title I, sec. 102, October 21, 1998, 112 Stat. 2681-752, 21 U.S.C. § 1801, et seq.

[41] Sec. 709 of the expired act authorized creation of the President's Council on Counter- Narcotics, which was never established.

statute into conformance with ONDCP's practice of directing up to 60% of campaign advertising to adults who influence youth, such as parents, teachers, clergy, and mentors.

Requirements for the Use of Campaign Funds

The new reauthorization act adds to existing law certain requirements regarding the use of campaign funds. For example, it requires that not more than $1.5 million can be spent on creative services per fiscal year. This limit can be increased to $2 million to meet urgent campaign needs with advance approval of the House and Senate Appropriations Committees. Most creative services, however, will continue to be donated, as at present.

Testing and Evaluation of Advertising

The new act requires that all ads be tested for effectiveness before they are aired. This requirement may be waived under certain circumstances. The act requires that the effectiveness of the campaign be evaluated by April 20 of each year by an independent entity. The evaluation must be based on specified survey research measures of drug use and other relevant studies to be determined by the Director.

Purchase of Advertising Time and Space

The new reauthorization act requires that at least 77% of appropriated campaign funds be used to purchase advertising time and space. The act further states that in any fiscal year for which less than $125 million is appropriated for the campaign, at least 72% must be spent on advertising time and space. In any fiscal year for which more than $195 million is appropriated, at least 82% must be spent on advertising time and space.

Division of Responsibilities and Functions

The new reauthorization act adds to current law a description of the separate duties of the Director, the Partnership for a Drug-Free America (PDFA), and the media buying contractor as follows:

Responsibilities of the Director

The Director is responsible for implementing a media campaign that focuses on the purposes set forth in the act and for approving (1) the overall campaign strategy, (2) all advertising and promotional material used in the campaign, and (3) the plan for the purchase of advertising time and space for the campaign.

Responsibilities of the Partnership for a Drug-Free America.

The Partnership for a Drug-Free America (PDFA) develops and recommends strategies to achieve the goals of the campaign, including addressing national, regional, and local drug threats, such as methamphetamine and ecstasy. The PDFA is also responsible for creating all advertising to be used in the campaign, except advertisements that are

- provided by other nonprofit entities under the matching requirement;
- intended to respond to high priority or emergent campaign needs that cannot timely be obtained at no cost (not including production costs and talent reuse payments), provided that any such advertising material is reviewed by the PDFA;

- intended to reach a minority, ethnic, or other special audience that cannot be obtained at no cost (not including production costs and talent reuse payments), provided that any such advertising material is reviewed by the PDFA; or
- any other advertisements that the PDFA is unable to provide or if the Director determines that another entity is more appropriate, in which case the Director must notify the House and Senate committees of jurisdiction, in writing, not less than 30 days prior to letting the contract.

Responsibilities of the Media Buying Contractor.

The Director contracts with a media buying contractor who plans and purchases advertising time and space for the campaign. The contractor cannot provide any service or material, or conduct any function or activity, that the Director determines should be provided by the PDFA.

Prohibition of Ads for Partisan Political Purposes

The expired act prohibits the expenditure of campaign funds ``for partisan political purposes." The new reauthorization act expands this language to read: ``For partisan political purposes, or express advocacy in support of or to defeat any clearly identified candidate, clearly identified ballot initiative, or clearly identified legislative or regulatory proposal." This provision is significant because the Director has been accused by some of using media campaign ads to oppose medical marijuana and other drug reform voter initiatives at state and local levels.

The new act also adds a prohibition against funding any advertising containing a primary message intended to promote support for the media campaign or to solicit private sector contributions to the campaign. All campaign ads must contain primary messages intended to reduce or prevent illicit drug use.

No-Cost Matching Requirement

The new reauthorization act continues the campaign's matching requirement under which media companies paid by the campaign to run antidrug ads are required to donate an equal amount of advertising time or space or other in-kind contributions to the antidrug effort, thereby doubling the campaign's ``firepower."

The new act requires that at least 70% of such no-cost match advertising directly relates to the substance abuse prevention message of the media campaign. The required percentage increases to 85% in any fiscal year in which less than $125 million is appropriated to the campaign. [42] The remaining ads still have to include a clear antidrug message, although it does not have to be the primary message of the match advertising.

Sponsorship Identification

S. 2560 (sec. 504(3)) would have exempted ads that are donated to the campaign under the matching requirement from the sponsorship identification provisions contained in section

---

[42] The campaign was appropriated less than $125 million in both FY2005 ($119 million) and FY2006 ($100 million). For a table showing detailed funding information since the campaign's inception in 1998, see CRS Report RS21490, War on Drugs: The National Youth Anti-Drug Media Campaign, by Mark Eddy.

317 of the Communications Act of 1934. [43] The Advertising Council's request for a waiver of this requirement was denied by the Federal Communications Commission (FCC) in November2002. [44] This provision, which provoked controversy, would have nullified the FCC order. (H.R. 2829, as introduced, had a similar provision (sec. 10(e)(4)), but it was dropped at markup by the full Government Reform Committee.) The new reauthorization act contains no such provision.

Financial and Performance Accountability

The new reauthorization act requires the Director to implement audits and reviews of the costs incurred by campaign contractors and subcontractors pursuant to sec. 304C of the Federal Property and Administrative Services Act of 1949 (41 U.S.C. § 254d). An audit must also be conducted to determine whether these campaign costs are allowable under sec. 306 of the same act. Employees of Ogilvy & Mather, the firm that previously held the contract for purchasing advertising time and space for the media campaign, were charged with over-billing the government for its services. [45] This audit requirement attempts to prevent overcharges in the future.

Report to Congress. [46]

The Director must submit annually a report to Congress that describes

- the campaign strategy and whether specific objectives of the campaign were accomplished;
- steps taken to ensure that the campaign operates in an effective and efficient manner consistent with the campaign's overall strategy and focus;
- plans for the purchase of advertising time and space;
- policies and practices implemented to ensure that federal funds are used responsibly to purchase advertising time and space and eliminate the potential for waste, fraud, and abuse; and
- all contracts entered into with a corporation, partnership, or individual working on behalf of the campaign.

Prevention of Marijuana Use

The act contains congressional findings on the harmfulness of marijuana and authorizes the Director to emphasize the prevention of youth marijuana use in the campaign's advertisements and other activities. This provision brings the media campaign's statutory language in line with what the campaign has been doing in recent years.

---

[43] Sec. 317 states that all matter broadcast by a station in exchange for consideration from any person shall, at the time the matter is broadcast, be announced as paid for or furnished by that person. 47 U.S.C. 317

[44] Federal Communications Commission, Order FCC 02-268, released November 7, 2002.

[45] U.S. General Accounting Office, Anti-Drug Media Campaign: Aspects of Advertising Contract Mismanaged by the Government; Contractor Improperly Charged Some Costs, GAO-01-623, June 2001.

[46] Due to a drafting error, this reporting requirement is repeated from sec. 203 of the new reauthorization act. In this instance, however, it is missing three reporting elements that are contained in the earlier version.

Prevention of Methamphetamine Abuse [47]

The new reauthorization act requires the Director to expend not less than 10% of funds appropriated for the campaign in a fiscal year on advertisements and grants specifically intended to reduce the use of methamphetamine. After FY2007, if the Director certifies in writing to Congress that domestic methamphetamine laboratory seizures (as reported to DEA's El Paso Intelligence Center) have decreased by at least 75% from the 2006 level, the Director may apply the anti-methamphetamine funds to advertisements specifically intended to reduce the use of other drugs, as the Director considers appropriate.

Authorization of Appropriations

The new reauthorization act authorizes appropriations for the media campaign in the amounts of $195 million each for FY2007 and FY2008 and $210 million each for FY2009 through FY2011.

Authorization of Appropriations for ONDCP (Sec. 601)

The new reauthorization act amends current law to authorize, except where the bill authorizes specific amounts, the appropriation of such sums as may be necessary for FY2006 through FY2010.

Termination Date for ONDCP (Sec. 602)

During consideration of ONDCP reauthorization in the 109th Congress, the agency's sunset provision proved controversial. H.R. 2829 (sec. 3) would have repealed the sunset provision contained in law (sec. 715) (21 U.S.C. § 1712), which technically terminated ONDCP on September 30, 2003. [48] The House bill contained no new termination provision, thereby authorizing ONDCP indefinitely. During floor consideration of H.R. 2829, Representative Paul offered an amendment to add a five-year sunset provision to H.R. 2829, but the amendment was defeated 85-322.

All three of the previous ONDCP authorizing acts contained five-year sunset provisions. S. 2560 (sec. 602) would have stuck to custom and extended ONDCP for five years, terminating the agency on September 30, 2010. It was the Senate's approach that prevailed and was carried over into H.R. 6344. The new reauthorization act, therefore, extends the life of ONDCP through the end of FY2010.

Designation of U.S. Anti-Doping Agency (Secs. 701-703)

The new reauthorization act designates the U.S. Anti-Doping Agency as the U.S. representative responsible for coordinating with other anti-doping organizations involved in the coordination of amateur athletic competitions that are recognized by the U.S. Olympic

---

[47] This provision was added to H.R. 2829 by a floor amendment offered by Reps. Rehberg, Boozman, Steve King, Capito, Souder, and Graves.

[48] Despite this sunset provision, Congress continued to fund the agency through annual appropriations.

Committee to ensure the integrity of amateur athletic competitions, the health of the athletes, and the prevention of use of performance enhancing drugs, or performance-enhancing genetic modifications accomplished through gene-doping, by U.S. amateur athletes. This provision was taken from S. 2560 (Title VII), which incorporated the language of S. 529. [49] The act also authorizes appropriations for the U.S. Anti-Doping Agency. [50]

Drug-Free Communities Act Reauthorization (Secs. 801-805)

The new act reauthorizes the Drug-Free Communities Support Program, [51] a grant program funded by ONDCP and administered by the Substance Abuse and Mental Health Services Administration (SAMHSA), an agency of the U.S. Department of Health and Human Services. It amends the Drug-Free Communities Act of 1997 (21 U.S.C. 1524(a)) to reauthorize the program through FY2012. It authorizes appropriations for the program in the amounts of $109 million for FY2008, $114 million for FY2009, $119 million for FY2010, $124 million for FY2011, and $129 million for FY2012.

The new act requires that not more than 3% of the funds appropriated for the program may be used by ONDCP to pay for administrative costs. The agency delegated to carry out the program may use up to 5% of the funds allocated for grants for administrative costs.

The new act states that a grantee cannot be suspended or terminated from the program without first being afforded a fair, timely, and independent appeal. This provision arose out of a controversy in 2005 when a number of community anti-drug coalitions unexpectedly lost their funding. The Director must submit a report to Congress, within 60 days of enactment, that details the appeals process required by this provision.

The new act increases the maximum value of individual grants that can be awarded under this program in a fiscal year from $100,000 to $125,000 and states that the Director cannot impose any eligibility criteria on new applicants or renewal grantees that are not provided for in statute.

The Director must grant $2 million for each fiscal year from 2008 through 2012 to the Community Anti-Drug Coalitions of America to provide for the continuation of the National Community Anti-Drug Coalition Institute.

National Guard Counterdrug Schools (Sec. 901)

The new reauthorization act statutorily authorizes, for the first time, the operations of five counterdrug schools operated by the National Guard, requires an annual report to Congress on their activities, and authorizes appropriations to the Department of Defense of $30 million for each fiscal year from 2006 through 2010. [52]

---

[49] Only the proposed authorizations differed between the two bills.

[50] For more on this subject, which is not directly related to ONDCP, see CRS Report RL32894, Anti-Doping Policies: The Olympics and Selected Professional Sports, by L. Elaine Halchin.

[51] Reauthorization of this program was included in S. 2560, as introduced.

[52] These provisions, which are not directly related to ONDCP, were introduced as S. 1785 in the 109th Congress and were subsequently incorporated into the text of S. 2560, from which they made their way into H.R. 6344.

National Methamphetamine Clearinghouse (Sec. 1001) [53]

The new reauthorization act contains the National Methamphetamine Information Clearinghouse Act of 2006, which establishes, within the Department of Justice (DOJ), [54] an information clearinghouse to be known as the National Methamphetamine Information Clearinghouse (NMIC). The act also creates a National Methamphetamine Advisory Council, consisting of 10 members appointed by the Attorney General to three-year terms. At least three of the members must represent law enforcement agencies, at least four must be from nonprofit organizations that provide services related to methamphetamine, and one must represent the Department of Health and Human Services. Advisory council members will not be compensated for their council duties, but they will receive travel and per diem expenses.

Clearinghouse Requirements and Review

The NMIC is created to promote information sharing of successful law enforcement, treatment, environmental, social service, and other programs related to the production, use, or effects of methamphetamine and of grants available for such programs. It will provide a toll-free number and a website for information on the short- and long-term effects of methamphetamine use, methamphetamine treatment programs and programs for drug endangered children, and grants for methamphetamine-related programs. It will allow a qualified entity to submit items to be posted on the website regarding successful public or private programs or other useful information related to the production, use, or effects of methamphetamine. (A ``qualified entity'' is defined as a state or local government, school board, or public health, law enforcement, nonprofit, or other nongovernmental organization that provides services related to methamphetamine.) The website will include a restricted section, accessible only by law enforcement organizations, that contains successful strategies, training techniques, and other information that the advisory council determines helpful to law enforcement agency efforts to combat the production, use, or effects of methamphetamine.

Within 30 days of submission of an item by a qualified entity, the advisory council must review an item submitted for posting on the website to evaluate and determine whether the item meets the requirements for posting and, in consultation with the Attorney General, to determine whether the item should be posted in a restricted section of the website. Within 45 days of submission of an item, the Council will post the item on the website or notify the entity that submitted the item of the reason for not posting it and of any modifications that could be made that would allow it to be posted.

Authorization of Appropriations

The act authorizes to be appropriated $500,000 for FY2007 to establish the clearinghouse and council and such sums as are necessary for the operation of the clearinghouse and council for each of fiscal years 2007 through 2009. [55]

---

[53] This provision was added by a floor amendment to H.R. 2829 offered by Reps. Chabot, Boswell, Calvert, Cannon, and Larsen. The language was somewhat modified for inclusion in H.R. 6344.

[54] H.R. 2829 would have created the clearinghouse within ONDCP. S. 2560 placed it in DOJ.

[55] H.R. 2829 would have authorized an appropriation of $1 million for FY2007 to establish the clearinghouse and the advisory council, and would have authorized funding necessary for their operation for each fiscal year through FY2011. S. 2560, on the other hand, would have authorized $2 million to establish the clearinghouse and the advisory council and funding necessary for their operation through FY2010.

Repeals (Sec. 1101)

The new reauthorization act repeals section 710 of the expired act, which provided for the establishment of a Parents Advisory Council on Youth Drug Abuse, which is no longer active. It also repeals section 6073 of the Forfeiture Amendments Act of 1988 (21 U.S.C. 1509), establishing the Treasury Department's Special Forfeiture Fund, which once provided funds to ONDCP but no longer exists.

Controlled Substances Act Amendments (Sec. 1102)

The new reauthorization act amends section 303(g)(2) (21 U.S.C. 823(g)(2)) of the Controlled Substances Act relating to registration requirements of practitioners who dispense narcotic drugs to individuals for maintenance or detoxification treatment. This provision is unrelated to ONDCP and its drug-control programs.

Report on Intelligence Sharing (Sec. 1103) [56]

The new reauthorization act requires the Director to submit to Congress, within 180 days of enactment, a report evaluating existing and planned law enforcement intelligence systems used by federal, state, local, and tribal law enforcement agencies responsible for drug trafficking and drug production enforcement. The report must address

- the current law enforcement intelligence systems used by federal, state, and local law enforcement agencies;
- the compatibility of such systems in ensuring access and availability of law enforcement intelligence to federal, state, local, and tribal law enforcement agencies;
- the extent to which federal, state, local, and tribal law enforcement agencies are sharing law enforcement intelligence information needed to assess current threats and to design appropriate enforcement strategies; and
- the measures needed to ensure and promote effective information sharing among law enforcement intelligence systems operated by federal, state, local, and tribal law enforcement agencies responsible for drug trafficking and drug production enforcement.

South American Heroin Strategy (Sec. 1104) [57]

The new reauthorization act requires the Director, in coordination with the Secretary of State, to submit to Congress, not more than 90 days after enactment, a comprehensive

---

[56] This report requirement originated in the Senate Reauthorization bill in the 108th Congress (S. 1860, sec. 307) and reappeared in S. 2560 (sec. 1103) in the 109th Congress.

[57] This provision originated as an amendment proposed by Rep. Mica to H.R. 2086, the House reauthorization bill in the 108th Congress.

strategy that addresses the increased threat from South American heroin, especially Colombian heroin and the emerging threat from opium poppy cultivation in Peru. The act requires that the strategy include efforts to eliminate the problem at the source. They would also require interdiction and precursor chemical controls, demand reduction and treatment, alternative development programs, efforts to inform and involve local citizens, and assessment of the specific level of funding and resources necessary to simultaneously address the threats from South American heroin and from Colombian and Peruvian coca. Classified or sensitive information would be presented to Congress separately from the rest of the strategy.

Model State Drug Laws (Sec. 1105) [58]

The new reauthorization act authorizes an appropriation of $1.5 million for each fiscal year 2007 through 2011 to provide for a 501(c)(3) corporation to advise states on establishing laws and policies to address alcohol and other drug issues, based on the model state drug laws developed by the President's Commission on Model State Drug Laws in 1993, and to revise such model state drug laws and draft supplementary model state laws to take into consideration changes in the alcohol and drug abuse problems in the state involved.

Study of Iatrogenic Addiction (Sec. 1106) [59]

The new reauthorization act requires the Director to request the Institute of Medicine of the National Academy of Sciences to conduct a study examining certain aspects of iatrogenic addiction to opioid analgesic drugs in Schedules II and III of the Controlled Substances Act (21 U.S.C. 812). The act defines iatrogenic addiction as

> an addiction developed from the use of an opioid analgesic by an individual with no previous history of any addiction, who has lawfully obtained and used the drug for a legitimate medical purpose by administration from, or pursuant to the prescription or order of, an individual practitioner acting in the usual course of professional practice.

The study shall assess the current scientific literature to determine, if possible,

- the rate of iatrogenic addiction associated with the appropriate use of prescription opioid analgesics;
- the impact of iatrogenic addiction associated with these drugs on the individual, the prescriber, other patients, and society in general;
- the comparative abuse liability of these prescription drugs when used properly by the ultimate user for a legitimate medical purpose;
- the types of prospective or retrospective studies that should be undertaken to determine the rate of iatrogenic addiction associated with the appropriate use of opioid analgesics; and

---

[58] This provision was added to H.R. 2829 by a floor amendment offered by Rep. Lungren.

[59] This provision was added to H.R. 2829 by a floor amendment offered by Rep. Lynch.

- a feasible timeline for conducting and reporting such studies, should the current state of the scientific literature be insufficient to determine the rate, impact, and comparative abuse liability of these drugs.

A report on the status of the study must be submitted to Congress within one year of the date of enactment of the act.

Strategy to Stop Internet Drug Advertising (Sec. 1107)

The new reauthorization act requires the Director, within 120days of enactment, to submit to Congress a strategy to stop advertisements that provide information about obtaining scheduled prescription drugs over the Internet without a lawful prescription.

Report on Diversion of Prescription Drugs (Sec. 1108)

The new reauthorization act requires the Director, in consultation with the Secretary of Health and Human Services, to submit to Congress, within 90 days of enactment, a report that includes a plan to conduct a study on the illegal diversion and inappropriate uses of prescription drugs. The report would include

- methods to utilize surveys to provide appropriate baseline data on the diversion and abuse of scheduled prescription drugs to evaluate the extent and nature of potential problems associated with inappropriate uses of prescription drugs in order to guide corrective actions to reduce such problems, without unintentionally hindering access to these drugs for legitimate medical purposes; and
- a scientifically based analysis of the relative contribution of both innate and acquired genetic factors, environmental factors, psychological factors, and drug characteristics that contribute to addiction to prescription drugs.

Afghan Heroin Strategy (Sec. 1109)

The new reauthorization act requires the Director to submit to Congress, within 90 days of enactment, a comprehensive strategy that addresses the increased threat from Afghan heroin. The strategy must include opium crop eradication efforts; the destruction of heroin and raw opium stockpiles and of heroin production and storage facilities; interdiction and precursor chemical controls; demand reduction and treatment; alternative development programs; measures to improve cooperation and coordination between relevant federal, foreign, and international agencies; and an assessment of the amount of funding and resources necessary to reduce the production and trafficking of heroin. Classified or sensitive information would be presented to Congress separately from the rest of the strategy.

Southwest Border Counternarcotics Strategy (Sec. 1110)

Within 120 days of enactment and every two years thereafter, the new reauthorization act requires the Director to submit to Congress a Southwest Border Counternarcotics Strategy. This report would set forth the government's strategy for preventing the illegal trafficking of drugs across the international border between the United States and Mexico, state the specific roles and responsibilities of the relevant National Drug Control Program agencies for implementing the strategy, identify the specific resources required to enable the relevant drug control agencies to implement the strategy, and include a strategy to end the construction of tunnels under the border. [60] The Director shall issue the strategy in consultation with the heads of the relevant National Drug Control Program agencies. The strategy cannot change existing agency authorities or the laws governing interagency relationships, but it may include recommendations about changes to such authorities or laws. Classified or sensitive information will be submitted to Congress separately from the rest of the strategy.

Mycoherbicide Study (Sec. 1111)

The new reauthorization act requires the Director to submit to Congress, within 90 days of enactment, a report that includes a plan to conduct, on an expedited basis, a scientific study of the use of mycoherbicides as a means of illicit drug crop elimination. The report will be prepared by an appropriate government scientific research entity and must include a complete and thorough scientific peer review. The study must contain an evaluation of the likely human health and environmental impacts of mycoherbicides derived from fungus naturally existing in the soil. [61]

H.R. 2829 would have required the report to include a plan to conduct controlled scientific testing in a major drug producing nation of a mycoherbicide naturally existing in the producing nation. This was changed in H.R. 6344 to require that the study be conducted in U.S. territory and not in any foreign country. The change was prompted by public opposition to this provision, which proved to be controversial. [62]

State Precursor Chemical Control Law Study (Sec. 1112)

The new reauthorization act requires the Director to conduct, in consultation with the National Alliance for Model State Drug Laws, a study of state laws with respect to precursor chemical controls. The Director must submit to Congress, not later than six months after the date of enactment, a report on the results of the study. The report must include a comparison

---

[60] The provision on tunnels was added to H.R. 2829 by a floor amendment offered by Rep. Filner. It also requires the Director to recommend criminal penalties for persons who construct or use such tunnels.

[61] The requirement that the report look at the effects of mycoherbicides on human health and the environment was added to H.R. 2829 by the adoption of an amendment offered by Rep. Cummings at the Government Reform Committee markup of H.R. 2829 on June 16, 2005. The overall provision was originally proposed by Rep. Burton.

[62] See, for example, ``Repeating Mistakes of the Past: Another Mycoherbicide Research Bill," a report by the Drug Policy Alliance, available at *[http://www.drugpolicy.org]*.

of the state laws studied, the effectiveness of each such law, and a list of best practices observed with respect to such laws.

Study of Drug-Endangered Children Programs (Sec. 1113)

The new reauthorization act requires the Director to submit to Congress, no later than six months after the date of enactment, a report on methamphetamine related activities conducted by state drug endangered children programs. The study must include an analysis of the best practices of the activities studied and recommendations for establishing a national policy to address the problems of children whose physical, mental, or emotional health are at risk because of the production, use, or effects of methamphetamine by another person.

Drug Court Hearings at Alternative Sites Study (Sec. 1114) [63]

The new reauthorization act require the Director to conduct a study on drug court programs that conduct hearings in nontraditional public places, such as schools, so that students see the consequences of drug abuse by nonviolent offenders, thereby serving as a strong deterrent and promoting demand reduction. The Director must include a report on this study with the Drug Control Strategy that is due to Congress on February 1, 2007. The report must include an evaluation of the results of the study and such recommendations as the President considers appropriate.

Report on Tribal Participation in HIDTAs (Sec. 1115) [64]

Within one year of the bill's enactment, the new reauthorization act requires the Director to submit a report to Congress on the representation of tribal governments in the High Intensity Drug Trafficking Areas (HIDTA) Program. The report must include

- a list of tribal governments represented in the program and a description of their participation,
- an explanation of the rationale for the level of representation by tribal governments, and
- recommendations by the Director on methods for increasing the number of tribal governments represented in the HIDTA Program.

Report on School Drug Testing (Sec. 1116)

The new reauthorization act requires the Director, within 120days of enactment, to submit a report to Congress on drug testing in schools. The report must include a list of

[63] This provision was added to H.R. 2829 by a floor amendment offered by Rep. Boozman.

secondary schools that have initiated drug testing after attending a conference on school drug testing sponsored by ONDCP.

Report on ONDCP Performance Bonuses (Sec. 1117)

The new act requires the Director, within 120 days of enactment, to submit a report to Congress on performance bonuses awarded at ONDCP. The report must include a list of employees who received performance bonuses, and the amount of such bonuses, for the period beginning on October 1, 2004, and ending on the date of submission of the report.

Sponsorship Identification in Advertisements (Sec. 1118) [65]

The new reauthorization act requires that every advertisement or other communication that ONDCP pays for, either directly or through a contract, shall include a prominent notice stating that it was paid for by ONDCP. This requirement includes advertisements disseminated in any form and includes communications by individuals in any form, including speech, print, or any electronic means. This provision prevents, among other things, the distribution of so-called ``video news releases'' by ONDCP --- a practice that ONDCP says it has stopped. [66]

Identification of sponsorship of broadcast matter is required by sec. 317 of the Communications Act of 1934. [67] The Advertising Council had earlier requested a waiver of this requirement so that advertisements donated to ONDCP's media campaign under the matching requirement would not have to be identified as having been sponsored by ONDCP. The Federal Communications Commission (FCC) denied the request in November 2002. [68]

In the 108th Congress, there was a legislative attempt to nullify the 2002 FCC order. The ONDCP reauthorization bills in both the Senate (S. 1860, sec. 404(3)) and the House (H.R. 2086, sec. 10(e)(4)) contained provisions to exempt advertisements donated to the National Youth Anti-Drug Media Campaign under the matching requirement from being identified as sponsored by ONDCP. (The provision in the House bill was dropped at markup by the full Government Reform Committee.) This provision in the new reauthorization act will have broader applicability, extending beyond the media campaign to all public announcements by ONDCP.

---

[64] This provision was added to H.R. 2829 by a floor amendment offered by Rep. Renzi.

[65] This section was added to H.R. 2829 by an amendment offered by Ranking Member Waxman at the Government Reform Committee markup on June 16, 2005.

[66] House Government Reform Committee Report, p. 69.

[67] Sec. 317 (47 U.S.C. § 317) states that all matter broadcast by a station in exchange for consideration from any person shall, at the time the matter is broadcast, be announced as paid for or furnished by that person.

[68] Federal Communications Commission, Order FCC 02-268, released November 7, 2002.

Awards for Coerced Abstinence Programs (Sec. 1119) [69]

The new reauthorization act require the Director to make competitive awards to fund demonstration programs by eligible local partnerships to coerce abstinence, through the use of drug testing and sanctions, of chronic hard drug users living in the community under the supervision of the criminal justice system.

Use of Award Amounts

The amounts awarded to eligible partnerships will be used to

- support the efforts of the agencies, organizations, and researchers included in the eligible partnership;
- develop and field a drug testing and graduated sanctions program for chronic hard-drug users living in the community under criminal justice supervision; and
- assist chronic hard-drug users by strengthening rehabilitation efforts through job training, drug treatment, or other services.

Definition of Eligible Partnership

The term ``eligible partnership'' is defined as a working group whose application to the Director

- identifies the roles played, and certifies the involvement of, three or more agencies or organizations, which can include state or local agencies (such as those carrying out police, probation, prosecution, courts, corrections, parole, or treatment functions), federal drug control agencies, and community-based organizations;
- includes a qualified researcher;
- includes a plan to administer drug tests at least twice a week to recovering addicts living in the community while under the supervision of the criminal justice system, and to swiftly and certainly impose a known set of graduated sanctions for noncompliance with community-release provisions relating to drug abstinence (whether imposed as a pretrial, probation, or parole condition or otherwise);
- includes a strategy for responding to a range of substance use and abuse problems and a range of criminal histories;
- includes a plan for integrating data infrastructure among the agencies and organizations included in the eligible partnership to enable seamless, real-time tracking of hard-drug users under criminal justice supervision; and
- includes a plan to monitor and measure the progress toward reducing the percentage of the population of hard-drug users under criminal justice supervision who, upon being summoned for a drug test, either fail to show up or test positive for drugs.

---

[69] This section was added to H.R. 2829 at the House Judiciary Committee markup by adoption of an amendment offered by Rep. Schiff. ``Coerced abstinence'' is an idea propounded by Mark A.R. Kleiman, Professor of Public Policy at the School of Public Affairs, University of California at Los Angeles, and a constituent of Rep. Schiff. See his ``Controlling Drug Use and Crime Among California's Drug-Involved Offenders: Testing, Sanctions, and Treatment,'' available at [http://www.spa.ucla.edu/faculty/kleiman/ Controlling_Drug_Use.pdf]

Reports to Congress

Not later than June 1, 2009, the Director must submit to Congress an interim report identifying the best practices in coercing abstinence in chronic hard-drug users, including the best practices identified through the activities funded under this section. Not later than June 1, 2010, the Director must submit to Congress a final report on the best practices in coercing abstinence in hard-drug users as identified by the demonstration programs.

Authorization of Appropriations

The act authorizes an appropriation for this awards program in the amount of $4.9 million each for FY2007 through FY2009. [70]

Policy Relating to Syringe Exchange Programs (Sec. 1120) [71]

The new reauthorization act amends current law (sec. 703(a)) (21 U.S.C. §1702(a)) by adding at the end the following statement:

> When developing the national drug control policy, any policy of the Director relating to syringe exchange programs for intravenous drug users shall be based on the best available medical and scientific evidence regarding their effectiveness in promoting individual health and preventing the spread of infectious disease, and their impact on drug addiction and use. In making any policy relating to syringe exchange programs, the Director shall consult with the National Institutes of Health and the National Academy of Sciences.

While Representative Souder, the act's sponsor, has often stated that he does not advocate needle exchange programs, he supported this amendment at the Government Reform Committee markup because he does believe that policy relating to the issue should be backed by the results of scientific studies. This was reiterated in the Government Reform Committee report on H.R. 2829, which plainly states that ``in adopting this amendment the Committee in no way endorses the use of such programs"(p. 70).

PROVISIONS OF H.R. 2829 NOT INCLUDED IN H.R. 6344

General Counterdrug Intelligence Plan

Not later than 120 days after enactment and every two years thereafter, H.R. 2829 (sec. 6(l)) would have required the Director, with the concurrence of the Director of National Intelligence, to submit to congress a General Counterdrug Intelligence Plan to improve coordination and eliminate unnecessary duplication among the federal counterdrug intelligence centers, activities, and agencies. The report would have to articulate clear and specific mission statements for each counterdrug intelligence center, system, and activity;

---

70 The annual authorization is reduced from the $10 million amount proposed in H.R. 2829, as amended.

71 This section was added to H.R. 2829 by an amendment offered by Ranking Member Waxman and modified by the Government Reform Committee at markup on June 16, 2005.

specify each federal, state, and local entity that participates in each counterdrug center, system, and activity; specify the means by which proper oversight of such centers, systems, and activities would be assured; specify the means by which counterdrug intelligence and information would be forwarded effectively to all levels of officials responsible for U.S. counterdrug policy; and specify mechanisms to ensure that state and local law enforcement agencies would be apprised of counterdrug intelligence and information acquired by federal law enforcement agencies. (The last counterdrug intelligence plan was prepared in 2000 and is considered outdated.)

Southwest Border Violence Study [72]

H.R. 2829 (sec. 6(o)) would have required the Director to submit to Congress, within 180 days of enactment and annually thereafter, a study of persons kidnapped, killed, or missing along the border between the United States and Mexico. The study would have reported on the specific impact on U.S. citizens of border violence related to drug trafficking and included recommendations on methods to solve the offenses and reduce their occurrence. To conduct this study, the bill would have authorized an appropriation of $1 million for each fiscal year from 2007 through 2011.

Assessment of Youth Drug Use [73]

Not later than one year after enactment, H.R. 2829 (sec. 6(p)) would have required the Director to complete an assessment of report materials, studies, and statistics to determine the extent to which children aged 12 to 17 experiment with and regularly use alcohol, cigarettes, prescription drugs without a prescription, marijuana, and other illicit drugs; and the extent to which they have access to intervention services or programs, including drug testing, counseling, rehabilitation, legal representation, and other services or programs associated with prevention, treatment, and punishment of substance abuse. The period studied would have been the five- year period before enactment.

Synthetic Drugs Strategy

The House bill (sec. 6(r)) would have required the Director to submit to Congress, not later than 120 days after the date of enactment, the National Synthetic Drugs Action Strategy outlined in the National Synthetic Drugs Action Plan submitted by the Director in October 2004.

---

[72] This provision was added to H.R. 2829 by a floor amendment offered by Rep. Cuellar.

[73] This provision was added to H.R. 2829 by a floor amendment offered by Rep. Jackson- Lee.

Methamphetamine Strategy [74]

No later than 90 days after the date of the enactment, the Director would have been required by the House bill (sec. 6(u)) to submit to Congress a comprehensive strategy that addressed the increased threat from methamphetamine. The strategy would have included interdiction and precursor chemical controls, demand reduction and treatment, alternative development programs, efforts to prevent the diversion of precursor chemicals on an international level, and an assessment of the level of funding and resources necessary to reduce significantly the production and trafficking of methamphetamine.

Awards for Shutting Down Illicit Drug Markets [75]

H.R. 2829 (sec. 14) would have required the Director to make competitive awards to fund demonstration programs by eligible local partnerships for the purpose of shutting down local illicit drug market hot-spots and reducing drug-related crime through evidence-based, strategic, problem-solving interventions that deter drug dealers or alter the dynamic of drug sales. The amounts awarded to eligible partnerships would have been used to support the efforts of the agencies, organizations, and researchers included in the eligible partnership; develop and field a directed and credible deterrent threat; and strengthen rehabilitation efforts through job training, drug treatment, or other services. Not later than June 1, 2009, the Director would have been required to submit to Congress an interim report identifying the best practices in drug market eradication. Not later than June 1, 2010, the Director would have submitted to Congress a final report on the best practices in drug market eradication as identified by the demonstration programs. The bill would have authorized appropriations for this awards program in the amount of $10 million each for FY2007 through FY2009.

International Summit on Methamphetamine Threat [76]

The House bill (sec. 20) would have required the Director, in consultation with the Secretary of State, the Attorney General, the Secretary of Homeland Security, the Secretary of Health and Human Services, and the United States Trade Representative, to convene, within 12 months of enactment, an international summit on the threat of methamphetamine and synthetic drug precursor chemicals. The Director would seek the participation and involvement of government leaders at the highest level from all countries that are direct sources of precursor chemicals and from all countries that are affected by methamphetamine production, trafficking, and use. The purpose of the summit would have been to intensify and coordinate an effective international response to prevent methamphetamine production and precursor diversion. The Director would have been required to encourage the negotiation, drafting, and ratification of multilateral or bilateral agreements that contain

---

[74] This provision was added to H.R. 2829 by a floor amendment offered by Rep. Hooley.

[75] This section was added to H.R. 2829 at the House Judiciary Committee markup by adoption of an amendment offered by Rep. Schiff.

[76] This provision was added to H.R. 2829 by a floor amendment offered by Reps. Baird, Cardoza, and Hooley.

information-sharing treaties concerning provisions for precursor importation and exportation and additional provisions for annual assessments of the medical and scientific needs of each signatory country. The bill would have authorized an appropriation of $1 million for this purpose.

Report on HHS Sponsorship of Harm Reduction Conference [77]

The Director would have been required by H.R. 2829 (sec. 22) to submit to Congress, no later than 30 days after enactment, a report explaining the rationale and circumstances that led to the sponsorship by the Department of Health and Human Services of, and the participation by HHS employees in, the First National Conference on Methamphetamine, HIV, and Hepatitis Science and Response, conducted by the Harm Reduction Coalition and the Harm Reduction Project in August 2005 in Salt Lake City. The report would have included a description of ONDCP management and reporting systems that are in place, or that would be put in place, to ensure that the policy of the federal government is consistently supportive of efforts to prevent the use of methamphetamine. This provision reflected the position of some Members of Congress that the harm reduction approach to drug use, which has been widely implemented in Europe and elsewhere, is an evil to be stamped out, not an alternative policy worthy of consideration.

Report on the Methamphetamine Epidemic

H.R. 2829 (sec. 27) would have required the Director to prepare, within 120 days of enactment, a report on methamphetamine usage in the United States. The report would have described methamphetamine usage by zip code based on information obtained from industrial and school drug testing and on seizures of clandestine laboratories.

Reauthorization Bills in the 108th Congress

The agency's authorization expired on September 30, 2003, [78] putting its reauthorization on the agenda of the 108th Congress. Bills were introduced in both the House of Representatives (H.R. 2086) and the Senate (S. 1860) to extend ONDCP for another five years.

---

[77] This provision was added to H.R. 2829 by a floor amendment offered by Rep. Graves.

[78] Since the expiration of its authorization, activities of ONDCP were carried out under authority provided by appropriations.

The House Bill, H.R. 2086

House Government Reform Subcommittee Hearings

To prepare for its consideration of the House ONDCP reauthorization bill, the Subcommittee on Criminal Justice, Drug Policy, and Human Resources held a series of three hearings on ONDCP and its programs early in the first session of the 108th Congress. At the first hearing, on March 5, 2003, ONDCP Director Walters testified on his agency's recently released National Drug Control Strategy for 2003. [79]

The subcommittee's second hearing, held on March 27, 2003, focused on the National Youth Anti-Drug Media Campaign. [80] The media campaign was originally created and authorized separately from ONDCP's reauthorizing statute by the Drug- Free Media Campaign Act of 1998. [81] The media campaign's authorization expired at the end of FY2002, but it continued to be funded through appropriations measures. [82]

Two of ONDCP's other programs, the High Intensity Drug Trafficking Areas Program and the Counterdrug Technology Assessment Center, were the subjects of the subcommittee's third and final hearing on April 8, 2003. ONDCP Deputy Director for State and Local Affairs Scott Burns and Drug Enforcement Administration Chief of Operations Roger Guevara, along with several state and local law enforcement officials, testified at this hearing. [83]

Introduction of H.R. 2086 and Subcommittee Markup

On May 14, 2003, Subcommittee Chairman Souder introduced H.R. 2086, the Office of National Drug Control Policy Reauthorization Act of 2003. At markup the next day, the bill was ordered reported, as amended, to the full Government Reform Committee.

Committee Hearing and Markup

The full Government Reform Committee held a hearing and scheduled a markup for May 22, 2003. Director Walters testified at the hearing portion of the committee meeting. [84] The markup scheduled to follow the Director's testimony was postponed, however, due to disagreements between the committee's majority and minority Members over certain provisions in the bill. These disagreements were later resolved and a rescheduled markup was

---

[79] U.S. Congress, House Committee on Government Reform, Subcommittee on Criminal Justice, Drug Policy and Human Resources, ONDCP Reauthorization and the National Drug Control Strategy for 2003, hearing, 108th Cong., 1st sess., March 5, 2003 (Washington: GPO, 2003).

[80] U.S. Congress, House Committee on Government Reform, Subcommittee on Criminal Justice, Drug Policy and Human Resources, ONDCP Reauthorization: The National Youth Anti-Drug Media Campaign, hearing, 108th Cong., 1st sess., March 27, 2003 (Washington: GPO, 2003).

[81] P.L. 105-277, Division D, Title I, Sec. 102, October 21, 1998, 112 Stat. 2681-752, 21 U.S.C. § 1801 et seq.

[82] Further information on the media campaign and analysis of its impact on youth drug use in the United States can be found in CRS Report RS21490, War on Drugs: The National Youth Anti-Drug Media Campaign, by Mark Eddy.

[83] U.S. Congress, House Committee on Government Reform, Subcommittee on Criminal Justice, Drug Policy and Human Resources, ONDCP Reauthorization: The High Intensity Drug Trafficking Areas Program and CTAC, hearing, 108th Cong., 1st sess., April 8, 2003 (Washington: GPO, 2003).

[84] U.S. Congress, House Committee on Government Reform, H.R. 2086, The Office of National Drug Control Policy Reauthorization Act of 2003, hearing on H.R. 2086, 108th Cong., 1st sess., May 22, 2003 (Washington: GPO, 2003).

held on June 5, 2003, when the full committee approved an amendment in the nature of a substitute offered by Representative Souder. [85]

One point of disagreement concerned a provision that would have allowed the ONDCP Director to use funds appropriated for the National Youth Anti-Drug Media Campaign to oppose efforts in the states, including referenda and legislative proposals, to legalize the use of any controlled substance. Instead, the amended version of H.R. 2086 would have forbidden any media campaign funds from being used for ``partisan political purposes or advocacy in support of or to defeat any clearly identified candidate, clearly identified ballot initiative, or clearly identified legislative or regulatory proposal." This was an expansion of the language in current law that simply prohibits use of media campaign funds ``for partisan political purposes." This wording was expanded in an attempt to stop the Director and other ONDCP officials from publicly campaigning against medical marijuana ballot initiatives in the states and to curtail ONDCP's alleged use of media campaign ads to persuade voters to oppose such initiatives.

At markup, Representative Waxman, the committee's ranking Member, offered an amendment to eliminate the requirement in current law (sec. 704(b)(12)) that the Director ``take such actions as necessary to oppose any attempt to legalize the use of a substance (in any form) that is listed in schedule I ... and has not been approved for use for medical purposes by the Food and Drug Administration." Arguing against the amendment, Representative Souder stated his belief in the importance of the Director speaking out against any efforts that would violate federal law, notwithstanding that the issue under debate involved efforts to change federal law, not break federal law. The amendment was rejected by voice vote and the provision remains in current law, unchanged by the new reauthorization act.

House Judiciary Committee Actions

The House Judiciary Committee, to which H.R. 2086 was also referred, considered the bill on July 9, 2003, and ordered it reported, as amended, on July 14, 2003.

H.R. 2086 Passes the House

The House passed the measure, without amendment, by voice vote under suspension of the rules, on September 30, 2003. [86] The following day, the measure was received in the Senate and referred to the Committee on the Judiciary. H.R. 2086 received no further consideration and died at the close of the 108th Congress. It laid the groundwork, however, for the ONDCP reauthorization bills that would be introduced in the 109th Congress.

---

85 U.S. Congress, House Committee on Government Reform, Office of National Drug Control Policy Reauthorization Act of 2003, report to accompany H.R. 2086, 108th Cong., 1st sess., H.Rept. 108-167, part 1, June 19, 2003 (Washington: GPO, 2003).

86 ``Office of National Drug Control Policy Reauthorization Act of 2003," *Congressional Record, daily edition, vol. 149* (September 30, 2003), pp. H8962-H8972.

The Senate Bill, S. 1860

The Senate's ONDCP reauthorization bill was introduced on November 14, 2003, by Senators Hatch, Biden, and Grassley and was referred to the Judiciary Committee.[87]

Structure and Major Provisions of S. 1860.

The part of the Senate bill that would have reauthorized ONDCP and the media campaign (Titles I through V) followed the structure of the House proposal, although it differed from H.R. 2086 in many of its details. Like the House bill, S. 1860 would have amended ONDCP's Reauthorization Act of 1998. It also would have amended the Drug-Free Media Campaign Act of 1998; however, unlike the House bill, it would have left it as a separate statute. The remaining titles of S. 1860 contained additional drug-control measures, including treatment provisions, that were unrelated to ONDCP and that were not found in H.R. 2086. S. 1860 saw no action beyond introduction and committee referral, and the bill died at the close of the 108th Congress. Many of its provisions, however, were incorporated into both H.R. 2829 and S. 2560, the House reauthorization bills in the 109th Congress.

[87] *Sen. Hatch, et al., introductory remarks, Congressional Record*, daily edition, vol. 149 (November 14, 2003), pp. S14811-S14815.

In: The War on Drugs,: Winning, Losing or Treading Water ISBN 978-1-59454-235-0
Editor: Nelson V. Arcos

Chapter 2

WAR ON DRUGS: THE NATIONAL YOUTH ANTI-DRUG MEDIA CAMPAIGN *

Mark Eddy

SUMMARY

Authorization of the National Youth Anti-Drug Media Campaign, a multi-media federal program to persuade America's youth not to use drugs, expired at the end of FY2002. H.R. 2829 (passed by the House on March 13, 2006) and S. 2560 (reported by the Senate Judiciary Committee on May 25, 2006) would reauthorize the media campaign, along with the other programs run by the Office of National Drug Control Policy (ONDCP). H.R. 5576, the House-passed appropriations bill that funds ONDCP, proposes $100 million for the campaign for FY2007. The media campaign's effectiveness has been questioned, and the program has engendered its share of controversy. Nevertheless, ONDCP, the office of the "drug czar," is optimistic that recent changes in campaign strategy will help to reduce illegal drug use by young people.

BACKGROUND

Although it accounts for less than 1% of the federal drug-control budget, the National Youth Anti-Drug Media Campaign is, for many Americans, the most visible aspect of the war on drugs. This is by design. The campaign's strategy is based on the belief that its efforts to persuade young people not to use illegal drugs will be effective only if its messages are seen repeatedly by large numbers of youth and by the adults who influence them — such as parents, teachers, clergy, and mentors. According to congressional testimony in 2003, the

* Excerpted from CRS Report RS21490, dated July 3, 2006

campaign's broadcast, print, and Internet ads reach about 90% of all teens at least four times per week at a cost to taxpayers of less than $8 per teenager per year.[1]

Congressional Research Service: The Library of Congress

The media campaign was authorized by the Drug-Free Media Campaign Act of 1998.[2] This law, less than two pages in length, instructed the Director of the Office of National Drug Control Policy (commonly referred to as the "Drug Czar") to "conduct a national media campaign ... for the purpose of reducing and preventing drug abuse among young people in the United States." The antidrug media campaign is an attempt at behavior change, forms of which have been used in other government campaigns and are used by nongovernmental organizations and commercial marketers. It seeks to reinforce existing antidrug attitudes in youth and adults and reverse the attitudes of those who have positive ideas about illegal drugs, thereby reducing the number of young Americans who use illegal drugs.

The media campaign is a public-private partnership. Most of the campaign's advertisements have been produced by the Partnership for a Drug Free America (PDFA), a nonprofit organization that recruits advertising agencies to develop creative concepts on a pro bono basis. Appropriated media campaign funds are then used to cover the costs of actually making the antidrug ads. The Partnership itself receives minimal federal funding. Its relationship with the Office of National Drug Control Policy (ONDCP) has made PDFA the single largest public service initiative in the history of advertising.

In addition to media ads, the campaign has a non-advertising component consisting of public outreach and specialized supporting communications efforts. These include the operation of antidrug websites, meetings with news and entertainment writers and editors to encourage them to promote antidrug messages, and a corporate sponsorship program under which leading corporations insert antidrug messages into their own communications with their customers and the public.

Program Funding

The Drug-Free Media Campaign Act authorized appropriations to ONDCP of $195 million for each fiscal year from 1999 through 2002 — a total of $975 million — to run the campaign. The Administration had originally proposed a somewhat less generous $175 million per year budget — for a total of $875 million — although subsequent budget requests were for larger amounts. Actual appropriations through FY2002 of $930 million amounted to $55 million more than originally proposed and $45 million less than the authorized level.

Although the authorization expired at the end of FY2002, the Administration has continued to request funding for the campaign, and Congress has continued to provide appropriations at levels less than requested in the President's annual budget request and less

---

1 The facts cited in this paper, unless otherwise noted, are drawn from U.S. Congress, House Committee on Government Reform, ONDCP Reauthorization: The National Youth Anti-Drug Media Campaign, 108th Cong., 1st sess., Mar. 27, 2003 (Washington: GPO, 2003).

2 P.L. 105-277, Division D, Title I, Sect. 102, Oct. 21, 1998; 112 Stat. 2681-752; 21 U.S.C.1801.

than appropriated in previous years (see Table 1). Congress has reduced funding for the media campaign every year since FY2001, from $185 million in that year's budget to $100 million in FY2006, an overall cut of 47%. Nevertheless, over the nine years of the campaign's existence, Congress has appropriated nearly $1.5 billion to the media campaign.

The President's budget submission for FY2004 provided the following comment about the campaign (*Appendix*, p. 1053):

> In 2002, the Office of Management and Budget (OMB) conducted a systematic review of more than 200 Federal programs to assess their performance in a number of areas. The National Youth Anti-Drug Media Campaign has not demonstrated the results sought and does not yet have adequate performance measures and related goals. The OMB recommended actions include (1) continued emphasis on developing acceptable performance measures and goals; (2) allowing sufficient time for the effects of recent ONDCP actions to be realized before pursuing changes to the program; (3) seeking no funding increases for the program; and (4) making FY2005 funding contingent upon improved results.

Congressional skepticism about the program persists, as evidenced by declining levels of funding for the campaign.

Table 1. Media Campaign Appropriations, by Fiscal Year (dollars in millions)

Fiscal Year	Authorized	Administration Request	House Passed	Senate Passed	Final Appropriation
1998	$195.0	$175.0	$195.0	$110.0	$195.0
1999	195.0	195.0	185.0	110.0	185.0
2000	195.0	185.0	195.0	96.5	185.0
2001	195.0	185.0	185.0	98.7	185.0
2002	195.0	185.0	180.0	185.0	180.0
2003	—	180.0	170.0	100.0	150.0
2004	—	170.0	150.0	100.0	145.0
2005	—	145.0	120.0	100.0	120.0
2006	—	120.0	120.0	95.0	100.0
2007	—	120.0	100.0	TBD	TBD

Source: Table prepared by Congressional Research Service (CRS) from Administration budget requests and from appropriation bills. (Amounts shown are pre-rescission; rescissions were 0.38% in FY2000, 0.22% in FY2001, 0.65% in FY2003, and 0.59% in FY2004.)

Early Implementation of the Campaign

Phase I of the campaign, January-July 1998, consisted of a 12-city test pilot of ads addressed to various ethnic and geographic audiences. Audience awareness surveys and focus groups were conducted. Phase II, August 1998-July 1999, moved the campaign's testing and evaluation to the national stage with antidrug ads on television, radio, print, and outdoor media. Internet sites for youth, parents, and community partners were launched. Partnerships were begun with corporations, community antidrug coalitions, and state and local governments. Research efforts continued.

In 1999, after conducting a series of panels composed of national experts in public health, social marketing, advertising, and youth behavior change, ONDCP organized Phase III of the campaign. The decision was made to target the campaign's prevention efforts toward youths aged 9 to 18 but with an emphasis on so-called "tweens," those aged 11 to 13 (7th and 8th graders). National surveys showed that drug use first began at the ages of 11 to 13, but was not yet widespread. It was believed that focusing on these younger youth would be the most effective strategy. "Stopping drug use before it starts" became a familiar refrain of then-Drug Czar Barry McCaffrey. Phase III commenced in August 1999 with all elements in place, including additional partnerships with national media, entertainment, and sports organizations as well as civic, professional, and community groups.

The Matching Requirement and an Early Controversy

The campaign's authorizing legislation has a matching requirement. Media companies that are paid by the campaign to run antidrug ads are required to donate an equal amount of advertising time or space or other in-kind contributions to the antidrug effort. ONDCP contracts with the Advertising Council to run this National Media Match Program, which has garnered $447 million worth of pro bono TV and radio time for public service announcements (PSAs). In addition to the campaign's core ads, the matching requirement can be met by airing the PSAs of other agencies or groups — such as the YMCA — whose programs reinforce ONDCP's youth drug prevention strategy.

Early in the program, ONDCP began giving credit toward the matching requirement to television networks whose programs contained antidrug story lines. The networks could then reclaim the credited time it owed to the government and resell it to commercial advertisers at the going rate. Some magazines participating in the campaign also were credited with meeting the matching requirement by printing stories or editorials with antidrug content. Under this scheme, the networks earned $21.8 million in FY1999 by selling airtime that, in the absence of the credits for antidrug messages embedded in their programs, would have been donated to the campaign under the matching requirement.[3]

This practice was publicized in January 2000, in the online magazine *Salon*, by freelance reporter Daniel Forbes, who also claimed that, in some cases, ONDCP was reviewing scripts

---

[3] U.S. Congress, House, Committee on Commerce, Subcommittee on Telecommunications, Trade, and Consumer Protection, The White House, the Networks and TV Censorship, hearing, 106th Cong., 2nd sess., Feb. 9, 2000 (Washington: GPO, 2000), p. 40.

and suggesting changes to make shows conform to the campaign's antidrug message.[4] The next day, the story appeared on the front page of the *Washington Post*[5] and was picked up by other media outlets, resulting in congressional hearings at which ONDCP officials denied influencing the content of TV shows and magazine articles. Following the controversy, FY2001 appropriations language prohibited the practice of crediting media outlets on the basis of story content[6] At least one law review article has deemed the practice unconstitutional[7].

OVERSIGHT AND EVALUATION

The campaign's authorizing and appropriations language both require rigorous evaluation of the program. ONDCP has allocated more than $50 million for research and evaluation of the program. The National Institute on Drug Abuse (NIDA) manages the Phase III evaluation process for ONDCP and awarded the prime evaluation contract to Westat, Inc. Results are derived from a nationally representative household survey of youths and parents. In May 2002, NIDA released a Westat evaluation report that found little evidence that the youth campaign had had direct, favorable effects between 2000 and 2001 on drug use by young Americans, although it was found to modify parental behavior.[8] In its subsequent November 2002 report, Westat stated:

> There is little evidence of direct favorable Campaign effects on youth. There is no statistically significant decline in marijuana use to date, and some evidence for an increase in use from 2000 to 2001. Nor are there improvements in beliefs and attitudes about marijuana use between 2000 and the first half of 2002. Contrarily, there are some unfavorable trends in youth anti-marijuana beliefs. Also there is no tendency for those reporting more exposure to Campaign messages to hold more desirable beliefs.[9]

Congressional appropriators, informed by these and other evaluations of the media campaign, have frequently expressed concern about the campaign. For example, after noting that total appropriations since the inception of the campaign had exceeded $1 billion, the FY2003 appropriations conference report stated: "The conferees are deeply disturbed by the lack of evidence that the National Youth Anti-Drug Media Campaign has had any appreciable impact on youth drug use.... If the campaign continues to fail to demonstrate effectiveness,

---

[4] Daniel Forbes, "Prime-Time Propaganda," *Salon*, Jan. 13, 2000. Forbes' stories on this issue can be accessed in the archives of Salon.com.

[5] Howard Kurtzand Sharon Waxman, "White House Cut Anti-Drug Deal with TV," *Washington Post*, Jan. 14, 2000, p. A1.

[6] U.S. Congress, Conference Committees, 2000, Making Omnibus Consolidated and Emergency Supplemental Appropriations for Fiscal Year 2001, conference report to accompany H.R. 4577, H.Rept. 106-1033, 106th Cong., 2nd sess. (Washington: GPO, 2000), pp. 390-391.

[7] Ariel Berschadsky, "White House Anti-Drug Policy: Statutory and Constitutional Implications," Cardozo Arts and Entertainment Law Journal, vol. 19, 2001, p. 199.

[8] Vanessa O'Connell, "Drug Czar Says Ad Campaign Has Flopped," Wall Street Journal, May 14, 2002, p. B1.

[9] Robert Hornik, et al., Evaluation of the National Youth Anti-Drug Media Campaign: Fifth Semi-Annual Report of Findings Executive Summary (Rockville, MD: Westat, Nov. 2002), p. xi.

then the Committees will be compelled to reevaluate the use of taxpayer money to support the Media Campaign."[10]

A controversial series of ads, which began running during the 2002 Super Bowl, painted drug users as implicit supporters of terrorism by indirectly providing money to terrorists. These ads were criticized as misleading and ineffective in media stories. Some critics contended that it is drug prohibition laws — not drug users — that make possible huge, illegal drug profits, some of which might be used to fund acts of terrorism. Moreover, the ads target young, infrequent users who do not account for the vast bulk of drug use — and therefore drug revenues. These ads, which are no longer run, also created friction between ONDCP and PDFA, with PDFA considering the ads off-target.

Changes in Strategy

ONDCP Director John P. Walters convened a task force in February 2002 to examine strategic issues affecting campaign performance. The group agreed on significant changes in campaign strategy. Recognizing that the sharpest increase in drug use occurs among youth aged 14 to 16 (9th and 10th graders), the campaign's focus was shifted from "tweens" to these older teens. More rigorous testing of ads was also decided upon. In the past, not all ads were tested before they ran. Now, all TV ads would be thoroughly tested against more demanding standards before being aired. There would also be earlier involvement by ONDCP in the advertising development process.

The release of Westat's May 2002 evaluation resulted in another important change. It was decided that the campaign would concentrate its efforts against marijuana. Walters said in a hearing that "it is clear that we cannot expect to make progress toward our goal of reducing youth drug use until we significantly reduce the use of marijuana, the preponderant drug of choice among youth." [11] H.R. 2829 (sec. 12(a)) would reinforce this anti-marijuana focus of the campaign with its congressional findings on the harmfulness of the drug and its provision that "the Director [of ONDCP] may emphasize prevention of youth marijuana use" in the advertising and other activities of the media campaign.

Two more changes were revealed by ONDCP Chief of Staff Chris Marston at the House hearing in March 2003. [12] Previously, 60% of campaign ad expenditures had been directed at adults, 40% at youth. Marston announced a reversal of that ratio. He also said that the campaign would introduce the theme of treatment in its ads, beginning with an emphasis on early intervention, in an attempt to reach youth who use drugs on a regular basis or who are suspected of using drugs. Taken together, according to Marston's testimony, all of these changes "mark a substantially new and essentially re-directed Media Campaign."

---

[10] U.S. Congress, Conference Committees, 2003, Making Further Continuing Appropriations for the Fiscal Year 2003, and for Other Purposes, conference report to accompany H.J.Res. 2, H.Rept. 108-10, 108th Cong., 1st sess. (Washington: GPO, 2003), pp. 1345-1346.

[11] U.S. Congress, Senate Committee on Appropriations, Subcommittee on Treasury and General Government, Effectiveness of the National Youth Anti-Drug Media Campaign, special hearing, 107th Cong., 2nd sess., June 19, 2002 (Washington: GPO, 2002), p. 14. Actually, alcohol, followed by tobacco, is the most prevalent drug used by America's youth, and such drug use, while legal for adults, is not legal for youth.

[12] U.S. Congress, House Committee on Government Reform, ONDCP Reauthorization: The National Youth Anti-Drug Media Campaign, 108th Cong., 1st sess., Mar. 27, 2003 (Washington: GPO, 2003).

REAUTHORIZING LEGISLATION IN THE 109TH CONGRESS

H.R. 2829 and S. 2560, bills to reauthorize ONDCP, would extend the media campaign and authorize appropriations. H.R. 2829, as amended, passed the House on March 13, 2006, and has been sent to the Senate. S. 2560 was reported by the Senate Committee on the Judiciary on May 25, 2006. For analysis on how these bills would affect the media campaign, see CRS Report RL32352, *War on Drugs: Reauthorization of the Office of National Drug Control Policy*, by Mark Eddy.

In: The War on Drugs: Winning, Losing or Treading Water ISBN 978-1-59454-235-0
Editors: Nelson V. Arcos

Chapter 3

SAFE AND DRUG-FREE SCHOOLS AND COMMUNITIES ACT: PROGRAM OVERVIEW AND REAUTHORIZATION ISSUES *

Gail McCallion

SUMMARY

The Safe and Drug-Free Schools and Communities Act (SDFSCA), Title IV-A of the Elementary and Secondary Education Act (ESEA), is the federal government's major initiative to prevent drug abuse and violence in and around schools. It was most recently reauthorized by the ESEA, as amended by the No Child Left Behind Act (P.L. 107-110), in January of 2002. Like all No Child Left Behind Act programs, it is being considered for reauthorization in the 110th Congress.

The SDFSCA supports two major grant programs — one for states and one for National Activities. State Grants are distributed to the states, the District of Columbia, and Puerto Rico, by a formula that allocates 50% of the funds on the basis of school-aged population, and 50% in proportion to ESEA Title I, Part A, concentration grants for the preceding fiscal year. State governors are permitted to use up to 20% of their state's grant for comprehensive activities that deter youth from using drugs and committing violent acts in schools. National Activities grants are awarded by the Secretary for a variety of National Activities to prevent substance abuse and support violence prevention. States award grants to local educational agencies (LEAs) using a formula that allocates 40% of an LEA's grant on the basis of school enrollment and 60% on the basis of an LEA's relative share of total Title I-A grants for the preceding fiscal year. The statute permits LEAs to use funds for a wide variety of activities intended to enhance violence prevention efforts and reduce drug and alcohol abuse.

For FY2008, $513 million was appropriated for the SDFSCA. The majority of these funds are provided for State Grants ($295 million), with the remaining funds ($219 million) supporting National Activities. For FY2009, the Administration has requested $282 million

---

* Excerpted from CRS Report RL34496, dated May 19, 2008

for the SDFSCA. Under this proposal, appropriations for State Grants would be reduced to $100 million, and appropriations for National Activities would be decreased to $182 million. In justifying the requested reduction in State Grant appropriations, the Administration has argued that the structure of the State Grants program is flawed and spreads funding too broadly to support quality interventions.

Many issues are likely to be considered during reauthorization of the SDFSCA program. Issues discussed in this report include the Administration's proposal, recommendations of the Safe and Drug-Free Schools and Communities Act Advisory Board, recommendations of the Secretaries of the U.S. Department of Education (ED) and the U.S. Department of Health and Human Services (HHS), and the U.S. Department of Justice (DOJ), following the Virginia Tech tragedy, and issues of potential concern to Members of Congress.

OVERVIEW

The Safe and Drug-Free Schools and Communities Act (SDFSCA), Title IV-A of the Elementary and Secondary Education Act (ESEA), is the federal government's major initiative to prevent drug abuse and violence in and around schools. The SDFSCA supports two major grant programs — one for states and one for National Activities. It was most recently reauthorized by the ESEA, as amended by the No Child Left Behind Act (P.L. 107-110), in January of 2002. Like all No Child Left Behind Act (NCLB) programs, it is being considered for reauthorization in the 110th Congress.[1]

State Grants

The SDFSCA supports two major grant programs — one for States and one for National Activities. Of the funds authorized for State Grants, 1% or $4.75 million (whichever is greater), is reserved for Guam, American Samoa, the Virgin Islands, and the Commonwealth of Mariana Islands; and the same amount is reserved for the Secretary of the Interior to administer programs for Indian youth. In addition, 0.2% is reserved to provide programs for Native Hawaiians. The remaining funds are distributed to the states, the District of Columbia, and Puerto Rico, by a formula that allocates 50% of the funds on the basis of school-aged population, and 50% in proportion to ESEA Title I, Part A, concentration grants for the preceding fiscal year.[2] States are guaranteed to receive the greater of one-half of one percent of the total allotted to all states, or the amount the state received for FY2001. State governors are permitted to use up to 20% of their state's grant allocation for comprehensive activities that deter youth from using drugs and committing violent acts in schools.

[1] The SDFSCA was initially enacted in 1994 in response to concerns about increased school violence and drug use among school-aged youth. This legislation extended, amended and renamed the Drug-Free Schools and Communities Act of 1988 (DFSCA), extending the DFSCA's mission of drug abuse prevention to include violence prevention. For more detailed information on the historyof this program, see CRS Report RL30482, The Safe and Drug-Free Schools and Communities Program: Background and Context, by Edith Fairman Cooper.

[2] CRS Report RL33731, Education for the Disadvantaged: Issues for ESEA Title I-A Under the No Child Left Behind Act, by Wayne C. Riddle.

Of funds remaining after the governor's share, states are permitted to use up to 3% of their allotment on state administrative activities, and up to 5% of their allotment on other state activities. States must use 93% of their allotment to make formula grants to local educational agencies (LEAs). Practically, this requirement of allocating 93% of state allotments to LEAs means that states must reserve less than the maximum percentage set-aside for state administration or other state activities.

Governors' Grants

Governors are to use their grants for comprehensive activities targeted to children and youth not normally served by State Educational Agency (SEA) or LEA programs, or to children and youth that need special services or additional resources (such as children and youth who are in juvenile detention, runaways or homeless, pregnant or parenting youth, or school dropouts.) Governors award these funds as discretionary grants to LEAs, community based organizations (CBOs), other private or public entities, or consortia thereof. Governors may reserve up to 3% of their grant for administrative costs.

Local Educational Agency Grants

States award grants to LEAs according to a formula that allocates 40% of an LEA's grant on the basis of school enrollment[3] and 60% on the basis of an LEA's relative share of total Title I-A grants for the preceding fiscal year. To receive an SDFSCA grant, all LEAs are required to submit an application to their SEA that includes a detailed explanation of the LEA's comprehensive plan for drug and violence prevention.[4] The LEA must also provide assurances that the LEA or the schools to be served have appropriate policies in place to prohibit, among other things, the illegal possession of weapons and that the school has prevention activities designed to create and maintain a safe, disciplined, and drug-free environment. An assurance must also be included that the LEA or schools to be served have a crisis management plan for responding to violent or traumatic events on school grounds.[5] LEAs may reserve up to 2% of their award for administrative costs. No more than 40% of an LEA's award after reservations may fund school security activities. Of that amount, no more than 50% may be used for security activities other than hiring and training security personnel.

The statute permits LEAs to use funds for a wide variety of activities.[6] Because the list of specifically authorized activities is quite lengthy, these activities have been grouped here into six broad categories.

1. Security Activities

- Acquiring and installing metal detectors and related devices
- Reporting criminal offenses committed on school property

---

[3] Allocations are based on relative enrollments in public and private nonprofit elementary and secondary schools within the LEA's boundaries compared to total such enrollment for all LEAs within the state.

[4] ESEA, Section 4114(d).

[5] ED maintains a website that provides links to resources of potential use to school leaders developing a crisis management plan. More information is available at [http://www.ed.gov/ admins/lead/safety/emergencyplan/index.html].

[6] ESEA, Section 4115.

- Developing and implementing comprehensive school security plans or obtaining technical assistance on such plans
- Supporting safe zones of passage for students to and from school
- Hiring and mandatory training, based on scientific research, of school security personnel

2. Student Testing and Data Reporting

- Drug testing and locker checks (consistent with all legal requirements)
- Establishing or implementing a system to transfer suspension and expulsion records to other schools

3. Education Activities

- Drug and violence prevention activities designed to reduce truancy
- Violence prevention and education activities to reduce victimization due to prejudice and intolerance
- Alternative education programs for violent or drug abusing students, particularly students who have been or are at risk of being suspended or expelled
- Developing and implementing character education programs as part of drug and violence prevention that takes into account the views of students' parents
- Providing for community service and service learning projects

4. Counseling, Mentoring and Other Student Support Activities

- Expanded and improved school-based mental health services including early identification of violence and illegal drug use, assessment, and counseling services for students, parents, families, or school personnel by qualified providers
- Conflict resolution programs, including peer mediation programs and youth anti-crime and anti-drug councils and activities
- Counseling, mentoring, referral services, and other student assistance practices and programs, including assistance from qualified mental health service providers
- Programs that encourage students to confide in and seek advice from trusted adults regarding violence and illegal drug use
- Establishing and maintaining a school safety hotline
- Programs that respond to the needs of students who are faced with domestic violence or child abuse

5. Training and Monitoring of School Personnel

- Professional development and training in prevention education, early identification and intervention, mentoring, or rehabilitation referral, for school personnel, parents and interested community members
- Conducting background checks on all school personnel and prospective employees to see whether they have been convicted of a crime that bears upon the employee's fitness
- Creating an action plan and providing training to school personnel on how to prevent youth suicide

6. Family, Community, and Emergency Activities

- Activities involving families, communities, and drug and violence prevention providers that set expectations and explain the consequences of illegal drug use and violence
- Dissemination of drug and violence prevention information to schools and the community
- Community-wide planning and organizing activities which may include gang activity prevention

Reporting Requirements

The SDFSCA requires states to establish a Uniform Management Information and Reporting System (UMIRS) for the collection and reporting of information related to school safety and drug prevention.[7] Under this system, states must collect and make publicly available the following information:

- truancy rates;
- the frequency, seriousness, and incidence of violence and drug-related offenses resulting in suspensions and expulsions in elementary and secondary schools in the state;
- the types of curricula, programs, and services provided by the state's chief executive officer, the state educational agency (SEA), LEAs, and other recipients of funds under the act; and
- the incidence and prevalence, age of onset, perception of health risk, and perception of social disapproval of violence and drug use by youth in schools and communities.

The first 2 items must be collected and reported on a school-by-school basis; states determine the frequency of data collection. The SDFSCA also includes a gun-free schools provision that requires all states receiving ESEA funds to have a law imposing at least a one-year expulsion for any student who brings a firearm to school. Each state must report data collected from LEAs on any such incidents to the Secretary annually.[8]

States are also required to submit a report annually on the progress they have made on their identified performance measures; this information is submitted as part of the Consolidated State Performance Report required by NCLB. LEAs are required to submit information which is needed by the state to complete this report. States must make this information available to the public. In addition, the statute requires NCES to collect data on the incidence and prevalence of illegal drug use and violence in elementary and secondary schools. NCES does collect data regarding crime and violence occurring in schools.[9] NCES does not collect data on drug use in schools because three surveys are already collecting this data: The Centers for Disease Control and Prevention's (CDC) *Youth Risk Behavior Survey*,

[7] ESEA, Section 4112(c)(3).

[8] ESEA Title IV-A, Subpart 3. The chief administering officer of a local educational agency may modify this expulsion requirement on a case-by-case basis. In addition, the LEA may provide the student with educational services in an alternative setting (Section 4141).

HHS's *National Survey on Drug Use and Health (formerly the National Household Survey on Drug Abuse)*, and the HHS-funded University of Michigan *Monitoring the Future* study.

Program Performance

The U.S. Department of Education (ED) is currently conducting a study on the extent to which LEAs are implementing research-based drug and violence programs; and whether the programs are being implemented consistently with that research. Data for this study were collected from a nationally representative sample of school districts for the 2004-2005 school year; follow-up data are being collected for the 2007-2008 school year. These two questions also serve as Government Performance and Results Act (GPRA) measures for the State Grant program. (Assessment of progress on meeting these goals cannot be made until 2007-08 data are collected and analyzed).

There are five other GPRA measures for the State Grants Program. These five are the percentage of students in grades 9-12 who were offered, sold, or given an illegal drug on school property during the past 12 months; the percentage of students in grades 9-12 who used marijuana one or more times during the past 30 days; the percentage of students in grades 9-12 who had five or more drinks of alcohol in a row one or more times during the past 30 days; the percentage of students in grades 9-12 who were in a physical fight on school property one or more times during the past 12 months; and the percentage of students in grades 9-12 who carried a weapon such as a gun, knife, or club on school property one or more times during the past 30 days. The 2005 targets (the latest data available) for the first 3 indicators were exceeded; the remaining two indicators did not meet their 2005 targets (but the results were not statistically significant). However, these data do not compare participants in SDFSCA programs to non-participants, rather they are nationally representative data from the CDC's Youth Risk Behavior Surveillance System.[10][10]

In addition, ED is conducting a national evaluation of the impact of a particular intervention on reducing middle school violence. This evaluation is assessing the impact of combining a curriculum-based program (Responding in Peaceful and Positive Ways) with a whole school program (Best Behavior), that among other things, is intended to improve teachers' classroom management skills. This evaluation is to compare disruptive, aggressive and violent incidents in 20 middle schools randomly assigned to participate in this program to 20 other middle schools serving as the control group. The first year of data were collected for the 2005-2006 school year. Three years of data are to be collected; results from the study are expected to be released in 2010.

[9] Currently it conducts a survey of school principals called School Survey on Crime Safety and it has a supplement (School Crime Supplement) to the U.S. Dept. of Justice's (DOJ) National Crime Victimization Survey of students ages 12 through 18.

[10] The program has also been evaluated with the Office of Management and Budget's (OMB) Program Assessment Rating Tool (PART) twice. The OMB issued the PART to help assess the management and performance of executive agency programs. In 2002, the SDFSCA State Grants program was rated "ineffective," in 2006, the program was rated "results not demonstrated."

National Activities

The SDFSCA provides general authority to the Secretary to award grants for a variety of National Activities to prevent substance abuse and support violence prevention. The following programs are currently receiving SDFSCA funding under National Activities.

- **Alcohol Abuse Reduction.** Grants to LEAs to develop and implement innovative and effective programs to reduce alcohol abuse in secondary schools. ED may transfer up to 20% of the appropriation for alcohol abuse reduction to the Substance Abuse and Mental Health Services Administration (SAMHSA) of HHS to provide technical assistance to grantees. Grantees are required to implement one of the programs that SAMHSA has determined to be effective in reducing underage alcohol abuse.
- **Mentoring Programs.** Grants are provided to LEAs, non-profit community based organizations (CBOs), or partnerships thereof, to support mentoring programs for children at risk of: educational failure; dropping out of school; involvement in criminal or delinquent activities; or for children who lack positive role models. Priority is to be given to programs that are school-based. Funding must be used for (but is not limited to) training and hiring mentors and other staff, and disseminating outreach materials. However, mentors may not be paid out of grant funds.
- **Impact Evaluation.** Currently impact evaluation funds are used for the study, described above, on the extent to which LEAs are implementing research-based drug and violence programs, and whether they are being implemented consistently with the research based model. Other evaluations are being financed by general National Activities funding.
- **Project Serv (School Emergency Response to Violence).** This program provides education-related services to LEAs that have been disrupted by a violent or traumatic crisis. Project Serv funds may be used for a wide variety of activities, including mental health assessments, referrals, and services for victims and witnesses of violence; enhanced school security; technical assistance on developing a response to the crisis; and training for teachers and staff in implementing the response. Appropriations for this program are requested on a no-year basis; funds remain available for obligation at the federal level until needed. Thus, funds can be carried over from year to year in the event that there are no school-related crises in a given year.
- **Drug Testing.** Supports drug testing programs for K-12 students; funds are also awarded to Institutions of Higher Education for drug prevention and campus safety.
- **Readiness and Emergency Management for Schools.** Previously called the *Emergency Response and Crisis Management Grant Program*. This competitive grant program provides funds to LEAs to strengthen and improve their emergency response and crisis plans at the district and school levels. LEAs are required to form partnerships and collaborate with community organizations, local law enforcement agencies, heads of local government, and offices of public safety, health, and mental health as they review and revise these plans. Plans are required to be coordinated with state or local homeland security plans and must support the implementation of

the National Incident Management System (NIMS). Grants may be used for training school safety teams and students, conducting facility audits, informing families about emergency response policies, implementing an Incident Command System (ICS), conducting drills and simulation exercises, preparing and distributing copies of crisis plans, and, to a limited extent, for purchasing school safety equipment. Grantees under this program may receive support in managing and implementing their projects and sustaining their efforts over time from the Emergency Response and Crisis Management Technical Assistance Center.[11]

- **SDFSCA Advisory Committee.** This committee was created by ED's Secretary, Margaret Spellings in June of 2006. The Committee was given a mandate to examine several specific issues and has issued a report providing its responses and recommendations (discussed below).
- **Safe Schools/Healthy Students (SS/HS) Grant Program.** The SS/HS is funded jointly by ED and the U.S. Department of Health and Human Services, Substance Abuse and Mental Health Services Administration (SAMHSA). The program is administered by ED, SAMHSA, and the U.S. Department of Justice (DOJ). The SS/HS initiative is a discretionary grant program that provides services for students, schools, and communities with federal funding via LEAs, to implement an enhanced, coordinated, comprehensive plan of activities, programs, and services that focus on healthy childhood development and the prevention of violence and alcohol and drug abuse. Grantees are required to establish partnerships with local law enforcement, public mental health, and juvenile justice agencies/entities.

Additionally, specifically authorized programs that previously have received SDFSCA National Activities funding are

- National Coordinator Program (funded from 1999-2004).
- Community Service Grant Program (funded in 2002 and 2003).

Specifically authorized programs that have never received SDFSCA National Activities funding are

- Hate Crimes Prevention,
- School Security and Technology Resource Center, and
- National Center for School and Youth Safety.

[11] Additional information is available at [http://www.ercm.org/] and [http://www.ed.gov/programs/dvpemergencyresponse/resources.html].

Funding

For FY2008, $513 million was appropriated for the SDFSCA.[12] The majority of these funds are provided for State Grants ($295 million), with the remaining funds ($219 million) supporting National Activities. For FY2009, the President has requested $282 million for the SDFSCA. Under this proposal, appropriations for State Grants would be reduced to $100 million and appropriations for National Activities would be decreased to $182 million. In justifying the requested reduction in State Grant appropriations, the Administration has argued that the structure of the State Grants program is flawed and spreads funding too broadly to support quality interventions.[13]

Reauthorization Issues

The following discussion of SDFSCA reauthorization issues and proposals is divided into 4 sections. Firstly, the Administration's proposal for a major restructuring of the SDFSCA program is discussed. Secondly, recommendations of the Safe and Drug-Free Advisory Committee are summarized. This Committee was convened by Secretary Spellings in June of 2006 to examine a variety of issues — including the SDFSCA state grants program and data collection. Thirdly, the findings of the Secretaries of ED and HHS, and the Attorney General, regarding proposals to improve violence prevention in light of the Virginia Tech incident are summarized. Finally, major reauthorization issues that are likely to be considered by Congress are addressed.

The Administration's FY2009 Reauthorization Proposal

The Administration has proposed restructuring the SDFSCA program by significantly decreasing the role of State Grants and refocusing National Activities. The Administration argues that currently State Grants are not targeted to LEAs most in need of funding, and that the grants received by LEAs are often too small to fund a quality program:

> SDFSC State Grants provide more than half of local educational agencies (LEAs) with allocations of less than $10,000, amounts typically too small to mount comprehensive and effective drug and school safety programs.[14]

Funding for State Grants would be reduced in FY2009 to $100 million (FY2008 funding equals $294.8 million) and would no longer be distributed by states to LEAs by formula. The Administration proposes that SEAs use these funds to provide training, technical assistance

---

12 The House passed an amendment to the FY2008 Labor HHS Education Appropriations bill that would shift $46.5 million in funding from Reading First to the SDFSCA program, in order to maintain FY2008 funding ($513 million) at roughly the FY2007 level.

13 U.S. Department of Education. Justifications of Appropriation Estimates to the Congress: Fiscal Year 2009, Volume I.

14 U.S. Department of Education. Justifications of Appropriation Estimates to the Congress: Fiscal Year 2009, Volume I, p. F-20.

and information on effective programs to LEAs. States could also use funds to provide competitive grants to a limited number of LEAs.

National Activities would be funded in FY2009 at $182 million (FY2008 funding was $218.6 million) and reorganized into a single flexible grant program focusing on four broad areas: emergency planning; preventing violence and drug use, school culture and climate; and emerging needs. According to the Administration most of these grants would provide direct support to LEAs

> ... in sufficient amounts to make a real difference, for targeted projects that address key national concerns and are structured in a manner that permits grantees and independent evaluators to measure progress, hold projects accountable, and determine which interventions are most effective. [15]

Related programs authorized under ESEA provisions other than Title IV include Mentoring, Physical Education, Elementary and Secondary School Counseling, and Civic Education. All four would be eliminated under the Administration's proposal.[16] In addition, Character Education would no longer be a distinct program with its own authority (currently it is authorized by ESEA Title V-D, Subpart 3), but it would continue to receive funding under the National Grants Program in the FY2009 proposal.

The SDFSCA Advisory Committee Recommendations

The SDFSCA Advisory Committee was created in June 2006 by ED Secretary, Margaret Spellings.[17] The Committee is made up of representatives from several Federal agencies, state and local government representatives, and individuals with relevant expertise. The Committee was asked by the Secretary to examine the SDFSCA State Grants Program, the NCLB unsafe school choice option (discussed briefly below), and the collection of safety data. Following the Virginia Tech tragedy, the Secretary asked the Committee to also examine three additional issues: trauma; nonpublic schools; and urban/rural challenges.

On June 11, 2007, the Committee issued a report with its findings and recommendations regarding the issues it was charged with examining.[18] The Committee held six meetings, conducted six conference calls, and heard testimony from 38 witnesses. The Committee's recommendations are summarized below by issue (recommendations on trauma, nonpublic schools and urban/rural challenges are incorporated within the discussion of the other issues).

State Grant Issues

According to the Committee's report:

---

[15] U.S. Department of Education. Justifications of Appropriation Estimates to the Congress: Fiscal Year 2008, Volume I, p. F-15.

[16] Physical Education and Elementary and Secondary School Counseling are authorized by ESEA, Title V, Part D, Fund for the Improvement of Education. Civic Education is authorized by ESEA, Title II, Part C, Subpart 3.

[17] It is authorized by ESEA, Section 4124.

[18] U.S. Department of Education, Safe and Drug-Free Schools and Communities Advisory Committee, Enhancing Achievement And Proficiency Through Safe And Drug-Free Schools, Washington, D.C., June 2007.

Underlying all of the Committee's recommendations is the need for clearer standards for all recipients of grant funds, including the Governors portion of the program. [19]

The Committee expressed support (with some reservations) for allowing states to use a larger share of SDFSCA state grants for state purposes, in particular, to provide technical assistance and help with data collection to LEAs. There was also support for making changes to the Governors funds. Proposals included making the funds contingent on the collection of data on school safety and drug abuse, or shifting the funds back to the states.

The Committee noted that presently there is no consensus at the federal or state level on the definition of safety and drug and alcohol problems, and as a consequence no consensus on desired outcomes or measures of effectiveness. The Committee report stated: "...at all levels, the current implementation of the State Grants Program has not required the use of data to determine needs." It recommended that ED provide states and LEAs with clear measurable outcomes of success, encourage improved program assessment, and provide clear guidelines on effective prevention programs. These changes would require collection of uniform data on key indicators of safety and drug and alcohol abuse from all schools and LEAs.

Because of limited federal funding for the SDFSCA program, the Committee recommended that there be more incentives incorporated into the program to foster local partnerships, possibly including a requirement for local matching funds. In addition, there was significant support among the Committee members for changing the program from the current system of allocating funds to all LEAs by formula), to a system in which funds are controlled by states and grants are awarded competitively to LEAs to fund priority needs.

The Committee recommended increased emphasis be placed on program compliance with the SDFSCA "Principles of Effectiveness," and on the identification and testing of promising innovative programs. It encouraged ED to develop separate guidelines for rural and urban schools appropriate to the unique challenges faced by each in implementing drug and alcohol prevention programs and safety efforts. And, it recommended the development of explicit guidelines on the requirements LEAs must meet in working with nonpublic schools. In addition, the Committee recommended that cooperation among the Federal agencies providing support for drug and alcohol prevention and increased safety be improved and enhanced.

Unsafe School Choice Option (USCO)

USCO is authorized by the ESEA, Title IX-E-2, Section 9532, not as part of the SDFSCA. It requires states to establish statewide policies under which any student who attends a persistently dangerous public elementary or secondary school, or who becomes a victim of a violent crime while in or on the grounds of the public elementary or secondary school he or she attends, must be offered the opportunity to transfer to another public school within the same LEA. (For information on USCO see CRS Report RL33371, *K-12 Education, Implementation Status of the No Child Left Behind Act of 2001 (P.L. 107-110).*) The Committee found the USCO "has not been as effective as the need it addresses requires." The Committee made several recommendations for improvements including the following.

---

[19] Ibid.

- Allowing, in addition to consideration of violent incidents, other indicators (such as substance abuse, bullying, gang activity, racism) of school safety to be factored into the determination of whether a school is safe.
- The provision, by ED, of training for administrators, teachers and other school personnel on how best to assist students who are victims or victimizers, including transfer options.
- Reexamination of the term "persistently dangerous." The Committee felt that this terminology stigmatizes schools and unduly penalizes schools that accurately report violent incidents. It recommended using more neutral terminology; for example, schools might be put on a "watch list" and given priority for SDFSCA state grant funding. The Committee also recommended assistance be provided to schools experiencing significant safety problems.
- The provision, by ED, of guidelines for schools with safety problems on ways to improve safety including information on best practices. ED could also provide support and technical assistance to these schools.
- Improving the ability of schools to cope with potential tragedies by educating school personnel on how these events can affect students and on how to identify warning signs that a student needs intervention (such as counseling). ED could provide assistance by distributing information on best practices and providing training on how to identify and refer students at risk for assistance early on.

Data Requirements

The Committee recommended that serious consideration should be given to what data are most important and whether it is possible for states and LEAs to collect it. Data collection could be coordinated by agencies working on alcohol and drug abuse and safety to minimize the burden on states and LEAs. ED could play an important role in coordinating data collection by federal agencies so that only one set of data are being collected. Coordination between federal agencies and state and local governments would also be useful. Consideration should be given to formulating a uniform set of questions for states and LEAs to use for program evaluation.

The Secretary's Recommendations

Following the Virginia Tech tragedy, President George W. Bush asked Secretary Margaret Spellings, Secretary Mike Leavitt of the Department of Health and Human Services and Attorney General Alberto Gonzales of the Department of Justice to meet with local officials and experts across the country, and to report on their findings on issues raised by the tragedy. On June 13, 2007, the group issued its report that included the following findings regarding important issues in need of local, state, and federal action.

- Information sharing is critical in instances such as the Virginia Tech tragedy. However, there is confusion among education, public safety, and mental health staff regarding what information can be shared on individuals who are a threat to themselves or others.

- Information regarding individuals who may not legally own a gun is crucial, but currently is not always accurate and complete.
- Prevention of future tragedies requires improved awareness and communication.
- People with mental illnesses must get the services they need — currently some feel that there are insufficient resources available to meet this need, especially at colleges and universities.
- Make better use of current knowledge of best practices in emergency preparedness and violence prevention. Disseminate information on examples of successful programs, and facilitate their implementation.[20]

Reauthorization Status in the 110th Congress

As of the date of this report there has been no action on legislation to reauthorize the No Child Left Behind Act in the U.S. House of Representatives or the U.S. Senate. A draft House reauthorization bill was circulated for public comment, but a bill has not yet been introduced. Some of the major SDFSCA reauthorization issues that may to be considered by Congress include the following.

- Whether (absent significant increases in appropriations) the funding level for the program is sufficient to support the allocation of funds to all LEAs by formula. Currently more than half of LEAs receive SDFSCA grants of less than $10,000. Questions have been raised regarding whether such small grants can support effective programs.
- Although the last reauthorization adjusted the formula to put more emphasis on awarding grants on the basis of poverty, some argue that switching to competitively awarded LEA grants would allow for better targeting of school districts most in need of SDFSCA funds.
- Strengthened data collection and reporting requirements. Currently Uniform Management Information and Reporting System (UMIRS) data is collected by each state relying upon state definitions of required data items. As a consequence data are not comparable across states. States are required to report these data to the public, but the frequency of collection and reporting is determined by each state. ED has recently issued a publication providing definitions of UMIRS reporting items titled *The Uniform Data Set: A Guide to Measures for the Uniform Management Information and Reporting System*. It would require states to report some required data items using these definitions, to the extent feasible. ED may accelerate these efforts once the data requirements adopted in a reauthorized program are known. During reauthorization the issue of uniform data standards may be considered. Reauthorization legislation may require annual reporting of these data to ED, as well as to the public.

---

[20] Michael Leavitt, Margaret Spellings, and Alberto Gonzales, Report To The President On Issues Raised By The Virginia Tech Tragedy. June 13, 2007.

- An increased emphasis on programs to prevent bullying and harassment (believed to be key to violence prevention). Bullying is a serious problem at many schools; in 2005, approximately 28% of 12 to 18 year old students reported that they were bullied at school in the last six months.[21]
- Provision of comprehensive mental health programs. The Virginia Tech tragedy and similar events heightened awareness that access to mental health services is an important component of preventing school violence.
- How to improve performance measures for the program. ED is currently collecting data on the extent to which LEAs are implementing research based programs, and if the implementation of those programs is consistent with the research based model. ED has collected data for 2005, which is serving as the base year. Targets for these measures have been set for 2008; these data are not yet available. In addition, ED collects data for five measures tabulating the percentage of students in grades 9-12 who (1) were offered, sold, or given an illegal drug on school property during the past 12 months; (2) had 5 or more drinks in a row during the past 30 days, (3) were in a physical fight on school property during the past 12 months, or (4) carried a weapon on school property one or more times during the past 30 days. These data are from the CDC's Youth Risk Behavior Surveillance Survey, which is based on a nationally representative biennial sample of students in grades 9-12. However, given the scope of SDFSCA programs under current funding levels, only a small percentage of students in grades 9-12 can be served by comprehensive violence and drug abuse prevention programs. As a consequence, some believe these national measures do not accurately reflect the program's performance.
- Emergency Management. Legislation to reauthorize the SDFSCA may increase the emphasis on enhancing local emergency planning for all potential hazards in and around schools through a variety of mechanisms, including increased cooperation with first responders, and relevant local, state, and federal agencies. A recent Government Accountability Office (GAO) report found that most school districts would benefit from more federal guidance in developing emergency plans.[22] Its recommendations for ED (in cooperation with the Department of Homeland Security and HHS, as appropriate) included developing procedures for continuing student education during a prolonged school closure due to an emergency; the examination and identification of successful practices for evacuating and sheltering students and

---

[21] Dinkes, R., Cataldi, E., and Lin-Kelly, W. (2007), *Indicators of School Crime and Safety*. National Center for Education Statistics, U.S. Dept. of Education and Bureau of Justice Statistics, U.S. Dept of Justice. Washington, D.C.

[22] GAO-07-609, EMERGENCY MANAGEMENT: Most School Districts Have Developed Emergency Management Plans, but Would Benefit from Additional Federal Guidance. U. S. Government Accountability Office, June 2007.

staff with special needs during emergencies; identifying the impediments to collaboration in emergencies between LEAs, first responders, and community partners, and the development and dissemination of strategies to enhance such cooperation.

In: The War on Drugs: Winning, Losing or Treading Water ISBN 978-1-59454-235-0
Editor: Nelson V. Arcos

Chapter 4

MARIJUANA FOR MEDICAL PURPOSES: A GLIMPSE OF THE SUPREME COURT'S DECISION IN UNITED STATES V. OAKLAND CANNABIS BUYERS' COOPERATIVE AND RELATED LEGAL ISSUES *

Charles Doyle

SUMMARY

There is no medical necessity defense against prosecution for the federal crimes of cultivating or distributing marijuana, even in places where state law recognizes such a defense. So said the Supreme Court in *United States v. Oakland Cannabis Buyers' Cooperative*, 532 U.S. 483, 486 (2001). Although there may be some question as to their vitality, the Court left undecided issues involving a necessity defense for possession and possible commerce clause, enactment clause, and due process clause challenges. In *Gonzales v. Raich*, 125 S.Ct. 2195 (2005), the Court held that Congress's' power under the commerce clause enabled it to enact a regulatory scheme that extended to the purely local cultivation and possession of marijuana for medical purposes. There are proposals in this Congress to reverse the impact of the Court's decisions.

Background

The federal Controlled Substances Act (the Act) outlaws the cultivation, distribution, or possession of marijuana. The ban is a component of federal and state schemes which regulate the sale and possession of drugs and other controlled substances. The State of California has created a medical necessity exception to its marijuana prohibitions. The Oakland Cannabis Buyers Cooperative (the Coop) was one of the entities which dispensed marijuana to patients qualified to receive it under state law.

* Excerpted from CRS Report RS20998 dated June 14, 2005

Federal authorities sued to enjoin cultivation and distribution of marijuana in violation of federal law by the Coop and its suppliers. The federal district court granted a preliminary injunction, which the Court of Appeals overturned for failure to consider an implicit medical necessity defense.

The necessity or "choice of evils" defense has been recognized under various circumstances by a number of other lower federal appellate courts. The Supreme Court seemed to verify its vitality, at least indirectly, when it described the prerequisites for the defense to an escape charge: "where a criminal defendant is charged with escape and claims that he is entitled to an instruction on the theory of duress or necessity, he must proffer evidence of a bona fide effort to surrender or return to custody as soon as the claimed . . . necessity has lost its coercive force."

Supreme Court's Coop Decision

The Coop argued that necessity, as a common law defense, was an implicit exception to the Act's prohibitions. No member of the Supreme Court agreed. In fact, the Court questioned the very existence of a federal necessity defense, although as the concurring opinion points out, the case holds no more than that there is no necessity defense to the federal proscription on the cultivation or distribution of marijuana.

On the basic point, the members of the Court were of one mind — Congress in the Act addressed and rejected the very exception for which the Coop sought recognition. Congress outlawed manufacturing or distributing controlled substances except as authorized in the Act. The only authorized exception for Schedule I controlled substances, such as marijuana, is government approved research; the Coop did not argue that it was engaged in government approved research; there is no other explicit exception for marijuana.

But the federal necessity defense is a creature of common law, frequently assumed if rarely cited by name, and Congress did not reject it by name. Yet Congress did limit Schedule I to those controlled substances with "no currently accepted medical use." It assigned marijuana to Schedule I. Thus, "[i]t is clear from the text of the Act that Congress has made a determination that marijuana has no medical benefits worthy of an exception. The statute expressly contemplates that many drugs <have a useful and legitimate medical purpose and are necessary to maintain the health and general welfare of the American people,' §801(a), but it includes no exception at all for any medical use of marijuana. Unwilling to view this omission as an accident, and unable in any event to override a legislative determination manifest in a statute, [the Court] reject[ed] the Cooperative's argument."

The clarity of Congress's' rejection of a medical necessary defense doomed the Coop's invocation of the constitutional avoidance doctrine, a canon of statutory construction available only in cases of ambiguity. The Court declined to consider the constitutional issues which might have called for avoidance in the face of an ambiguity because the lower court had not raised them.

Constitutional Issues

Although the Court set them aside, the Coop's brief presented commerce clause, enactment clause and due process clause questions. The commerce clause, in conjunction with the enactment or necessary and proper clause, empowers Congress to enact legislation regulating interstate and foreign commerce. Congress passed the Act, at least in part, as an exercise of its powers under the common clause.

Congress's' commerce clause powers are substantial but not unlimited. The Court summarized the scope of those powers in *Lopez* and *Morrison*, two instances where the commerce clause was found insufficient to support a claim of legislative authority. "First, Congress may regulate the use of the channels of interstate commerce. Second, Congress is empowered to regulate and protect the instrumentalities of interstate commerce, or persons or things in interstate commerce, even though the threat may come only from intrastate activities. Finally, Congress's' commerce authority includes the power to regulate those activities having a substantial relation to interstate commerce, . . . *i.e.*, those activities that substantially affect interstate commerce."

Recognizing that the boundaries of this last category of commerce clause power, intrastate activity with an interstate impact, are not always easily identified, *Morrison* and *Lopez* identified some of the signs which reveal that a regulated activity may in fact have no significant impact on interstate commerce. "First, [they] observed that §922(q) [the section at issue in *Lopez*] was a criminal statute that by its terms has nothing to do with commerce or any sort of economic enterprise, however broadly one might define those terms . . . . The second consideration . . . that we found important . . . was that the statute contained no express jurisdictional element which might limit its reach to a discrete set of firearms possessions that additionally have an explicit connection with or effect on interstate commerce . . . . Third, we noted that neither §922(q) nor its legislative history contains express congressional findings regarding the effects upon interstate commerce of gun possession in a school zone . . . . Finally, our decision in *Lopez* rested in part on the fact that the link between gun possession and a substantial effect on interstate commerce was attenuated."

The Coop argued that "[o]nly the cultivation and distribution of cannabis in exchange for money or barter can be considered commerce, but even such commerce here is exclusively intrastate and therefore not within the power of Congress to regulate commerce among the states." Yet the Act, including its proscriptions on the cultivation, distribution and possession of marijuana, appears to be within the Congress's commerce clause powers as described in *Lopez* and *Morrison*. They identify as indicative of criminal statutes beyond the clause's reach those which purport to punish activities that have "nothing to do with commerce or any sort of economic enterprise." As the Coop's very name (Oakland Cannabis *Buyers'*) indicates, cultivation, distribution, or possession of marijuana almost always involves or is closely linked to some form of commercial activity — particularly if distribution requires the participation of physicians and health care insurers. Even marijuana grown at home for personal medical use might find its way within a regulatory scheme under the commerce clause. *Lopez* and *Morrison* cite with approval *Wickard v. Filburn* in which the Court upheld the regulation of wheat grown locally for home consumption as a rationale component of the regulation of the interstate wheat market.

In *Gonzales v. Raich*, the Court followed the path laid out in *Wickard*. It had "no difficulty concluding that Congress had a rational basis for believing that failure to regulate the intrastate manufacture and possession of marijuana would leave a gaping hole in the CSA" in light of "the enforcement difficulties that attend distinguishing between marijuana cultivated locally and marijuana grown elsewhere" as well as "concerns about diversion into illicit channels." In the mind of the Court "when it enacted comprehensive legislation to regulate the interstate market in a fungible commodity, Congress was acting well within its authority to 'make Laws which shall be necessary and proper' to 'regulate Commerce . . . among the several States.' That the regulation ensnares some purely intrastate activity is of no moment."

Even if Congress had lacked the legislative authority to ban cultivation, distribution and possession of marijuana under the commerce clause, its legislative authority to implement our various treaty obligations for the suppression of illicit controlled substances would probably be sufficient.

When Congress enjoys legislative subject matter jurisdiction, such as the power to regulate interstate and foreign commerce, it may nevertheless elect to pass laws which exceed what is constitutionally "proper" under the implementary necessary and proper or enacting clause. For instance, legislation is not "proper for carrying into execution" constitutionally vested powers, such as those under the commerce clauses, when it seeks to "compel the states to enact or enforce a federal regulatory program" or to when it issues "directives requiring the states to address particular problems, [or] command[s] the states' officers, or those of their political subdivisions, to administer or enforce a federal regulatory program.

The Coop argued that Congress is not acting in the necessary and proper exercise of its legislative authority when it acts in total derogation of rights which the people of a given state have identified as fundamental unenumerated constitutional rights. The contention may have helped spur the three concurring members of the Court to urge at least a rule of construction that would recognize a medical necessity defense for marijuana possession. The majority's sweeping dicta and the accompanying footnote which sparked Justice Stevens' comments, however, may reflect the fact that at least five members of the Court found the "necessary and proper" argument unpersuasive.

Of course, the Coop's Ninth Amendment fundamental-unenumerated-rights argument is closely akin to its substantive due process contentions, i.e., that "these patients have a fundamental right to be free from government interdiction of their personal self-funded medical decision, in consultation with their physician, to alleviate their suffering through the only alternative available to them."

The due process clause "provides heightened protection against government interference with certain fundamental rights and liberty interests. . . .[I]n addition to the specific freedoms protected by the Bill of Rights, the liberty specially protected by the due process clause includes the rights . . . to bodily integrity and to abortion . . . [and in all likelihood] to refuse unwanted lifesaving medical treatment." The Court, however, has been reluctant to expand the concept of substantive due process, and has specifically refused to consider physician assisted suicide among the fundamental liberties so protected.

Glucksberg seems to pose a major obstacle to recognition of a right to use marijuana for medicinal purposes, for it appears to have refused to acknowledge the right which the Coop claims. The Coop claims patients have "a fundamental right to be free from government interdiction of their personal self-funded medical decision, in consultation with their physician, to alleviate their suffering." *Glucksberg* found that terminally ill patients facing the prospect of a painful death have no due process right to the assistance of their physicians to secure and assist in the administration of painless but fatal substances to alleviate their suffering.

Beyond this, the *Glucksberg* expansion tests are not particularly helpful. They require that those rights within the ambit of due process protection consist of "those fundamental rights and liberties which are, objectively, deeply rooted in this Nation's history and tradition, and implicit in the concept of order liberty, such that neither liberty nor justice would exist if they were sacrificed." The history of the Coop's asserted right is arguably exactly the opposite. It is a history replete with government regulation of the practice of medicine, of the distribution and use of medicinal products, of controlled substances, and of marijuana in particular.

Federal regulation of marijuana as a crime control measure dates back from the Marihuana Tax Act of 1937, by which time every state in the Union already regulated its sale. The Act was modeled after the more general Harrison Narcotics Act of 1914 under which opium and other narcotics were regulated. Congress passed the earlier Food and Drug Act of 1906 "to prevent the manufacture, sale or transportation of adulterated, misbranded or poisonous, or deleterious foods, drugs, medicines, or drugs and for regulating the traffic therein," 34 Stat. 768 (1906). In more general terms, "the practice of medicine . . . has a long history of being regulated to protect the public safety."

Glucksberg's dicta seems to further undermine any contention that due process substantially restricts the federal government's authority to refuse to legalize marijuana for medical use. There, the Court cited *United States v. Rutherford*, for the observation that "Congress could reasonably [determine] to protect the terminally ill, no less than other patients, from the vast range of self-styled panaceas that inventive minds can devise." Here, Congress appears to have done just that. It has concluded that marijuana is highly addictive and has no accepted medical use, but permits reclassification of marijuana and its subsequent use when and if its medicinal benefits can be demonstrated under the procedures of the Controlled Substances Act.

Finally, although the issue was not raised in *Oakland Cannabis Buyers' Cooperative*, the lower federal courts initially appeared divided over whether the First Amendment right to free speech shields physicians who prescribe or otherwise recommend marijuana to their patients. A court in the Northern District of California granted a preliminary injunction enjoining federal authorities from prosecuting physicians for such conduct. The order also prohibited federal authorities from revoking the physicians registration to prescribe controlled substances and from excluding them from Medicare/Medicaid participation for such conduct. The court subsequently made the injunction permanent in an unpublished opinion. It found serious questions as to whether the federal enforcement policy permitted a content-based restriction on speech and whether it was unconstitutionally vague.

A court in the District of Columbia, on the other hand, refused to issue a similar injunction. From the D.C. court's perspective, "there are no First Amendment protections for speech that is used as an integral part of conduct in violation of a valid criminal statute." Therefore, "even though state law may allow for the prescription or recommendation of medicinal marijuana within its borders, to do so is still a violation of federal law. . . . The fact that speech or writing is the mechanism used by physicians to carry out such a task does not make the conduct less violative of federal law. The First Amendment does not prohibit the federal government from taking action against physicians whose prescription or recommendation of medicinal marijuana violates the [Act]."

The Ninth Circuit muted the prospect of a conflict when it held that while the First Amendment precludes punishing doctors simply because they recommend that their patients use marijuana, it did not preclude punishment of a doctor who intends his patient to use the recommendation to acquire marijuana in violation of federal law.

Related Legislative Activity

State medical marijuana initiatives have provoked a mixed response in Congress including proposals to:

- require the Attorney General to revoke the controlled substance registration of any practitioner who recommended marijuana for medical purposes;
- bar those who recommend marijuana for medical purposes from participating in Medicare and state health care programs;
- clarify and increase the penalties applicable to Controlled Substance Act violations by registrants;
- make mandatory, in those states with a medical marijuana exception, the discretionary denial of federal benefits for those convicted of controlled substance offenses;
- make it clear that Controlled Substance Act provisions continue to apply notwithstanding the massage of state medical marijuana laws;
- provide that the Controlled Substance Act shall supersede any state law with which it differs;
- study the impact of the California and Arizona medical marijuana initiatives;
- create a federal medical marijuana exception to the Controlled Substances Act and the Federal Food, Drug and Cosmetic Act in the states with medical marijuana laws;
- prohibit use of funds appropriated for the District of Columbia to conduct any ballot initiative to legalize or reduce the penalties for violations involving Schedule I controlled substances;
- prohibit use of funds appropriated for the District of Columbia to enact or implement any law to legalize or reduce the penalties for violations involving Schedule I controlled substances (and prohibiting the D.C. medical marijuana referendum from taking effect)(Barr Amendment); and
- prohibit the recipients of transit grants from promoting the legalization or medical use of schedule I controlled substances, like marijuana.

In the 108th Congress, Congressmen Farr (H.R. 1717) and Frank (H.R. 2233) offered bills creating a medical marijuana exception in states where the exemption is recognized. And both the House and Senate versions of the D.C. appropriations legislation for FY2004 include the Barr Amendment (H.R. 2765, §123/S. 1583, §126).

Thus far in the 109th Congress only successor to Congressman Frank's proposal H.R. 2087, has appeared.

In: The War on Drugs: Winning, Losing or Treading Water ISBN 978-1-59454-235-0
Editor: Nelson V. Arcos

Chapter 5

DRUG CONTROL: INTERNATIONAL POLICY AND APPROACHES *

Raphael Perl

SUMMARY

Efforts to significantly reduce the flow of illicit drugs from abroad into the United States have so far not succeeded. Moreover, over the past decade, worldwide production of illicit drugs has risen dramatically: opium and marijuana production has roughly doubled and coca production tripled. Street prices of cocaine and heroin have fallen significantly in the past 20 years, reflecting increased avail-ability. The effectiveness of international narcotics control programs in reducing consumption is a matter of ongoing concern. Despite apparent national political resolve to deal with the drug problem, inherent contra-dictions regularly appear between U.S. anti-drug policy and other national policy goals and concerns. Pursuit of drug control policies can sometimes affect foreign policy interests and bring political instability and economic dislocation to countries where narcotics production has become entrenched economically and socially. Drug supply interdiction programs and U.S. systems to facilitate the international movement of goods, people, and wealth are often at odds. U.S. international narcotics policy requires cooperative efforts by many nations which may have domestic and foreign policy goals that compete with the requirements of drug control. The mix of competing domestic and international pressures and priorities has produced an ongoing series of disputes within and between the legislative and executive branches concerning U.S. international drug policy. One contentious issue has been the Congressionally-mandated certification process, an instrument designed to induce specified drug-exporting countries to prioritize or pay more attention to the fight against narcotics businesses. Current law requires the President, with certain exceptions, to designate and withhold assistance from countries that have failed demonstrably to meet their counter narcotics obligations. P.L. 106-246, "Plan Colombia," a $1.3 billion military assistance-focused initiative to provide emergency supplemental narcotics assistance to Colombia, was signed into law July 13, 2000. Recently,

* Excerpted from CRS Report IB88093 dated February 2, 2006

U.S. policy toward Colombia has focused increasingly on containing the terrorist threat to that country's security. The Bush Administration's FY2005 budget request continues a policy, begun in FY2002, to request authority for the State and Defense Departments to supply assistance to Colombia for counterterrorism purposes. For instance, U.S.-supplied helicopters and intelligence could be used to support military operations against guerrillas financed by drugs as well as against drug traffickers themselves. See CRS Report RL32337, *Andean Counterdrug Initiative (ACI) and Related Funding Programs: FY2005 Assistance.*

An issue likely to achieve increased attention in the 109th Congress is that of sky-rocketing opium poppy cultivation in Afghanistan and whether to press for aerial crop eradication against the wishes of the local Afghan leadership. See CRS Report RL32686, *Afghanistan: Narcotics and U.S. Policy.*

Drug control approaches addressed in this issue brief include:

- Expansion of efforts to reduce foreign production at the source.
- Expansion of interdiction and enforcement activities to disrupt supply lines.
- Expansion of efforts to reduce worldwide demand.
- Expansion of economic disincentives for international drug trafficking.

MOST RECENT DEVELOPMENTS

On January 28, 2006, President Evo Morales of Bolivia appointed Felipe Caceres, a coca leaf grower, to head his government's fight against drug trafficking — escalating concern in U.S. policy circles that Morales will follow through on his pre-election pledge to roll back U.S. efforts to curb coca production in Bolivia. U.S. counter narcotics programs in Bolivia were funded at $79.2 million in FY2006 (alternative development and law enforcement). The Administration's FY2007 request is expected to be somewhat less.

A report released by the Government Accountability Office (GAO-06-200) argues for the development of better counter-drug performance measures by government agencies and warns that the diversion of military assets to Iraq and Afghanistan is likely to hamper the ability of U.S. law enforcement to intercept drug shipments in the future. Proponents of strong drug interdiction policies have long been concerned that the nation's focus on anti-terror objectives will detract from resources and political will needed to combat foreign source illicit drug production and trafficking.

BACKGROUND AND ANALYSIS

Problem

More than 14 million Americans buy illicit drugs and use them at least once per month, spending by most conservative estimates over $60 billion annually in a diverse and fragmented criminal market. Such drugs are to varying degrees injurious to the health, judgment, productivity and general well-being of their users. The 2002 *National Drug*

Control Strategy (hereafter *Strategy*) of the White House Office of National Drug Control Policy (ONDCP) estimates the total costs of drug abuse to American society to be approximately $160 billion. The major components of this total are health care costs ($14.9 billion), workplace productivity losses ($110.5 billion) and losses related to crime, the criminal justice system, and social welfare ($35 billion). According to the *Strategy* more than 60% of the inmates in the federal prison system are drug law violators; moreover, the addictive nature and high price of most illegal drugs contribute significantly to the incidence of violent crime and property crime in the United States. Additionally, the U.S. illicit drug market generates billions of dollars in profits. Such profits provide international drug trafficking organizations with the resources to effectively evade and compete with law enforcement agencies, to penetrate legitimate economic structures, and, in some instances, to challenge the authority of national governments.

Calculated in dollar value terms, at least four-fifths of all the illicit drugs consumed in the United States are of foreign origin, including virtually all the cocaine and heroin and most of the marijuana, according to the ONDCP *Strategy* and the U.S. Drug Enforcement Administration (DEA) 2002 report, *Drug Trafficking in the United States*. According to DEA, the methamphetamine market is supplied predominantly from laboratories in both the United States and Mexico while most of the hallucinogens and illegally marketed psychotherapeutic drugs and "designer" drugs are of domestic U.S. origin.

Drugs are a lucrative business and a mainspring of global criminal activity. According to a 2002 estimate by the State Department's Bureau of International Narcotics and Law Enforcement Affairs (INL), as much as 930 tons of cocaine could have been produced from coca leaf grown in South America in 2001. If sold internationally at an average U.S. street price per gram of $100, the drug would yield a gross value of $93 billion, a figure exceeding the Gross National Income of three-quarters of the world's nations. A November 2002 study by the United Nations Office on Drugs and Crime estimated the net regional earnings of the illicit drug industry in the Caribbean at $3.3 billion, or about half the Gross National Income of Jamaica or Trinidad. Little is known about the distribution of revenues from illicit drug sales, but foreign supply cartels exercise considerable control over wholesale distribution in the United States and illicit proceeds are often laundered and invested through foreign banks and financial institutions.

In December 2002, the Chief of Operations of the U.S. Drug Enforcement Administration (DEA) told a Congressional panel that the number of hard-core heroin users in the United States had increased to "almost a million" from an estimated 630,000 in 1992. The DEA Heroin Signature Program, which identifies the sources of that drug seized by U.S. federal authorities, found that 56% of the seized heroin was of Colombian origin.

The federal anti-drug initiative has two major elements: (1) reduction of demand and (2) reduction of supply. Reduction of demand is sought through education to prevent dependence, through treatment to cure addiction and through measures to increase prices and risk of apprehension at the consumer level. Reduction of supply (which currently accounts for about 53% of the federal anti-drug control budget, according to the *Strategy*) is sought by programs aimed at destabilizing the operations of illicit drug cartels at all levels and severing their links to political power, and by seizing their products, businesses, and financial assets. As most illicit drugs are imported, a major interdiction campaign is being conducted on the U.S. borders, at ports of entry, on the high seas, and along major foreign transshipment routes and at production sites. An international program of source crop eradication is also being pursued. As reported in the *Strategy*, approximately 18% of the requested federal drug control budget of $11.7 billion for FY2004 is for interdiction and 9.2% is for international assistance programs. These ratios continue to remain relatively constant. The major international components of federal policies for the reduction of illicit supply are discussed below.

On or about March 7, 2005, the State Department released its annual International Narcotics Control Strategy Report (INCSR), a comprehensive assessment of the efforts of foreign nations to combat the illicit drug trade and drug related money laundering.

Current International Narcotics Control Policy

The primary goal of U.S. international narcotics policy is to reduce the supply of illicit narcotics flowing into the United States. A second and supporting goal is to reduce the amount of illicit narcotics cultivated, processed, and consumed worldwide. U.S. international narcotics control policy is implemented by a multifaceted strategy that includes the following elements: (1) eradication of narcotic crops, (2) interdiction and law enforcement activities in drug-producing and drug-transiting countries, (3) international cooperation, (4) sanctions/economic assistance, and (5) institution development. The U.S. State Department's Bureau of International Narcotics and Law Enforcement (INL) has the lead role coordinating U.S. international drug intervention and suppression activities.

In April 2001, the President requested $882 million in economic and counter narcotics assistance for Colombia and regional neighbors as part of an Andean Regional Initiative (ARI). The ARI proposal differed from the Plan Colombia program in two key areas: (1) spending on economic and social programs would be roughly equal to the drug control and interdiction components that had been the primary focus of Plan Colombia; and (2) more than half of the assistance was targeted to neighboring countries experiencing spillover effects from Colombia's civil conflict and from narco trafficking activities in that country. The enacted appropriations bill (P.L. 107-115) cleared by Congress on December 20, 2001, provided $783 million for the Initiative, a cut of $99 million from the President's request. Of the appropriation, not less than $215 million was to be apportioned directly to the Agency for International Development (AID) for economic and social programs. The enacted bill included conditions on the use of funds for purchase of chemicals for the aerial spraying program in Colombia, limited the number of U.S. civilian and military personnel involved in Colombia to 800, and blocked funding for restoration of flights in support of the Peruvian air interdiction program until a system of enhanced safeguards is in place. The State Department's request for its Andean Drug Counter Drug Initiative (ACI) for FY2003 and FY2004 totaled $731 million for each year respectively. The Administration requested $731 million for the Andean Counterdrug Initiative for FY2005, and $114 million for economic assistance programs. Congress also raised from 400 to 800 the level of U.S. military personnel and from 400 to 600 the level of civilian contractor personnel allowed to be deployed in Colombia, in response to an Administration request.

Eradication of Narcotic Crops

A long-standing U.S. policy regarding international narcotics control is to reduce cultivation and production of illicit narcotics through eradication. The United States supports programs to eradicate coca, opium, and marijuana in a number of countries. These efforts are conducted by a number of U.S. government agencies administering several types of programs. The United States supports eradication by providing producer countries with chemical herbicides, technical assistance and specialized equipment, and spray aircraft. The

U.S. Agency for International Development (AID) funds programs designed to promote economic growth and to provide alternative sources of employment for the people currently growing, producing, or processing illicit drugs. AID also provides balance of payments support (especially to the Andean countries) to help offset the loss of foreign exchange (from diminished drug exports) occurring as a result of U.S.-supported anti-drug programs. U.S. eradication policy receives informational support from the State Department's Office of Public Diplomacy and Public Affairs (formerly the U.S. Information Agency (USIA)) which publicizes the dangers of drug abuse and trafficker violence. In addition, AID sponsors drug education and awareness programs in 33 Latin American, Asian, and East European countries.

The eradication program in the Andes resulted in the elimination of an estimated 110,000 hectares of coca in Peru and Bolivia between 1995 and 2001, or almost 70% of the combined cultivated area in those countries. Nevertheless, cultivation in Colombia increased by 119,000 hectares or 234% over the same period.[1] The shift in cultivation has had implications for Colombia's civil conflict, putting more "taxable" resources into the hands of Colombia's leftist guerrillas. The State Department's International Strategy report for 2001 notes that "The Colombian syndicates, witnessing the vulnerability of Peruvian and Bolivian coca supply to joint interdiction operations in the late 1990s, decided to move most of the cultivation to Colombia's southwest corner, an area controlled by the FARC, the country's oldest insurgent group." This trend continues in Colombia today.

On January 2, 2005, the *Los Angeles Times* reported that the Bush Administration is split over how to respond to Afghanistan's skyrocketing opium poppy production. The debate reportedly centers over whether to push for large scale aerial eradication, or to leave the issue to the discretion of local officials. Central to the debate is what some view as potentially competing U.S. policy objectives in the war-torn nation, i.e., counterterrorism, counter-narcotics, and political stability.

Interdiction and Law Enforcement

A second element of U.S. international narcotics control strategy is to help host governments seize illicit narcotics before they reach America's borders. A related imperative is to attack and disrupt large aggregates of criminal power, to immobilize their top leaders and to sever drug traffickers' ties to the economy and to the political hierarchy. Training of foreign law enforcement personnel constitutes a major part of such endeavors. The Department of State funds anti-narcotics law enforcement training programs for foreign personnel from more than 70 countries. In addition, the Department of State provides host country anti-narcotics personnel with a wide range of equipment, and U.S. Drug Enforcement Administration (DEA) agents regularly assist foreign police forces in their efforts to destabilize trafficking networks. U.S. efforts to promote effective law enforcement against

[1] Note, however, that in Congressional testimony on July 10, 2003, Acting State Department INL Assistant Secretary Paul E. Simons announced that coca cultivation in Colombia during the year 2002 had declined

narcotics traffickers also include suggestions to nations on means to strengthen their legal and judicial systems. Finally, an important judicial tool against drug dealers is extradition. Since 1997, the U.S. government has successfully extradited at least 14 major traffickers from Colombia to face justice in the United States.

International Cooperation

Essentially all elements of U.S. international narcotics control strategy require international cooperation. By use of diplomatic initiatives, both bilateral and multilateral, the Department of State encourages and assists nations to reduce cultivation, production, and trafficking in illicit drugs. These bilateral agreements and international conventions have thus far been largely ineffective in reversing the growth of international narcotics trafficking, in part because they lack strong enforcement mechanisms and are not uniformly interpreted by member nations.

U.S. international narcotics control strategy also requires cooperation among governments to coordinate their border operations to interdict traffickers. To this end, the U.S. government has provided technical assistance for anti-drug programs in other countries. For FY2005, the State Department's international narcotics control budget request totaled $1.05 billion to assist programs globally, including$90.2 million for Bolivia, $115.4 million for Peru, $462.8 million for Colombia, and $25.8 million for Ecuador. Also requested was $69.4 million for interregional aviation support, to provide aircraft for anti-drug programs in other countries. The United States also participates in multilateral assistance programs through the U.N. International Drug Control Program and actively enlists the aid and support of other governments for narcotics control projects. The U.N. currently assists 67 developing countries through development, law enforcement, education, treatment, and rehabilitation programs. For FY2005, the Bush Administration requested $15 million for general anticrime/anticorruption programs and $5 million for narcotics control-related contributions to international organizations; the majority of the latter constituted the U.S. voluntary contribution to the U.N. drug control program.

Sanctions/Economic Assistance

A fourth element of U.S. international narcotics control strategy involves the threat of, or application of, sanctions against drug producer or trafficker nations. These range from suspension of U.S. foreign assistance to curtailment of air transportation. Current law on International Drug Control Certification Procedures (P.L.107-228, Section 706) requires the President to submit to Congress not later than September 15 of the preceding fiscal year a report identifying each country determined to be a major drug transit or drug producing country as defined in section 481(e) of the Foreign Assistance Act of 1961. In the report the President must designate each country that has "failed demonstrably" to meet its counter narcotics obligations. Designated countries would be ineligible for foreign assistance unless the President determined that that assistance was vital to the U.S. national interest or that the country had made "substantial efforts" to improve its counter narcotics performance. Previous certification requirements had established a 30- calendar day review process in which the

overall by more than 15%, a development he characterized as a "direct result of the robust U.S.-assisted aerial eradication program."

Congress could override the President's determinations and stop U.S. foreign aid from going to specific countries, but this process is no longer extant.

A multilateral [drug performance] evaluation mechanism (MEM) has also been established under the auspices of the Organization of American States (OAS). This mechanism is seen by many as a vehicle to undermine and facilitate abolishment of the existing U.S. sanctions-oriented unilateral certification process which is often viewed as an irritant to major illicit drug-producing countries, and which, opponents argue, does little to promote anti-drug cooperation.

U.S. sanctions policy has been augmented with programs of economic assistance to major coca producing countries (see "Use of Sanctions or Positive Incentives" and "Bush Administration Anti-Drug Strategy," below). For FY2005 the State Department requested for drug related alternative development: approximately$124.7 million for Colombia, $53.9 million for Peru, $41.7 million for Bolivia and $14.9 million for Ecuador.

On June 2, 2003, President Bush submitted to Congress a list of foreign narcotics kingpins subject to U.S. legislative efforts to deny such individuals and entities access to U.S. financial systems and to prohibit U.S. individuals and companies from doing business with these kingpins. For the first time, foreign "entities" such as the Colombia's FARC and United Self-Defense Forces (AUC) are included in the list.

Institution Development

A fifth element of U.S. international narcotics control strategy increasingly involves institution development, such as strengthening judicial and law enforcement institutions, boosting governing capacity, and assisting in developing host nation administrative infrastructures conducive to combating the illicit drug trade. Institution development includes such programs as corruption prevention, training to support the administration of justice, and financial crimes enforcement assistance.

Policy Approaches

Overview

The primary goal of U.S. international narcotics control policy is to stem the flow of foreign drugs into the United States. A number of approaches have been proposed to reshape

U.S. international narcotics control policy and implement it more effectively. Whatever ideas are ultimately selected will have to consider the scope of the drug problem. It is estimated that the illicit drug trade generates as much as half of the approximately $750 billion in illegal funds laundered internationally each year. Policymakers face the challenge of deciding the appropriate level of funding required for the nation's international narcotics control efforts within the context of competing budgetary priorities.

Another challenge facing the U.S. international narcotics control efforts concerns how to implement policy most effectively. Some observers argue that current U.S. policy is fragmented and overly bilateral in nature. These analysts suggest that to achieve success, policy options must be pursued within the context of a comprehensive plan with a multilateral emphasis on implementation. For example, they point out that some studies indicate that interdiction can actually increase the economic rewards to drug traffickers by raising prices for the products they sell. They agree, however, that interdiction as part of a coordinated plan can have a strong disrupting and destabilizing effect on trafficker operations. Some analysts suggest that bilateral or unilateral U.S. policies are ill-suited for solving what is in effect a multilateral problem. They cite the need for enhancing the United Nations' ability to deal effectively with the narcotics problem and for more international and regional cooperation and consultation on international narcotics issues. Proponents of bilateral policy do not necessarily reject a more multilateral approach. They point out, however, that such multinational endeavors are intrinsically difficult to arrange, coordinate, and implement effectively.

Between 1981 and 2001 The United States spent $8.57 billion on international narcotics control, mostly in Latin America. Yet estimated potential production of South American cocaine over the period increased from 140 to 170 tons to almost 870 tons, according to State Department and other U.S. government figures. According to ONDCP's *Strategy* the average price per pure gram of cocaine in 2000 was $212, approximately half what it was in 1981, and the average purity of a gram of street cocaine was 69% higher. For heroin the price and purity respectively were 77% lower and 147% higher in 2000 than in 1981. Some analysts believe, viewing such trends, that current efforts to reduce the flow of illicit drugs into the United States have essentially failed and that other objectives, policies, programs, and priorities are needed. Four major approaches which have been suggested, in various combinations as part of an overall effort, are set out below.

Expansion of Efforts to Reduce Production at the Source

This option involves expanding efforts to reduce the volume of narcotic plants and crops produced in foreign countries before the crops' conversion into processed drugs. Illicit crops may either be eradicated or purchased (and then destroyed). Eradication of illicit crops may be accomplished by physically uprooting the plants, or by chemical or biological control agents. Development of alternative sources of income to replace peasant income lost by non production of narcotic crops may be an important element of this option.

Proponents of expanded efforts to stop the production of narcotic crops and substances at the source believe that reduction of the foreign supply of drugs available is an effective means to lower levels of drug use in the United States. They argue that reduction of the supply of cocaine — the nation's top narcotics control priority — is a realistically achievable option.

Proponents of vastly expanded supply reduction options, and specifically of herbicidal crop eradication, argue that this method is the most cost-effective and efficient means of eliminating narcotic crops. They maintain that, coupled with intensified law enforcement, such programs will succeed since it is easier to locate and destroy crops in the field than to locate subsequently processed drugs on smuggling routes or on the streets of U.S. cities. Put differently, a kilogram of cocaine hydrochloride is far more difficult to detect than the 300 to 500 kilograms of coca leaf that are required to make that same kilogram. Also, because crops constitute the cheapest link in the narcotics chain, producers will devote fewer economic resources to prevent their detection than to concealing more expensive and refined forms of the product.

In addition, eradication successes have been recorded in individual countries. According to INL's *International Narcotics Control Strategy Report* of 2002, for example, Pakistan has reduced opium cultivation by more than 95% since 1995 and Taliban-controlled Afghanistan accomplished a similar feat in a single year, eliminating more than 62,000 hectares or 97% of the opium crop between 2000 and 2001. However, INL reports that cultivation surged beginning in 2002 under the relatively weak Afghan political authority that succeeded the Taliban, suggesting that an effective central government presence in drug crop areas is critical to the success of eradication projects.

Opponents of expanded supply reduction policy generally question whether reduction of the foreign supply of narcotic drugs is achievable and whether it would have a meaningful impact on levels of illicit drug use in the United States. They argue that aerial spraying in Colombia has failed to contain the spread of coca cultivation and point to drug syndicates' moving into opium poppy cultivation in Colombia and (more recently) Peru. Total Andean cultivation, in fact, has remained relatively stable in the past decade despite U.S. efforts, and because farmers are finding ways to increase productivity per unit of land according to INL figures. Critics also suggest that even if the supply of foreign drugs destined for the U.S. market could be dramatically reduced, U.S. consumers would simply switch to consumption of domestically-grown or synthetic drug substitutes. Thus, they maintain, the ultimate solution to the U.S. drug problem is wiping out the domestic market for illicit drugs, not trying to eliminate the supply in source countries.

Some also fear that environmental damage will result from herbicides. As an alternative, they urge development, research, and funding of programs designed to develop and employ biological control agents such as coca-destroying insects and fungi that do not harm other plants. Others argue that intensified eradication will push the drug crop frontier and the attendant polluting affects of narcotics industries farther into ecologically sensitive jungle areas, with little or no decrease in net cultivation. In addition, reports have surfaced in Colombia of toxic effects of herbicides on legal crops and on the health of animals and humans, although the veracity of such accounts is debated.

Others question whether a global policy of simultaneous crop control is politically feasible since many areas in the world will always be beyond U.S. control and influence. Such critics refer to continuously shifting sources of supply, or the so-called "balloon syndrome": when squeezed in one place, it pops up in another. Nevertheless, many point out that the number of large suitable growth areas is finite, and by focusing simultaneously at major production areas, substantial reductions can be achieved if adequate funding is provided.

Some also question the value of supply reduction measures since world production and supply of illicit drugs vastly exceeds world demand, making it unlikely that the supply surplus could be reduced sufficiently to affect the ready availability of illicit narcotics in the U.S. market. Such analysts also suggest that even if worldwide supply were reduced dramatically, the effects would be felt primarily in other nation's drug markets. The U.S. market, they argue, would be the last to experience supply shortfalls, because U.S. consumers pay higher prices and because U.S. dollars are a preferred narcocurrency.

Political and Economic Tradeoffs

Some suggest that expanded and effective efforts to reduce production of illicit narcotics at the source will be met by active and violent opposition from a combination of trafficker, political, and economic groups. In some nations, such as Colombia, traffickers have achieved a status comparable to "a state within a state." In others, allegations of drug-related corruption have focused on high-level officials in the military and federal police, as well as heads of state; In Mexico, according to a *Washington Times* report, smugglers often are protected by heavily-armed Mexican military troops and police who "have been paid handsomely to escort the drug traffickers and their illicit shipments across the border and into the United States." In addition, some traffickers have aligned themselves with terrorist and insurgent groups, and have reportedly funded political candidates and parties, pro-narcotic peasant workers and trade union groups, and high visibility popular public works projects to cultivate public support through a "Robin Hood" image. Because some constituencies that benefit economically from coca are well armed, if the United States were successful in urging foreign governments to institute widespread use of chemical/biological control agents, cooperating host governments could well face strong domestic political challenge and violent opposition from affected groups. Heavy military protection, at a minimum, would be required for those spraying or otherwise eradicating drug crops.

Some critics have argued, with respect to Colombia, that eradication campaigns can have the unintended effect of aggravating the country's ongoing civil conflict. Since Colombia's guerrilla groups pose as advocates of growers, spraying may broaden support for such groups, thereby contradicting the objectives of the government's counterinsurgency efforts in the affected zones. Such observers believe that Colombia's enforcement priorities should shift to targeting critical nodes in transportation and refining and, to the extent possible, sealing off traffic routes to and from the main coca producing zones. The argument is made that interdiction can disrupt internal markets for coca derivatives and that, compared to eradication; it imposes fewer direct costs on peasant producers and generates less political unrest.

For some countries, production of illicit narcotics and the narcotics trade has become an economic way of life that provides a subsistence level of income to large numbers of people from whom those who rule draw their legitimacy. Crop reduction campaigns seek to displace such income and those workers engaged in its production. In this regard, these campaigns may threaten real economic and political dangers for the governments of nations with marginal economic growth. Consequently, some analysts argue that the governments of such low-income countries cannot be expected to launch major crop reduction programs without the substitute income to sustain those whose income depends on drug production.

Use of Sanctions or Positive Incentives

Those promoting expansion of efforts to reduce production at the source face the challenge of instituting programs that effectively reduce production of narcotic crops and production of refined narcotics without creating unmanageable economic and political crises for target countries. A major area of concern of such policymakers is to achieve an effective balance between the "carrot" and the "stick" approach in U.S. relations with major illicit narcotics-producing and transit countries.

Proponents of a sanctions policy linking foreign aid and trade benefits to U.S. international narcotics objectives argue against "business as usual" with countries that permit illicit drug trafficking, production, or laundering of drug profits. They assert that this policy includes a moral dimension and that drug production and trafficking is wrong, and that the United States should not associate with countries involved in it. Such analysts maintain that U.S. aid and trade sanctions can provide the needed leverage for nations to reduce production of illicit crops and their involvement in other drug related activities. They argue that both the moral stigma of being branded as uncooperative and the threat of economic sanctions prod many otherwise uncooperative nations into action. They further stress that trade sanctions would be likely to provide a highly effective lever as most developing countries depend on access to U.S. markets.

Opponents of a sanctions policy linking aid and trade to U.S. international narcotics objectives argue that sanctions may have an undesirable effect on the political and economic stability of target countries, making them all the more dependent on the drug trade for income; that sanctions have little impact because many countries are not dependant on U.S. aid; that sanctions historically have little effect unless they are multilaterally imposed; and that sanctions are arbitrary in nature, hurt national pride in the foreign country, and are seen in many countries as an ugly manifestation of "Yankee imperialism." Finally, an increasing number of analysts suggest that if sanctions are to be fully effective, they should be used in conjunction with additional positive incentives (subject perhaps to an expanded certification/approval process) to foster anti-drug cooperation.

Alternatively, some suggest positive incentives instead of sanctions. They believe that narcotics-producing countries must be motivated either to refrain from growing illicit crops, or to permit the purchase or destruction of these crops by government authorities. Many argue that since short term economic stability of nations supplying illegal drugs may depend upon the production and sale of illicit narcotics, it is unrealistic to expect such nations to limit their drug-related activities meaningfully without an alternative source of income. The House Appropriations Committee report on the 1993 foreign operations appropriations bill suggested that when it comes to narcotics related economic development "there is too little emphasis in either actual funding or policy."

It has been suggested by some analysts that a massive foreign aid effort — a so-called "mini-Marshall Plan" — is the only feasible method of persuading developing nations to curb their production of narcotic crops. Such a plan would involve a multilateral effort with the participation of the United States, Europe, Japan, Australia, other industrialized nations susceptible to the drug problem, and the rich oil producing nations. The thrust of such a plan would be to promote economic development, replacing illicit cash crops with other marketable alternatives. Within the framework of such a plan, crops could be purchased or else destroyed by herbicidal spraying or biological control agents while substitute crops and markets are developed and assured.

Any such program would be coupled with rigid domestic law enforcement and penalties for non-compliance. Thus, it could require a U.S. commitment of substantially increased enforcement assets to be used against both growers and traffickers, and some observers assert it might require direct U.S. military involvement at the request of the host country. Significant coercion might be required, since drug crops typically produce a better cash flow than licit crops grown in the same region. For example, in Afghanistan a hectare of opium earns 30 to 45 times as much as a hectare of wheat at prevailing prices ($13,000 compared to $300 to $400). Even if the international community bought up the entire Afghan opium crop, the temptation to plant new opium could prove irresistible to farmers.

Critics have concerns regarding positive incentive concepts. They warn of the precedent of appearing to pay "protection" compensation, that is, providing an incentive for economically disadvantaged countries to go into the drug export business. They also warn of the open-ended cost of agricultural development programs and of extraterritorial police intervention. Finding markets for viable alternative crops is yet another major constraint. Some experts argue that typical conditions of drug crop zones, such as geographical remoteness, marginal soils and, in certain countries, extreme insecurity, tend to limit prospects for legal commercial agriculture. According to one report, the soils in Colombia's Putumayo Department, an important center of coca cultivation, are simply too poor to support the number of people currently farming in the province if all converted to growing legal crops. Such observers believe that a more promising strategy is to foster development of the legal economy in other locales, including urban settings, in order to attract people away from areas that have a comparative advantage in coca or opium production. In the view of these analysts, the best "substitute crop" for coca or opium could well be an assembly plant producing electronic goods or automobiles for the international market.

Expansion of Interdiction and Enforcement Activities to Disrupt Supply Lines/ Expanding the Role of the Military

Drug supply line interdiction is both a foreign and domestic issue. Many argue that the United States should intensify law enforcement activities designed to disrupt the transit of illicit narcotics as early in the production/transit chain as possible — well before the drugs reach the streets of the United States. This task is conceded to be very difficult because the United States is the world's greatest trading nation with vast volumes of imports daily flowing in through hundreds of sea, air, and land entry facilities, and its systems have been designed to facilitate human and materials exchange. This has led some analysts to suggest that the military should assume a more active role in anti-drug activities.

Some in Congress, in the late 1980s and prior to appropriations for FY1994, had urged an expanded role for the military in the "war on drugs." The idea of using the military is not novel. Outside the United States, U.S. military personnel have been involved in training and transporting foreign anti-narcotics personnel since 1983. Periodically, there have also been calls for multilateral military strikes against trafficking operations, as well as increased use of U.S. elite forces in preemptive strikes against drug fields and trafficker enclaves overseas.

The military's role in narcotics interdiction was expanded by the FY1990-1991 National Defense Authorization Act. The conference report (H.Rept. 100-989) concluded that the Department of Defense (DOD) can and should play a major role in narcotics interdiction. Congress, in FY1989 and FY1990-1991 authorization acts, required DOD to promptly provide civilian law enforcement agencies with relevant drug-related intelligence; charged the President to direct that command, control, communications, and intelligence networks dedicated to drug control be integrated by DOD into an effective network; restricted direct participation by military personnel in civilian law enforcement activities to those authorized by law; permitted the military to transport civilian law enforcement personnel outside the U.S. land area; expanded the National Guard's role in drug interdiction activities; and authorized additional $300 million for DOD and National Guard drug interdiction activities.

DOD's requested drug budget total for FY2005 was 852.7 million as compared to $908.6 million for FY2004 and as compared to $905.9 million for FY2003.

Despite the military's obvious ability to support drug law enforcement organizations, questions remain as to the overall effectiveness of a major military role in narcotics interdiction. Proponents of substantially increasing the military's role in supporting civilian law enforcement narcotics interdiction activity argue that narcotics trafficking poses a national security threat to the United States; that only the military is equipped and has the resources to counter powerful trafficking organizations; and that counter drug support provides the military with beneficial, realistic training.

In contrast, opponents argue that drug interdiction is a law enforcement mission, it is not a military mission; that drug enforcement is an unconventional war which the military is ill-equipped to fight; that a drug enforcement role detracts from readiness; that a drug enforcement role exposes the military to corruption; that it is unwise public policy to require the U.S. military to operate against U.S. citizens; and that the use of the military may have serious political and diplomatic repercussions overseas. Moreover, some in the military remain concerned about an expanded role, seeing themselves as possible scapegoats for policies that have failed, or are likely to fail.

Expansion of Efforts to Reduce Worldwide Demand

Another commonly proposed option is to increase policy emphasis on development and implementation of programs worldwide that aim at increasing public intolerance for illicit drug use. Such programs, through information, technical assistance, and training in prevention and treatment, would emphasize the health dangers of drug use, as well as the danger to regional and national stability. The State Department's Office of Public Diplomacy and Public Affairs and AID currently support modest efforts in this area. Some believe these programs should be increased and call for a more active role for the United Nations and other international agencies in development and implementation of such demand reduction programs.

Expansion of Economic Disincentives for Illicit Drug Trafficking

Proponents of this approach say that the major factor in the international drug market is not the product, but the profit. Thus, they stress, international efforts to reduce the flow of drugs into the United States must identify means to seize and otherwise reduce assets and profits generated by the drug trade. Some critics point out the challenges of tracking, separating out and confiscating criminal assets. These include the huge volume of all international electronic transfers — more than $2 trillion each day — and the movement of much illegal money outside of formal banking channels (through hawala-type chains of money brokers).

Policymakers pursuing this option must decide whether laws in countries where they exert influence are too lenient on financial institutions, such as banks and brokerage houses, which knowingly facilitate financial transactions of traffickers. If the answer is "yes," national leaders might then take concerted action to promote harsher criminal sanctions penalizing the movement of money generated by drug sales, including revocation of licenses of institutions regularly engaging in such practices. Finally, those supporting this option favor increased efforts to secure greater international cooperation on financial investigations related to money laundering of narcotics profits, including negotiation of mutual legal assistance treaties (MLATs).

The George W. Bush Administration's Anti-Drug Strategy

The direction of drug policy under President George W. Bush does not appear to be an immediate top foreign policy priority for the Administration. To date, issues of international terrorism and homeland security appear to command more attention. However, Bush administration officials are beginning to portray Colombia's counter-insurgency campaign as part of the broader worldwide campaign against terrorism. While Congress has stipulated that U.S. military aid to Colombia be dedicated to fighting drugs, support is reportedly growing in Congress and the Administration for providing direct support to Colombia's efforts to rein in the rebel groups. The extent of any such support — and whether it might involve the use of American combat forces — remains to be determined.

On or about February 23, 2005, the White House released its annual National Drug Control Strategy, [http://www.whitehousedrugpolicy.gov/publications/policy/ndcs05/]. Central to the international component of the strategy is disrupting the operations of drug traffickers "including destroying the economic basis of the cocaine production business in South America by fumigating the coca crop, seizing enormous and unsustainable amounts of cocaine from transporters, and selectively targeting major [drug] organization heads for law enforcement action and, ultimately, extradition and prosecution in the United States."

Possible issues of concern to Congress relating to international drug control policy include the following:

(1) Can the Plan Colombia and the Andean Regional Initiative as currently envisioned have a meaningful impact on reducing drug shipments to the U.S. or in reducing the current level of violence and instability in Colombia? To what degree can a counter-drug plan which does not aim to deal a decisive blow to insurgent operations in Colombia be expected to meaningfully curb drug production and violence there?

(2) To what degree might a more regional approach to the drug problem in Colombia prove more effective and how might such an expanded initiative be funded?

(3) How does U.S. involvement in anti-drug efforts in the Andean nations affect other aspects of American foreign policy in the region, and in Latin America generally? Does a concentration on drug-related issues obscure more fundamental issues of stability, governance, poverty , and democracy (i.e., to what degree are drugs a major cause, or result, of the internal problems of certain Latin American countries)? Might U.S. pursuit of drug control objectives conflict in certain ways with efforts to resolve Colombia's ongoing civil conflict, for instance by alienating large rural constituencies in contested regions of the country?

(4) In the case of Colombia and other nations where insurgents are heavily involved in the drug trade, how can the United States ensure that U.S. military aid and equipment is in fact used to combat drug traffickers and cartels, rather than diverted for use against domestic political opposition or used as an instrument of human rights violations? How great is the risk that such diversions could take place, and is the degree of risk worth the possible gains to be made against drug production and trafficking?

(5) How extensive is drug-related corruption in the armed forces and police of the Andean nations? What impact might such corruption have on the effectiveness of U.S. training and assistance to these forces?

(6) Will an active role for the military in counter-narcotics support to foreign nations (i.e. Colombia) result in U.S. casualties? If so, is there an exit strategy and at what point, if at all, might presidential actions fall within the scope of the War Powers Resolution; that is, does the dispatch of military advisers to help other governments combat drug traffickers constitute the introduction of armed forces "into hostilities or into situations where imminent involvement in hostilities is clearly indicated by the circumstances"? (The War Powers

Resolution requires the President to report such an introduction to Congress, and to withdraw the forces within 60 to 90 days unless authorized to remain by Congress.)

(7) Will the evolving strategy under the Bush Administration produce better results than previous strategies in reducing illicit drug use in the United States and in supporting U.S. narcotics and other foreign policy goals overseas? Is a proper balance of resources being devoted to domestic (the demand side) vs. foreign (the supply side) components of an overall national anti-drug strategy? Are efforts to reduce the foreign supply level futile while domestic U.S. demand remains high? Are efforts to reduce domestic demand fruitless as long as foreign supplies can enter the country with relative impunity?

(8) To what extent will the Administration's current priority in fighting terrorism affect implementation of antidrug policy? Has repositioning of equipment and resources to improve U.S. defenses against acts of terrorism, for example the shift of Coast Guard vessels from the eastern Pacific and the Caribbean to perform coastal patrols and port security functions, lowered defenses with respect to curbing drug flows? On the flip side of the issue, to what degree has committing anti-drug resources to support anti-terrorism objectives significantly enhanced the effectiveness of counterterrorism efforts?

(9) To what extent should U.S. military assistance programs in Colombia target groups that use narcotics operations to finance terrorist activities (including leftist guerrillas and paramilitaries), as opposed to the narcotics trafficking infrastructure itself?

Certification Status

In December 2001, legislation on "Modifications to the Annual Drug Certification Procedures" in the Foreign Operations, Export Financing and Related Programs Appropriations Act (P.L. 107-115, Section 591) was enacted that effectively waived the drug certification requirements for FY2002. It required the President to withhold assistance from the countries most remiss in meeting their international drug-fighting obligations, but permitted the President to determine what countries to put in the "worst offending" category and (under specified conditions) to provide U.S. foreign assistance to a designated country. Legislation on "International Drug Control Certification Procedures" in the Foreign Relations Authorization Act of September 2002 (P.L. 107-228) extended the waiver to FY2003, and subsequently provided for a *de facto* ongoing waiver. Such changes may reflect the fact that spokesmen from many countries have complained for years about the unilateral and non-cooperative nature of the drug certification requirements, and have urged the United States to end the process or at least to replace it with multilateral evaluation mechanisms. Acting under this legislation, President Bush made designations on a transitional basis for FY2002 and FY2003, and then made designations on the designated date for FY2004 and FY2005.

On February 23, 2002, the President designated Afghanistan, Burma and Haiti as having "failed demonstrably" in counter-narcotics efforts, but granted national interest waivers to Haiti and Afghanistan under the new government.

On January 31, 2003, he designated Burma, Guatemala, and Haiti, but granted national interest waivers to Guatemala and Haiti.

On September 15, 2003, he designated Burma and Haiti, but granted a national interest waiver to Haiti.

On September 15, 2004, he removed Thailand from the list of major illicit drug transit or producing countries, and designated Burma as having "failed demonstrably" in counter-narcotics efforts.

On September 15, 2005, President Bush issued the annual determination that lists major illicit drug producing or drug transit countries. The President identified 20 countries to be included on the so-called "majors list": Afghanistan, The Bahamas, Bolivia, Brazil, Burma, Colombia, Dominican Republic, Ecuador, Guatemala, Haiti, India, Jamaica, Laos, Mexico, Nigeria, Pakistan, Panama, Paraguay, Peru, and Venezuela. Burma was again singled out a county which had "failed demonstrably" to adhere to its obligations under international counter narcotics agreements. Venezuela was singled out as well as having failed demonstrably, but was granted a national interests waiver exempting it from U.S. aid and trade sanctions and possible access to loans from international financial institutions. China and Vietnam were removed from the list.

Plan Colombia

On July 13, 2000, U.S. support for Plan Colombia was signed into law (P.L. 106-246). Included was $1.3 billion in emergency supplemental appropriations in equipment, supplies, and other counter narcotics aid primarily for the Colombian military. The plan aimed to curb trafficking activity and reduce coca cultivation in Colombia by 50% over five years. Though focused on military and law enforcement initiatives, Plan components included helping the Colombian Government control its territory; strengthening democratic institutions; promoting economic development; protecting human rights; and providing humanitarian assistance. Included as well was $148 million for Andean regional drug interdiction and alternative development programs. Supporters of the Plan argued that without enhanced U.S. aid, Colombia risks disintegration into smaller autonomous political units — some controlled by leftist or rightist guerrilla groups that are heavily involved in drug trafficking and violent crime -for- profit activity. Other observers cautioned that narcotics-related assistance to Colombia can, at best, produce serious reductions in illicit drug production only within a multi-year timeframe. They warn against enhanced U.S. involvement in a conflict where clear- cut victory is elusive and to a large degree dependent on reduction of the so far intractable U.S. domestic appetite for illicit drugs. Still others warned of the so-called "spillover" effect of Plan Colombia on neighboring nations such as Ecuador where narcolinked insurgents and paramilitaries increasingly operate. For additional data on issues relating to Plan Colombia see CRS Report RL32774, *Plan Colombia, a Progress Report*, CRS Report RL30541, *Colombia: Plan Colombia Legislation and Assistance (FY2000-FY2001)*, and CRS Report RS20494, *Ecuador: International Narcotics Control Issues.*

Andean Regional Initiative

In April 2001, the Bush Administration unveiled an Andean Regional Initiative (ARI) as a successor to Plan Colombia, requesting $882 million for the program. Of these funds approximately 45% percent were intended for Colombia and the remainder for six regional neighbors of Colombia (Bolivia, Brazil, Ecuador, Panama, Peru, and Venezuela) affected by drug trafficking and drug- related violence. By contrast, Colombia received two-thirds of the funds allocated under Plan Colombia. In December 2001, Congress passed the Foreign Operations Appropriations bill for FY2002, allocating $783 million to the ARI. Of the $783 million, 49% were provided to Colombia and the rest to the other six countries. Of the Colombia funds, 36% were earmarked for economic and social and governance purposes and 64% for counter narcotics and security, a ratio largely reflecting the enforcement orientation of Plan Colombia. In the case of Peru and Bolivia, the economic and social share was significantly higher — 61% in both countries. For FY2003, the Bush Administration requested $980 million in ARI funding, of which 55% was for Colombia. The ARI request for FY2004 totaled $990.7 million of which $463 million was for State Department Andean Counterdrug Initiative (ACI) programs for Colombia. For FY2005, Congress appropriated $731 million for the ACI (of which $466.5 was for Colombia) and an additional $106.5 million for Foreign Military Financing (FMF) funding. (For further information, see CRS Report RL32337, *Andean Counterdrug Initiative (ACI) and Related Funding Programs: FY2005 Assistance*; CRS Report RL32021, *Andean Regional Initiative (ARI): FY2003 Supplemental and FY2004 Assistance for Colombia and Neighbors*; and CRS Report RS21213, *Colombia: Summary and Tables on U.S. Assistance, FY1989-FY2004.*

In: The War on Drugs: Winning, Losing or Treading Water ISBN 978-1-59454-235-0
Editor: Nelson V. Arcos

Chapter 6

ILLICIT DRUGS AND THE TERRORIST THREAT: CAUSAL LINKS AND IMPLICATIONS FOR DOMESTIC DRUG CONTROL POLICY *

Mark A.R. Kleiman

SUMMARY

The international traffic in illicit drugs contributes to terrorist risk through at least five mechanisms: supplying cash, creating chaos and instability, supporting corruption, providing "cover" and sustaining common infrastructures for illicit activity, and competing for law enforcement and intelligence attention. Of these, cash and chaos are likely to be the two most important.

Different drugs, different trafficking routes, and different organizations have different relationships to terrorist threats. Therefore it might be possible to improve domestic security by targeting drug law enforcement on those drugs, routes, and organizations with the strongest known or potential links to terror. However, doing so would require new analytic capacities and decision-making strategies for all the agencies involved in drug law enforcement and there is no assurance that the policies that best implement the mission of protecting Americans from drug abuse will also perform best in protecting the country from terrorism. Indeed, the interests of ideology-driven terrorists and money-driven drug traders can sometimes diverge, as when increased resources deployed against terrorists adversely affect the activities of drug traders with no ties to terrorists.

Any terrorist threats exacerbated by the illicit drug markets might be reduced by shrinking the markets themselves, both in physical volume and financial revenue. It is not clear that increased drug law enforcement alone can succeed in that respect; the cocaine and heroin markets have proven stubbornly resistant to vigorous enforcement efforts.

Reducing demand for illicit drugs can also shrink the markets. The total number of users is much less important in determining drug volumes and revenues than the behavior of a

---

* Excerpted from CRS Report RL32334, dated April 20, 2004

relatively small number of chronic, high-dose drug-takers. Most of that "hard core" group consists of people who are repeatedly arrested, not only for drug offenses but for a wide range of property, violent, and public-order offenses. Acting to reduce the population of hard-core user-offenders, through treatment, drug courts, or testing-and-sanctions programs, may offer a better prospect for reducing the size of the drug markets, and thus potentially the contribution of drug trafficking to the terrorist threat.

BACKGROUND

Some terrorist organizations, and the governments that harbor and support them, also engage in drug dealing, or otherwise profit from the traffic in illicit drugs. The Office of National Drug Control Policy (ONDCP) has created a series of controversial print and television advertisements that attempt to use the links between drugs and terrorism to dissuade current and potential drug users. An exhibit at the new Drug Enforcement Administration (DEA) Museum makes the same point.[1] The links between the two sets of phenomena are important considerations in formulating a drug control policy that also contributes to the campaign against terror. Drug supply and demand reduction might contribute to homeland security by reducing the availability of funds and other forms of support to terrorist organizations. Integrating the two sets of concerns, if that is to be done, may require reexaming relevant aspects of existing domestic and foreign policy strategies. This report addresses issues relating to the formulation and execution of drug control policy in the context of its implications for terrorism.

POTENTIAL LINKS BETWEEN DRUG TRAFFICKING AND TERRORISM

Drug trafficking — in source countries, transit countries, and consumer countries, including the United States — could contribute to the problems of terror in at least five distinct ways:

- Supplying cash for terrorist operations;
- Creating chaos in countries where drugs are produced, through which they pass, or in which they are sold at retail and consumed — chaos sometimes deliberately cultivated by drug traffickers — which may provide an environment conducive to terrorist activity;
- Generating corruption in law enforcement, military, and other governmental and civil-society institutions in ways that either build public support for terrorist-linked

[1] Office of National Drug Control Policy, "Drug Czar Announces Extension of Ads Linking Drugs, Terror: Walters Hails 'Most Successful Ads in History of Anti-Drug Media Campaign,'" press release, Feb. 26, 2002; Drug Enforcement Administration, "DEA and Giuliani Open National Museum Exhibit on Drugs and Terrorism," press release, Sept. 3, 2002. See [http://www.whitehousedrugpolicy.gov/news/press02/022702.html] and [http://www.usdoj.gov/dea/pubs/pressrel/pr090302.html].

groups or weaken the capacity of the society to combat terrorist organizations and actions;

- Providing services also useful for terrorist actions and movements of terrorist personnel and materiel, and supporting a common infrastructure, such as smuggling capabilities, illicit arms acquisition, money laundering, or the production of false identification or other documents, capable of serving both drug-trafficking and terrorist purposes; and
- Competing for law enforcement and intelligence attention.

In principle, any of these might be important. It is likely that the first two listed — cash and chaos — are the dominant mechanisms by which the illicit drug traffic winds up contributing to the problem of terrorism, but the data required for a truly quantitative assessment are not currently available (at least in the unclassified literature).

Cash

There is no consensus on the total amount of international financial flows associated with the illicit drug trade. A United Nations figure of $400 billion per year is often cited, and compared with world trade figures in various categories of licit goods (textiles, petroleum, and food, for example).[2]

In the single biggest drug market, that for cocaine, the United States is reported to consume about one-third of the world total in terms of bulk. Yet the dollar value of all U.S. illicit drug markets *combined* is less than $65 billion per year, according to a study by the Office of National Drug Control Policy.[3] If the U.S. market is truly in the range of $65 billion, and the U.S. accounts for no less than one-third of the world total, then the actual amount is no more than half as great as the U.N. estimates, or about $200 billion. (That figure would be smaller than the licit retail market in alcohol or tobacco products.)

However, even that lower figure does not represent funds potentially available to fund terrorism. That $200 billion would, if accurate, represent the total value of all illicit drugs, priced at the retail level. The vast bulk of that retail value consists of the illicit earnings of traffickers within the country in which the drugs are sold, not the revenues available to producers and international traffickers.

The import-export prices of illicit drugs represent only a small fraction — about a tenth, in the case of cocaine — of the prices paid by consumers.[4] Moreover, some drugs are consumed in the countries where they are produced, for example the substantial amount of methamphetamine and cannabis produced and consumed in the United States. So if the aggregate "street price" of all the illicit drugs sold in the world were approximately $200

---

[2] United Nations Office for Drug Control and Crime Prevention, World Drug Report 2000 (Oxford, New York: Oxford University Press, 2000), pp. 55- 59.

[3] Office of National Drug Control Policy, "National Drug Control Strategy," Feb. 2002, pp. 57; and Office of National Drug Control Policy, "What America's Users Spend on Illegal Drugs 1988-1998," Dec. 2000, pp. 1-5. (Hereafter cited as ONDCP, "What America's Users Spend on Illegal Drugs.")

[4] Charles F. Mansi, et al.(eds.), Informing America's Policy on Illegal Drugs: What We Don't Know Keeps Hurting Us (Washington: National Research Council, 2001), pp.153-156.

billion dollars, the total value of drug imports and exports might be in the $10-20 billion range.

Of that amount, it is believed that only a tiny fraction flows to terrorist groups. In particular, groups that live by "taxing" or facilitating the production of raw drug crops which is where terrorist groups are most likely to be involved, are dealing with drugs at the point in the supply chain where their value is least. For example, heroin sells at retail in the United States for approximately $1 per pure milligram;[5] thus a kilogram of heroin, broken down and sold at retail, fetches $1 million. The "landed price" of that kilogram when it arrives in the United States is about $100,000.[6] But the 10 kilograms of opium that can be converted into that kilogram of heroin sell in Afghanistan for about $5,000, a 20th of the import price, and about one half of 1% of the retail price.

The $10 billion U.S. annual retail heroin market thus generates about $1 billion in imports, of which roughly $50 million goes to poppy growers. Terrorists and others who might levy "taxes" on this illicit agricultural activity cannot be extracting more than a very small share of that amount. The ratios in the cocaine trade are comparable: the total value of the coca leaf that goes to make up the $35 billion annual U.S. cocaine market is about $150 million at the point where it is harvested, and the total value of cocaine imports no more than $5 billion as first landed in this country.[7]

However, even though only a tiny fraction of the world's drug dealing revenues goes to benefit terrorist groups, that relatively small amount could still be a large fraction of the world's terrorist revenues. Unfortunately, the amount of money required by terrorists to do enormous damage is relatively slight. The September 11 attacks are variously estimated to have cost between $500,000 and $2 million to carry out.[8] Even the higher of those estimates represents less than one hour's worth of revenue in the illicit market for cocaine in the United States, or about 1% of the annual value of the coca leaf that generates cocaine for the U.S. market. Therefore, the leakage of funds from drugs (or any other financial source, for that matter) into terror does not have to be substantial, measured as part of the drug trade, to constitute a large part of the funding of terror.

Similarly, the fact that most drug-dealing revenues are earned in consumer countries rather than source or transit countries does not necessarily mean that none of that money is available for the support of terrorism. Some of the revenues earned from transactions that take place in the United States may flow back to other countries where it is put to sometimes violent uses, as was the case with cocaine trafficking by the Medellin Cartel.[9] DEA reportedly has found that some of the revenues from a Midwestern methamphetamine and methamphetamine-precursor trafficking organization, some of whose personnel were

---

5 ONDCP, What American's Users Spend on Illegal Drugs (Table 6), p. 18.

6 U.S. Department of Justice, National Drug Intelligence Center (NDIC), Heroin Distribution in Three Cities, Document 2001-R0370-001, Nov. 2000, available at [http://www.usdoj.gov/ndic/pubs/648/la_econ.htm].

7 Jonathan P. Caulkins and Peter Reuter, "What Price Data Tell Us About Drug Markets," Journal of Drug Issues, vol. 28, no. 3 (1998), pp. 593-612 and R. MacCoun and Peter Reuter, Drug War Heresies: Lessons Learned from Other Vices, Times, and Places (Santa Monica, CA: RAND Corp., 2001), pp. 20-21.

8 Chris Baker, "Putting a Price Tag on Terror," Washington Times, Nov. 18, 2001, pp. A1($500,000 estimate), "Hard Evidence Would Help," Economist, Sept. 29, 2001, and The Canadian Foundation for Drug Policy, *How Drug Prohibition Finances and OtherwiseEnables Terrorism*, Introduction, p. 1 ($2 million estimate).

9 Kevin Jack Riley, *Snow Job*: *The War Against International Drug Trafficking*, (Greenwood Press, 1996), pp. 155-156.

nationals of Middle Eastern countries, was flowing into the coffers of terrorist organizations such as Hezbollah and Hamas.[10]

Unlike drug dealing, terrorism does not "naturally" generate money. Rather than flowing up from the bottom of the organization (starting with customers paying retail dealers, who then pay middlemen, who pay suppliers, who pay importers, who pay exporters), terrorist cash flows down the organization from organizers to foot soldiers (and their families). The money eventually comes from donors,[11] from extortion victims, from theft or robbery victims, and from illicit-market (including drug) transactions.

In the drug business, cash is seldom the factor that bounds how large an organization can grow; the limiting factors are people to buy from, people to sell to, the availability of drugs themselves (not ultimately scarce, but sometimes unavailable to those who would otherwise buy them), and opportunities to make relatively safe transactions.

Terrorist organizations, by contrast, may be cash-constrained. They vary enormously in their ability to solicit or extort contributions, and to steal or deal. An open question is how large the effect would be if it were possible to substantially reduce the money available to various kinds of terrorist groups from drug trafficking. The answer to that question may vary greatly from group to group; to the extent that

Al Qaeda, for example, is financed by the bin Laden family fortune or by fund-raising in Saudi Arabia, its dependence on drug revenues could be very slight. By contrast, drug revenues are undoubtedly important, perhaps central, to the financing both of the FARC[12] in Colombia and of the paramilitary forces opposing the FARC, as they were to the *Sendero Luminoso* ("Shining Path") in Peru.[13] Spanish authorities report that the March 2004 terrorist attacks on the Madrid train system that killed nearly200 people and injured 1,400 others were financed largely by sales of hashish (a marijuana derivative) and Ecstasy (MDMA).[14]

Chaos and Instability

Drug dealing can generate chaos and instability in source and transit countries by sustaining violence, both within and among groups of traffickers and between traffickers on the one hand and ordinary citizens and public authorities on the other. The growth of a criminal economy is also a potentially destabilizing factor. Drug law enforcement can create friction between law enforcement and military authorities on the one hand and ordinary citizens, including small farmers who illicitly grow drug crops, on the other. The secretive

---

10 Associated Press, "U.S. Drug Ring Tied to Aid for Hezbollah," *New York Times*, Sept. 3, 2002, p A16.

11 Some donors, no doubt, are deliberately financing terrorist activity. Others may be deceived by charitable appeals. Still others can be somewhere in between: giving money in "humanitarian" ways that may help support or endorse terrorist activity, for example by financing assistance to the families of terrorists who are killed.

12 The primary insurgent group in Colombia, called the Revolutionary Armed Forces of Colombia; the acronym is formed from the group's Spanish name, *Fuerzas Armadas Revolucionarias de Colombia.*

13 Testimony of DEA Administrator Asa Hutchinson, in U.S. Congress, Senate Committee on the Judiciary, *Narco-Terrorism: The Worldwide Connection Between Drugs and Terrorism, hearings*, 107th Cong., 2nd sess., Mar. 13, 2002, S.Hrg. 107-885 (Washington: GPO, 2001). See DEA's website at [http://www.dea.gov/pubs/cngrtest/ct031302p.html].

14 Dale Fuchs, "Spain Says Bombers Drank Water from Mecca and Sold Drugs," *New York Times*, Apr. 15, 2004, p. A3.

techniques of drug investigation can become entangled with the practice of authoritarian rule, as appears to have happened under the Fujimori[15] government in Peru.

In addition, traffickers can deliberately create chaos in order to weaken the ability of the institutions of government and civil society to interfere with their illegal business. In Colombia, for example, the Medellin Cartel attempted to use terror to deter the Colombian government from proceeding with vigorous law enforcement [16]measures.

The same effects can also take place in consumer countries. The retail drug traffic, especially when it grows violent, can be a powerful source of chaos, as many American neighborhoods discovered as the crack trade spread in the 1980s and early 1990s. It has been suggested, though not demonstrated, that drug trafficking has been used as a form of low-intensity conflict.[17] The theory is that forces hostile to a given country might attempt to introduce or aggravate drug addiction problems there as a means of attack.

Corruption and Intimidation

Large-scale drug trafficking frequently involves corrupt contacts between traffickers and officials, including elected officials, enforcement agents, prosecutors and judges, and military personnel. The corruption problem can be exacerbated by low public-sector wages. Both corruption and anti-corruption measures can be profoundly demoralizing, and can reduce the respect the public has for the agencies of government. Even when corruption does not actually exist, the perception of corruption can be corrosive. The resulting diminished public support for government agencies makes the anti-drug effort that much more difficult.

Once corruption becomes embedded in the practice of an agency, it may not remain restricted to its original domain; an army commander accustomed to taking bribes from drug traffickers may be less resistant to bribes from terrorist groups. (The opposite effect is also, of course, logically possible; the flow of corrupt money from drug trafficking may make the bribes terrorist groups are capable of paying seem too small to bother with from the viewpoint of officials used to larger bribes in the drug business.)

The complement to corruption is intimidation. The Medellin Cartel in Colombia famously offered officials a choice of *"plata o plomo"* (literally, "silver or lead"): those who refused corrupt cash risked violence against themselves and their families.[18] Agencies demoralized by drug-related intimidation may be less effective against terrorist groups.

Cover and Common Infrastructures

When it is impossible to conceal entirely the existence of illicit activity, more serious crimes can be disguised as less serious crimes as a way of avoiding enforcement attention or securing cooperation from accomplices willing to break some laws but not others. Terrorists

---

[15] Kevin G. Hall, "Military corruption dogs U.S. drug-fighting efforts in Peru," *Seattle Times*, Apr. 24, 2001, p. A8.

[16] Riley, 1996, p. 160.

[17] Douglas, Joseph D., *Red Cocaine: The Drugging of America and the West* (New Yorkand London: Edward Harle Limited, 1999).

[18] Ibid., p. 156.

might attempt to use the appearance, or even the actual practice, of drug trafficking as "cover" for themselves, their movements of contraband, or their preparations for terrorist actions. In addition, the existence of large illicit drug markets can facilitate terrorist activity by supporting a web of "service providers" — such as money launderers, providers of "cloned" cell phones, and makers of false identification documents — which terrorist groups can use, even though the terrorists themselves would not constitute a big enough market to keep such providers in business.

Another possibility is that terrorist material and personnel have moved, or will in the future move, disguised as illicit drugs, just as illicit drugs have been known to move disguised as other smuggled materials (e.g., diamonds). Unwitting accomplices and complicit officials may be less reluctant to participate in what they think is drug dealing than in helping carry out terrorist activity.[19]

It has been reported that some of the September 11 attackers used false identification obtained from an illicit commercial seller of such documents, a seller who did not know, or at least has not been charged with knowing, the end to which the results of his illegal activity would be put.[20] Whether that person's other clientele may have included drug traffickers has not been stated publicly (his primary market consisted of people defying the immigration laws), but there is no doubt that forbidden drug transactions (down to the level of alcohol purchases by underage drinkers) can and do make use of fraudulent documentation.

Drug traffickers need to consolidate cash they receive from further down their organizations into larger bundles and protect the resulting financial or physical assets from seizure, while terrorist organizers need instead to move money down their organizations to where it is spent. Therefore, the two sets of mechanisms may tend to remain quite distinct, except in cases where it is drug money earned in U. S. transactions that then flows into terrorist hands. Indeed, providers of illicit services to the drug trade have very strong incentives to avoid becoming entangled in terrorist acts.

After the September 11 attack, there was considerable speculation that terrorists might be making use of the same money-laundering services that support illicit drug transactions. This suggestion does not seem to have been borne out; it appears that a separate set of institutions (such as the informal *hawala* money-transfer networks), related to international remittances more than to drug dealing, may be in play.[21]

Competition for Enforcement Resources

The targeting of enforcement and intelligence resources sometimes involves choosing between counter-drug targets and counter-terror targets. Other things being equal, the larger the drug trafficking problem, the larger the resources required to combat it, and those resources may then be unavailable for use against terrorist targets. The extent to which new

---

[19] See Rick Mofina, "Canadian Diamonds Could Lure Terrorists: Police" St. John's Telegram, Ottowa, Canada, Aug. 24, 2002, p. A9 for a discussion of the methods used to smuggle drugs, precious gems, and other contraband.

[20] P. Shenen and D. Van Natta, "A Nation Challenged: The Investigation; U.S. Says 3 Detainees May Be Tied to Highjackings," *New York Times*, Nov. 1, 2001, p. A1.

[21] Douglas Frantz, "U.S.-Based Charity is Under Scrutiny," *New York Times*, June 14, 2002, p. A1.

funding and organizational restructuring will compensate for those "losses" is uncertain at this time.

The events of September 11 have already taken a toll on drug law enforcement. The Federal Bureau of Investigation has announced that a substantial fraction of the agents it had assigned to drug law enforcement will be reassigned to meet the threat of terrorism. The United States Customs Service has also redirected some of its investigative resources.[22] DEA agents are all devoted to drug law enforcement, but the share of the DEA in the total federal law enforcement budget is not fixed, and it is possible that the agency's growth will be slowed by the budgetary demands of the anti-terror effort.[23] It is also possible that some of the anti-terror effort by local law enforcement will employ resources that otherwise would have been devoted to drug law enforcement.

However, the extent of the competition should not be exaggerated; the two efforts have elements of joint production as well as competition. While investigative resources must be targeted against one threat or another, the activities of border inspection and air and sea interdiction are much less specific. Anything that makes it more difficult to smuggle contraband generally into the United States, for example, increases the challenge facing drug traffickers and terrorist groups alike; heightened scrutiny of passengers and freight in the immediate aftermath of September 11 led to temporary reductions in drug-smuggling volume.[24] On the other hand, some screening approaches are specific rather than generic; a Geiger counter will not detect drugs, and a Labrador will not alert on plutonium or anthrax spores.

The federal drug law enforcement effort, because of its size and international scope, can also contribute to the struggle against terror by extending the reach of complementary anti-drug enforcement mechanisms to a wider range of foreign agencies. The international consensus on the issue of illicit drug trafficking may allow the DEA (and investigators from other federal agents engaged in drug law enforcement) to obtain the cooperation of foreign agencies in ways that might otherwise be withheld from U.S. anti-terror units.

The links between some terrorists and drug trafficking may create exploitable vulnerabilities for the terrorist groups involved. Drug traffickers frequently offer information about one another to investigators, both to damage their commercial rivals and to build up their "favor banks" with enforcement agencies, either for general future use or as a way of avoiding being charged in a pending case.[25] Terrorist groups generally have much less occasion to employ such tactics. The intelligence-gathering value of drug law enforcement in the anti-terror effort has perhaps not been fully exploited. However, the secretive nature of the process of managing informants means that, even if it were being exploited, the results would not be evident to outside observers.

---

[22] R. Pear and P. Shenen, "Customs Switches Priority From Drugs to Terrorism," *New York Times*, Oct. 10, 2001, p. B11.

[23] Patrick J. Murphy et al., *Improving Anti-Drug Budgeting* (Santa Monica, CA: RAND Corp, 2000).

[24] Fox Butterfield, "Officials Report Drop in Drug Smuggling," *New York Times*, Sept. 28, 2001, p. A16.

[25] Even the drug cartels themselves are known to offer information to the authorities against one another as the case of Medellin Cartel head Pablo Escobar who believed that the Cali cartel had aided the government in his manhunt - Riley (1996), p. 172. For more on the role of informants, see Peter Reuter, *Licensed Criminals: Police and Informants*, RAND Document P-6820, 1982.

DRUG POLICY TO REDUCE THE TERRORIST THREAT

The Importance of Scale

Whichever aspect of the potential drug/terror connection we look at, the sheer scale of the illicit drug industry (measured in dollars) is an important determinant of the contribution it may make to terrorism. The correct weighting of drug control objectives against anti-terrorist objectives depends in part on how much drug trafficking actually contributes to the threat of terrorist action, and how much anti-drug efforts could do to reduce that contribution. Those factors, in turn, are likely to vary from drug to drug.

The Multiple Goals of Drug Control Policy

Drug control policy involves a variety of distinct, and sometimes competing, goals, other than combating terrorism.[26] A partial list might include

- reducing the prevalence of any illicit drug use, especially among children and teenagers;
- reducing addiction;
- reducing violence associated with drug trafficking;
- reducing crime associated with drug use;
- protecting neighborhoods from the disruptive effects of retail drug dealing;
- preventing the employment of juveniles in the drug traffic;
- protecting the public health from drug-related infectious diseases;
- protecting the children of drug users from being damaged by their parents' drug use;
- moderating the damage done by drug abuse to the health status, productivity, and family functioning of users; and
- reducing the prevalence of accidents due to intoxication.

The part of drug control policy concerned with reducing the drug contribution to terrorism will not necessarily serve all of these goals. That does not mean that the remaining goals should be abandoned, but it does imply that tradeoffs may need to be considered.

Moreover, all drugs are not likely to make the same contributions to the terrorism threat, either quantitatively or qualitatively. Ecstasy (MDMA) produced in the Netherlands and smuggled into the United States by Russian and Israeli organized-crime groups obviously poses a different set of issues than cocaine produced in FARC-dominated regions of Colombia.

Even the same drug may have very different implications for terrorism in different circumstances: where it comes from, how it travels, and which organizations traffic in it all make a difference. The United States gets the bulk of its heroin from poppies grown in

[26] For a further discussion of drug control policy issues, see Mark A. R. Kleiman, Against *Excess: Drug Policy for Results* (New York: Basic Books, 1992).

Colombia, a smaller amount from poppies grown in Southeast Asia, and relatively little from poppies grown in Southwest Asia, including Afghanistan. Most of the heroin produced from the Afghani poppy crop either stays in Asia or is trafficked into Europe. Thus in the period leading up to September 11, 2001, European heroin consumption potentially helped finance Al Qaeda activities, or helped support the Taliban regime which harbored Al Qaeda, but heroin consumption in the United States likely did not. U.S. heroin consumption may have contributed to the terrorist threat in Colombia, and perhaps in Mexico, but likely had very little impact on Afghanistan or its neighbors.[27] (Unlike petroleum, for example, which is traded in world markets, so that increased demand or decreased supply anywhere tends to raise prices everywhere, the illicit trade in heroin tends to be compartmentalized, so that prices for poppy can be high in Colombia but low in Afghanistan, or vice versa.) By contrast, anyone concerned with the terror problem in Colombia can afford to ignore Asian heroin consumption, because virtually no Colombian-source heroin makes its way to Asia.[28]

The international drug traffic involves large numbers of organizations of various sizes. Some may be connected to, or subject to extortion by, terrorist groups; others may not.[29] Drugs flow along many different pathways. Even for a given drug, country of origin, and trafficking route, there may still be crucial distinctions among trafficking organizations. Because different drug traffickers compete with one another, pressure put on any one translates into improved opportunities for the remainder. Thus effective enforcement against one smuggling route encourages the development of others, and alternatives developed under enforcement pressure may have greater connection to actual or potential terrorism than the ones they replace.

For example, cocaine and heroin from Colombia flows into the United States either by air and sea through the Caribbean and into South Florida, the Gulf Coast, and the East Coast, or overland through Central America and Mexico and across the Southwest Border.[30] Since these two routes compete with each other, pressure on either indirectly encourages the use of the other; the vast increase in enforcement pressure on the Caribbean route in the 1980s created the incentive for the development of the overland route. That probably reduced somewhat the possible contribution of drug-related money, chaos, and corruption to political violence in (e.g., the Dominican Republic), but increased those risks in Guatemala and Mexico. Without speculating as to whether that change represented a net gain or loss from a counter-terror perspective, it might be noted that published reports of the policy discussions regarding the build-up in Caribbean enforcement do not mention any discussion of the possible impacts of that move on Central American and Mexican political stability.

---

[27] U.S. Department of Justice, National Drug Intelligence Center (NDIC), National Drug Threat Assessment 2002, Document 2002-J0403-002, Dec. 2001, p. 19, available at [http://www.usdoj.gov/ndic/pubs07/716/index.htm].

[28] With Southeast Asia producingopiumin quantities sufficient to yield between 90 and 110 metric tons of heroin (NDIC measure cited above), there is no current need for import to the markets of China and Asia. Roughly 3 metric tons (6,600 pounds) made it to U.S. markets, according to NDIC.

[29] In Columbia, for example, the M-19 guerrilla movement has allegedly been "retained" by the drug cartels to provide protection and to carry out some of the bloodier retaliatory attacks on Columbian citizens and symbols of civil authority. The November 1985 attack on the Columbian Palace of Justice that resulted in more than 100 fatalities at a time when the Columbian Supreme Court was nearing a decision on the legality of extraditing drug suspects to the United States was attributed to this *ad hoc* alliance. Riley, 1996. p. 159-161).

[30] ONDCP, "Estimation of Cocaine Availability 1996-2000," Mar. 2002, pp. 18-20. Available at [http://www.whitehousedrugpolicy.gov/publications/pdf/cocaine2002.pdf].

In considering how to allocate our drug enforcement resources, policymakers may want to consider the effects on how the drugs flow. In addition to influencing the overall size of the market, enforcement can influence its composition and conduct. Organizations, drugs, and trafficking routes are not uniform in their potential contributions to terrorism. Insofar as enforcement concentrates differentially on those aspects of the drug trade most likely to be linked to terror, it may exert both direct effects, by dismantling some organizations, and indirect effects, by creating a relative competitive disadvantage for those organizations whose trafficking activity is most prone to support terrorism, which in turn will help shape traffickers' behavior.

Not every enforcement activity that reduces drug consumption reduces the demand for imported drugs. Enforcement against U.S. production of drugs that are also imported (for example, eradication of the domestic cannabis crop and crackdowns on domestic methamphetamine production) may shrink consumption of those drugs overall by making them more expensive and less available to U.S. consumers, but will tend to increase demand at the import level, creating new opportunities for overseas drug producers and traffickers. The net effect on the terrorist threat is not obvious. It would depend not only on how the resulting overseas production and import activity tied in with terrorism, but also on the details of the domestic production and trafficking that is displaced, some of which may be linked to terrorism.

The same is true of that part of the enforcement effort devoted to seizing drugs, as opposed to arresting traffickers or seizing non-drug assets. Drug seizures actually increase the demand for drug imports, thus potentially contributing to problems in source countries, because cocaine refiners must buy from coca producers enough leaf to produce the amount drug users buy and consume, plus the amount enforcement agencies seize and destroy. From the grower's viewpoint, a ton seized is no different from a ton consumed. If the seizure process were so efficient that traffickers stopped trying, leading to a physical shortage and massive price increases, the result might be to shrink the market overall, but the replacement cost of seized drugs is so small compared to the value of landing them successfully that traffickers seem to be willing to run very substantial seizure risks without being deterred.[31]

It is estimated that total cocaine seizures now amount to approximately one-quarter of the total amount of cocaine shipped to the United States,[32] but the price of cocaine remains near its all-time lows[33] and no physical shortages have been reported since the fall of the Medellin Cartel in 1989 produced a temporary (roughly six month) supply interruption.[34]

The incorporation of a counter-terror perspective into drug policy decision making could involve adding such considerations at every stage of the drug enforcement process. Enforcement initiatives that may seem justified from a purely drug control perspective may have to be reconsidered if their net effect on the terrorist threat would be in the wrong direction, as might be true, for example, in the case of some interdiction efforts.

---

[31] P. Reuter, G. Crawford, and J. Cave, *Sealing the Borders: Effects of Increased Military Efforts in Drug Interdiction* (Santa Monica, CA: RAND Corp., 1988).

[32] *Estimation of Cocaine Availability*, pp. 10-11.

[33] *What America's Users Spend on Illegal Drugs*, 2000, figure 9, p. 57.

[34] Even this shortage had limited impact on the domestic market. The price of cocaine per milligram, as calculated above, showed a significant increase at the retail (street) level in early 1990 but returned to previous levels within the year and then began to decline to current levels.

For example, the direct support the Taliban regime in Afghanistan received from drug trafficking (and indirect U.S. support for its counter-drug efforts) helped keep it in power during the time its territory was being used by Al Qaeda as a base from which to plot hostilities against the United States. In that case, then, the drug money that may have (indirectly) supported terrorism became a direct threat to the United States. (It is less clear whether any of the assistance provided by the United States to replace the incomes of poppy farmers put out of business by the Taliban's prohibition on poppy production[35] in practice helped keep the Taliban in power. The same applies to the other relief aid that flowed to Afghanistan in that period — though not directly to the Taliban government — from a variety of international sources, reportedly as a "reward" to the Taliban for the poppy ban.) On the other hand, drug trafficking also helped sustain some elements of the Northern Alliance that were allies of the United States in ousting the Taliban. Insofar as the goal is to protect the United States against terrorist acts, we need not merely to cut down on the drug-related contribution to terrorism generally, but to the drug-related contribution to terrorist groups that threaten us.

Shrinking the Drug Markets

In the most abstract terms, the scale of the illicit drug markets is determined by demand, price, and availability. The markets can be reduced by shrinking demand (in the technical economic sense of that term: reducing the amount of illicit drugs consumers are willing to buy at any given price), by increasing the retail prices of illicit drugs (and thus reducing the quantity consumed at any given level of demand), or by making drugs less available in ways other than raising prices (one way to think of this is in terms of increasing the time, risk, and inconvenience required for a consumer to find a supplier, a concept referred to in the drug abuse control literature as "search time.")[36]

Shrinking demand, reducing availability, and increasing price will all tend to reduce total physical and financial volume. It was formerly believed that raising drug prices would lead to increases in total revenues due to what was thought to be relatively inelastic demand by drug consumers; more recent evidence suggests strongly that demand for illicit drugs is more than unit-elastic, so that a price increase tends to produce a more-than-offsetting decrease in quantity purchased and thus a shrinkage in total revenues.[37] The fact that drug consumption at one point in time tends to increase effective demand at later points — because of the development both of social and personal habit patterns of drug use and of pharmacologically-based tolerance and dependency — reinforces this effect.

---

[35] U.S. Department of State, "Rocca Meets Taliban Representative in Islamabad," Aug. 2, 2001 at [http://usinfo.state.gov/topical/pol/terror/01080202.htm] and U.S. Department of State, "Rocca on $1.5 Million in Aid to Former Afghan Poppy Growers,"
Aug. 2, 2001 at [http://www.usembassy.it/file2001_08/alia/a1080204.htm].

[36] Peter Reuter and Mark A.R. Kleiman, "Risks and Prices: An Economic Analysis of Drug Enforcement," in Norval Morris and Michael Tonry, eds., *Crime and Justice: An Annual Review of Research, v. 7.* (Chicago: University of Chicago Press, 1986), pp. 301-306; and Jack K. Riley, *Crack, Powder Cocaine, and Heroin : Drug Purchase and Use Patterns in Six U.S. Cities,* ONDCP, 1997, pp. 14-21, at [http://www.ncjrs.org/pdffiles/167265.pdf].

[37] Jonathan P. Caulkins, "Estimating Elasticities of Demand for Cocaine and Heroin With Data from the Drug Use Forecasting System," unpublished Manuscript (1995), H. John Heinz III School of Public Policy and Management, Carnegie Mellon University.

The Difficulty of Raising Prices in Mature Markets

Perhaps the greatest surprise in the field of drug policy over the past generation has been the persistent failure of hard-drug prices to raise in the face of greatly expanded enforcement efforts. The scale of the drug enforcement enterprise, as measured by the number of traffickers in prison, has grown nearly 30-fold since 1980; even adjusting for the rise of heroin and cocaine volumes over that period, the increase in enforcement intensity (the ratio of enforcement effort to the size of the underlying market) has been roughly five-fold. Yet cocaine and heroin prices have actually fallen, in inflation-adjusted dollars, by approximately 80% each, and remain near their lowest levels.[38] Cannabis prices, which rose in the face of increased enforcement in the late 1970s and early 1980s, have also been drifting lower despite continued vigorous law enforcement efforts.[39]

There is considerable uncertainty about the reasons for the behavior of drug prices over the past two decades, and no consensus about what the course of drug prices would have been in the face of different policies. It may be the case that, beyond a certain size, drug markets become so resilient that enforcement has great difficulty influencing them. But there appears now to be little reason to think that any feasible increase in drug law enforcement effort could substantially increase prices. The Drug Enforcement Administration, which once used to refer to its price series as its "Performance Measurement System," no longer considers increasing drug prices as a gauge of its effectiveness.

Insofar as additional enforcement is not likely to substantially raise the prices of those drugs associated with terrorist activity, then bringing about such a price increase as a way of shrinking the volume in the drug markets cannot be listed as one of the more promising options for dealing with the threat posed by terrorist organizations.

The Difficulty of Reducing Availability in Mature Markets

There remain differences of opinion about the extent to which enforcement can have lasting effects on drug availability. The standard, skeptical view holds that retail-level enforcement — efforts directed at the dealers who make the final sale to drug users, and the immediate suppliers of those retail dealers, as opposed to higher-level traffickers — can only move markets around rather than actually shrinking them. That view is challenged by scattered success stories[40] and by dramatic differences in user-reported difficulty in purchasing drugs between New York (after its well-publicized crackdown on retail drug dealing) and other cities.[41]

Academic proponents of retail-oriented enforcement strategies emphasize the importance of disrupting the markets, rather than merely making many arrests, and argue in consequence for concentration, rather than dispersion, of retail enforcement activity. In yet-unpublished work, David Kennedy has begun to explore arrest-minimizing techniques for disrupting markets, in recognition of the fact that the cost of drug crackdowns in police and court

---

[38] *What America's Users Spend on Illegal Drugs*, 2000, pp. 57-58.

[39] Ibid., figure 12, p. 60

[40] For example, see M. Kleiman, *Crackdowns: The Effects of Intensive Enforcement on Retail Heroin Dealing,* in Marcia R. Chaiken (ed.), *Street Level Drug Enforcement: Examining the Issues* (Washington: National Institute *of Justice, 1988), and David M. Kennedy,* Closing the Market: Controlling the Drug Trade in Tampa, Florida, National Institute of Justice Program Focus, NCJ Number: 139963, April 1993.

[41] Riley, Table 21, 1997, pp. 19-20.

resources represent one of the most important barriers to their widespread use, and that the costs depend directly on the number of arrests made.

In theory, it might be possible to shrink drug volumes by systematically reducing retail availability. However, the efficacy of such a strategy depends on still-unproven claims about the capacities of law enforcement and about the effect of changes in retail availability on long-run drug consumption patterns, and especially of the consumption patterns of chronic high-dose illicit drug users, who collectively account for the vast bulk of illicit drug consumption.

If, as seems plausible, the level of violence were roughly proportional to some combination of the volume of transactions and the revenues of the industry, increasing search time would tend to decrease violence. On the other hand, a shrinking market might lead to increased levels of violent disputes among market participants, especially if dealers from a market forced out of existence by a crackdown attempt to poach on others' established sales territories. Since illicit drug prices now seem hard to influence, and since availability is directly determined by the numbers, social and spatial distribution, and behavior of retail sellers rather than that of large-scale distributors, it can be argued that retail-level drug law enforcement would be the most promising means of controlling non-drug crime.

However, in the absence of a well-worked-out and empirically tested theory of how the different levels of the drug traffic relate to each other — which may not be the same for all drugs, or for all times and places — one cannot rule out the possibility espoused by some enforcement officials and researchers, that enforcement directed at high-level dealers, particularly in source and transit zones, could, under some circumstances, decisively influence availability, and do so far more cost-effectively than retail-level strategies.[42]

For now, however, neither high-level nor retail-level enforcement can be considered highly likely to succeed in reducing the size of the drug markets. And, considered from the perspective of reducing terrorist threats, drug law enforcement may not be risk-free. Roughly 150,000 persons are sentenced to prison each year on drug charges — approximately one-quarter of the total influx to prison — and a comparable number are released. In addition to whatever effect prison might have in increasing propensities to violence generally, prisons are recruiting grounds for violent gangs with outside-the-walls affiliates and for extremist religious groups. While there have been no known attempts by overseas terrorist groups to recruit members in U.S. prisons or from among prison releasees, those populations would seem to be natural recruiting targets.[43] Even a very low success rate from such a large population could constitute a substantial increment to the potential supply of terrorists. Arguably, increasing the number of prisoners increases the number of potential terrorist recruits.

---

[42] B.D. Crane, A.R. Rivolo, and G.C. Comfort, *An Empirical Examination of Counterdrug Interdiction Program Effectiveness,* Institute for Defense Analysis, IDA paper, 1997, p. 3219; but see also Charles F. Manski, John V. Pepper, and Yonette Thomas, eds., Assessment *of Two Cost-Effectiveness Studies on Cocaine Control Policy,* Committee on Data and Research for Policy on Illegal Drugs, Committee on Law and Justice and Committee on National Statistics, Commission on Behavioral and Social Sciences and Education (Washington: National Academy Press, 1999).

[43] Chuck Colson, "Evangelizing For Evil In Our Prisons," *The Wall Street Journa*l, June 24, 2002, p. A16.

The Complexities of Demand Reduction.

The volume of the drug traffic, both physically and financially, which largely determines its potential contribution to terrorism, depends on drug users, who consume the drugs and pay for them, and in particular on high-dose, chronic drug users, who account for most of the total retail expenditure on illicit drugs.[44] That is the basis of the idea that drug demand reduction deserves a central place in policy thinking, in particular if the question is how to reduce the contribution of drug trafficking to terror.

"Demand reduction" names a goal, but does not name a single program, or group of programs. While prevention and treatment are often thought of as constituting the "demand side" of the anti-drug effort and enforcement the "supply side," matters on the ground are much less simple. First, the effective demand for any drug is in part a function of its retail availability; even consumers, who desire to acquire a drug, and have the money to pay for it, may be unable to buy if there is no seller geographically and socially convenient to them. From the viewpoint of large-scale drug suppliers, retail drug law enforcement, when it is successful in suppressing market activity rather than merely shifting it around, acts as a demand reduction measure. The same is true insofar as retail enforcement, and drug testing programs in various venues, act as deterrents to drug use.

The most familiar, and popular, demand reduction programs are drug abuse prevention programs, which include school-based, community-based, and mass-media efforts.[45] What they have in common is a goal of preventing, or at least retarding in time, the initiation of illicit drug use (and of the underage use of alcohol and tobacco). These programs are relatively inexpensive on a per-person basis and can therefore be applied to the entire population. When they are effective, they are extremely cost-effective as a means of reducing the number of illicit drug users. However, two factors may limit the capacity of such programs to make a substantial impact on the physical and financial flows in the illicit markets. First, even for the best prevention programs the measured effect sizes — the proportionate reduction in the number of persons engaging in the target behaviors — tend to be modest: a reduction in, for example, the rate of marijuana smoking in a seventh-grade cohort from 13% among "untreated" individuals to 10% among those exposed to a prevention program is considered a state-of-the-art result.[46] Second, most of those whose illicit drug use is prevented would never have become heavy users in any case, both because the transition from experimental use to heavy use is itself relatively infrequent and, possibly, because the very factors that make young people receptive to prevention messages may reduce their risks of progressing to heavy use even if they do initiate the consumption of illicit drugs.

The total number of illicit drug users is often considered the most important measure of the success of demand reduction efforts. But focusing on reducing the potential contribution of the drug problem to terrorism would shift the emphasis from the total number of drug users

---

44 Mark A.R. Kleiman, "Coerced Abstinence: A Neo-Paternalistic Drug Policy Initiative," in Mead, Lawrence A. ed., *The New Paternalism* (Brookings Institution Press, 1997), pp. 15-16.

45 J.P. Caulkins et al., *An Ounce of Prevention, a Pound of Uncertainty: The Cost-Effectiveness of School-Based Drug Prevention Programs* (Santa Monica, CA: RAND Corp., 1999), pp. 1-9.

46 Ibid., pp. 81-84. Mark A.R. Kleiman, "Addiction, Rationality, Behavior and Measures: Some Comments on the Problems of Integrating Econometric and Behavioral Economic Research," in Frank J. Chaloupka, Warren K. Bickel, Michael Grossman, and Henry Saffer, eds., *The Economic Analysis of Substance Use and Abuse: An Integration of Econometric and Behavioral Economic Research* (Chicago: The University of Chicago Press, 1999), pp. 242-247, National Bureau of Economic Research.

to the much smaller number of heavy users. Illicit drug users vary greatly in the quantities they consume, and therefore in the revenues they contribute to the illicit markets. A small fraction of all the users account for the vast bulk of total purchases, in accordance with "Pareto's Law," also known as the 80/20 rule, which finds that for many activities one-fifth of the number of persons involved account for four-fifths of the volume of transactions.[47] Shrinking the number of occasional users (except insofar as some of them would later have developed into heavy users) can make only a small contribution to reducing the volume of illicit drugs consumed. (The phenomenon is not limited to illicit drugs; alcohol consumption, which is more reliably known because sales are taxed and drinkers less unwilling to honestly describe their behavior than users of illicit drugs, follows the same pattern, with half of all alcohol consumed by the 10% heaviest drinkers and four-fifths of all alcohol consumed by the 20% heaviest drinkers.) In the case of cocaine, the entire population surveyed by the National Household Survey on Drug Abuse reports consuming no more than 10% of the actual volume of cocaine sold. Although account needs to be taken of the candor of individuals responding to a survey on illicit drug usage, the 10% figure still suggests the presence of a large "hidden" population of very heavy users who absorb the bulk of the cocaine sold.

The Arrestee Drug Abuse Monitoring (ADAM) system[48] (recently terminated by its sponsor, the National Institute of Justice) shows a very heavy concentration of drug use among property and violent crime offenders. The ADAM results, and other studies of offender populations, tend to confirm the existence of such a group of heavy users, not only for cocaine but for heroin and methamphetamine as well. This group of high-volume, persistent user-offenders, estimated at no more than about 3 million individuals, makes up the heart of the hard-drug markets. (Cannabis consumption also appears to be heavily concentrated, but chronic property and violent offenders represent a much smaller proportion of cannabis users than is the case for heroin, cocaine, or methamphetamine. Therefore, controlling offender drug use would have a smaller effect on the marijuana markets than on the markets for "hard" drugs.) Members of this population have average expenditures of more than $10,000 per year on cocaine and heroin,[49] which explains both their capacity to absorb so much of the supply and their concentration among offenders.

Shrinking the hard-drug markets thus depends largely on shrinking the consumption of this group of high-dose, chronic users, sometimes known as "hard-core" users and identified, not entirely accurately, with "addicts."

The best-known approach to doing so is providing more drug treatment services. Clear evidence from a wide range of studies indicates that high-volume drug users who enter and remain in treatment tend to make substantial reductions in their drug use while treatment lasts, and that the reductions tend to carry over into the post-treatment period. That appears to be true across virtually the entire range of treatment approaches. It is also the case that the number of treatment "slots" is exceeded by the number of persons estimated to be "in need of" drug treatment by various approaches. Some have concluded from those findings that

---

[47] Mark A.R. Kleiman, "Controlling Drug Use and Crime with Testing, Sanctions, and Treatment," in P.H. Heymann, and W.N. Brownsberger, eds., *Drug Addiction and Drug Policy* (Cambridge, MA: Harvard University Press, 2001), pp. 168-192.

[48] U.S. Department of Justice, National Institute of Justice, Arrestee Drug Abuse Monitoring Program (ADAM), 1999 Annual Report on Drug Use Among Adult and Juvenile Arrestees, June 2000, at [http://www.whitehousedrugpolicy.gov/publications/pdf/adam99.pdf].

[49] *What America's Users Spend on Illegal Drugs*, 2000, pp. 12-14.

increasing the number of hard-core users in treatment is the best approach to reducing the overall size of the drug problem, and have gone on to argue that increasing public funding for drug treatment programs is the most cost-effective approach to shrinking the drug markets.[50] To the extent that is the case, and to the limited extent that the drug markets help support terrorism, then drug treatment should be considered as one means of reducing terrorist risk.

Even under fairly conservative assumptions, it can be argued that increasing support for publicly paid drug treatment would have benefits well in excess of costs. However, it should be noted that funding is by no means the only barrier — perhaps it is not even the most important — to treatment participation. There has been considerable discussion of the "treatment gap," defined as the difference between the number of persons needing treatment and the number actually receiving it, and there is a belief that closing that gap with additional spending will greatly shrink the illicit markets. But neither of those ideas should be accepted without qualification, and expanding the supply of drug treatment is not the only, or necessarily the most effective or cost-effective, approach to reducing drug use among heavy drug users.

Treatment, too, can be analyzed in terms of supply and demand. While the need for treatment as defined by diagnostic criteria clearly outstrips current treatment capacity, it is much less clear that current capacity falls short of the actual number of users willing to undergo treatment. While most seriously impaired drug users would probably prefer to lead less disordered lives, that does not necessarily translate into a desire to give up drug use, still less the desire and determination to undergo, and remain with, the difficult process of recovery. Within the criminal justice system, as many as half of all those offenders assigned to treatment in lieu of criminal punishment never show up for a first treatment appointment, and a substantial proportion of those who do appear quickly to drop out. Increasing the demand for treatment is as difficult and as important as increasing its supply. (Improving treatment quality poses different challenges.)

While there are indeed waiting lists in some treatment programs, there are also programs unable to recruit enough clients to fill their allocated "slots." Rather than addressing a "treatment gap," it would be more accurate to talk of "treatment gaps," in the plural: shortfalls in the capacity to provide particular services, such as residential programs for mothers with small children.

One possible approach to increasing the effective demand for treatment is to use the pressure that the criminal justice system provides to *compel* user-offenders to enter into treatment and remain there. That is the common core of a wide mix of programs: both drug diversion programs, either discretionary with the court or, as with California's Substance Abuse and Crime Prevention Act ("Proposition 36"), mandated by law, and drug courts, which combine the diversion concept with direct supervision of the treatment process, and

---

[50] C.P. Rydell and S.S. Everingham, *Controlling Cocaine: Supply Versus Demand Programs*, (Santa Monica, CA: RAND Corp.); B.D. Crane, A.R. Rivolo, and G.C. Comfort, *An Empirical Examination of Counterdrug Inderdiction Program Effectiveness* (Alexandria, VA: Institute for Defense Analysis, 1997), p. 3219. David Boyum, *Costs and Benefits of Drug Treatment and Drug Enforcement : A Review of the CALDATA and RAND Studies*, 1995, ONDCP; Charles F. Manski, John V. Pepper, and Yonette Thomas eds., *Assessment of Two Cost-Effectiveness Studies on Cocaine Control Policy*, Committee on Data and Research for Policy on Illegal Drugs, Committee on Law and Justice and Committee on National Statistics, Commission on Behavioral and Social Sciences and Education (Washington: National Academy Press, 1999); and J.P. Caulkins, et al. *Response to the National Research Council's Assessment of RAND's Controlling Cocaine Study* (Santa Monica, CA: RAND Corp., 2000).

treatment compliance, by a judge who can impose sanctions on offenders who do not hold up their part of the diversion bargain. In addition, drug treatment can be, and often is, imposed as a condition of probation or parole, even for offenders who do not request, or receive, a formal diversion agreement in which punishment is suspended in favor of treatment.

However, the mandate to treatment, both under diversion programs and under probation and parole supervision, is frequently more nominal than real. Few community-corrections agencies are staffed or organized to monitor treatment compliance and deliver reliable sanctions for non-compliance. That is the advantage claimed by drug courts, but even judicial supervision has not proven to be a magic bullet. The voluntary nature of drug courts and diversion programs (offenders can, and some do, refuse the offer of diversion and accept instead the ordinary punishment for the crimes they are charged with) also limits their potential scope.

An alternative, or complementary, approach would be to use the powers of the criminal justice system in an attempt to compel desistance from illicit drug use directly, rather than trying to compel treatment attendance. It has been proposed that frequent drug tests for probationers and parolees, with reliable sanctions for continued drug use, could reach a larger population than the coerced-treatment approaches can, with comparable effectiveness in reducing drug use and much greater cost-effectiveness. There is some evidence that such programs can be effective, but there is also great difficulty in putting them into practice, given the procedural demands of imposing sanctions for probation violations (which tend to put an undesirable gap in time between the forbidden behavior and the sanction intended to deter it) and the organizational and funding challenges faced by probation departments, many of which have no more than a dollar a day to spend on supervising each of their clients.[51]

Even with all these difficulties, addressing the problem of drug use among hard-core user-offenders may in the view of many experts, represent the single best opportunity for reducing the volume of illicit drugs consumed in the United States. The threat of terrorism would provide one more reason to concentrate on this part of the drug problem.

CONCLUSION

American drug policy is not, and should not be, driven entirely, or even primarily, by the need to reduce the contribution of drug abuse to our vulnerability to terrorist action. There are too many other goals to be served by the drug abuse control effort. However, the links between the two issues are sufficiently clear that the institutions of drug abuse control would be wise to factor the impact of their activities on the terrorist threat into their decision-

[51] Mark A.R. Kleiman, "Controlling Drug Use and Crime with Testing, Sanctions, and Treatment," in P.H. Heymann, and W.N. Brownsberger eds., *Drug Addiction and Drug Policy* (Cambridge, MA: Harvard University Press, 2001), pp. 168-192; Mark A.R. Kleiman, "Coerced Abstinence: A Neo-Paternalistic Drug Policy Initiative," in Lawrence A. Mead, ed., *The New Paternalism* (Brookings Institution Press, 1997), pp. 15-16.; William N. Brownsberger, "Limits on the Role of Testing and Sanctions," in P.H. Heymann, and W.N. Brownsberger, eds., *Drug Addiction and Drug Policy.* (Cambridge, MA: Harvard University Press, 2001), pp. 193-205.; and Mark A.R. Kleiman, T. Tran, P. Fishbein, Maria-Teresa Magula, W. Allen, and G. Lacy, "Opportunities and Barriers in Probation Reform: A Case Study of Drug Testing and Sanctions," California PolicyResearch Center, *CPRC Brief*, vol. 14, no. 4, June 2002.

making. Such a focus could involve employing enforcement to reduce the opportunities that drug trafficking provides to terrorist groups, and focusing the demand control effort more on the issue of hard-core user-offenders.

In: The War on Drugs: Winning, Losing or Treading Water
Editor: Nelson V. Arcos
ISBN 978-1-59454-235-0

Chapter 7

DRUG TRAFFICKING AND NORTH KOREA: ISSUES FOR U.S. POLICY *

Raphael F. Perl

SUMMARY

At least 50 documented incidents in more than 20 countries around the world, many involving arrest or detention of North Korean diplomats, link North Korea to drug trafficking. Such events, in the context of credible, but unproven, allegations of large scale state sponsorship of drug production and trafficking, raise important issues for the United States and its allies in combating international drug trafficking. The challenge to policy makers is how to pursue an effective counter drug policy and comply with U.S. law which may require cutting off aid to North Korea while pursuing other high-priority U.S. foreign policy objectives including (1) limiting possession and production of weapons of mass destruction; (2) limiting ballistic missile production and export; (3) curbing terrorism, counterfeiting, and international crime; and (4) addressing humanitarian needs.

Reports that the Democratic People's Republic of North Korea (DPRK) maybe limiting some of its food crop production in favor of drug crop production are particularly disturbing given the country's chronic food shortages, though the acreage in question is comparatively small. Another issue of rising concern is the degree to which profits from any North Korean drug trafficking, counterfeiting, and other crime-for-profit enterprises may be used to underwrite the costs of maintaining or expanding North Korean nuclear and missile programs. As the DPRK's drug trade becomes increasingly entrenched, and arguably decentralized, analysts question whether the Pyongyang regime (or any subsequent government) would have the ability to effectively restrain such activity, should it so desire.

Since 2003, overall seizures of North Korean-linked methamphetamine and heroin are generally down, arguably in response to enhanced international attention paid to such activity in the wake of the April 2003 seizure of heroin carried on the North Korean Vessel the "Pong Su." Some suggest that this decline in seizures being identified as DPRK origin is because

* Excerpted from CRS Report RL32167, dated January 25, 2007

North Korean source methamphetamine is now regularly being mistakenly identified as "Chinese source" given growing links of Chinese criminal elements to North Korea's drug production/trafficking activities. In line with such a conclusion are press reports in late 2006 of the arrests in differing locations in China of North Korean nationals involved with Chinese criminals in the trafficking of methamphetamine. However, it is not clear from the reports whether the drugs were of DPRK origin or whether the North Koreans arrested had links with DPRK officials. Reduction of illicit drug seizures linked to the DPRK has also given rise to speculation that North Korea has cut back on, if not dramatically curbed, its drug trafficking activity, and is compensating from the loss of income in this arena by beefing up its production and trafficking of counterfeit brand cigarettes.

It remains clear, however, that regardless of the mix of DPRK criminal activities at any particular given point in time, income from DPRK criminal activity continues to play a pivotal role in overall DPRK finances.

BACKGROUND

Allegations of North Korean drug production, trafficking, and crime- for- profit activity have become the focus of rising attention in Congress, the press, and diplomatic and public policy for. As early as October 28, 1997, Senators Charles Grassley and Jessie Helms sent a letter to Secretary of State, Madeleine Albright, questioning why North Korea was not included in the State Department's March 1, 1997, annual International Narcotics Control Strategy Report (INCSR) as a country involved in illicit drug production and trafficking. The Senators noted that according to press reports, North Korea's opium production in 1995 was 40 metric tons (mt) (roughly comparable to Mexico's) and that they believed that this figure "clearly represents a figure of over 1,000 hectares," the threshold cropland figure for inclusion in the report and designation as a major drug producing country.[1]

The Department of State's response of December 12, 1997, cited an inability to obtain data to substantiate North Korean production levels. Subsequently, in October 1998, the conferees for the Fiscal Year 1999 Omnibus Appropriations Act directed the President to include in the (March 1, 1999) INCSR "...information regarding the cultivation, production, and transshipment of opium by North Korea. The report shall be based upon all available information."[2] A Senate Bill (S. 5), Section 1209 of the Drug Free Century Act, introduced January 19, 1999, proposed a statement of congressional concern that the Department of State had "evaded its obligations with respect to North Korea" under the Foreign Assistance Act and encouraged the President to submit any required reports. It was not acted upon by the Senate.

---

[1] North Korean climate and soil are relativelyinhospitable to poppy cultivation and fertilizer is reportedly in short supply. Rough calculations suggest that perhaps such conditions might yield roughly the equivalent of 10 kilograms of opium gum per hectare. Under such a formula, 40 metric tons of raw opium production would be roughly indicative of 3,000 to 4,000 hectares of poppy cultivation. Note also that the DPRK produces some licit opium. According to the International Narcotics Control Board (INCB), the DPRK reported cultivating 91 hectares of opium poppy in 1991 which produced 415 kg. of opium.

[2] H.R. 4328, P.L. 105-277, 112 Stat. 2681, signed into law October 21, 1998. For conference report language see *Congressional Record*, October 19, 1998, H11365.

The Department of State has consistently been cautious not to pin an ironclad label of "state sponsorship" on North Korean drug trafficking activity. To do so would arguably require the imposition of foreign aid sanctions on the Pyongyang regime, a move seen by many as (1) over prioritizing drugs vis-à-vis more pressing issues (i.e., nuclear proliferation) and (2) unwisely restricting the portfolio of Administration options for dealing with what has been called a rogue state.

Moreover, if the amount of North Korean illicit poppy cultivation cannot be verified, the 1,000 hectare threshold potentially triggering foreign aid cutoff under the Foreign Assistance Act of 1961 will not be met. Consistent with such policy concerns, the Department of State has maintained that although allegations of illicit drug activity "remain profoundly troubling.... [T]he United States has not been able to determine the extent to which the North Korean Government is involved in manufacturing and trafficking in illegal drugs."[3]

The provisions of the Foreign Assistance Act of 1961 referred to above require that countries cultivating 1,000 hectares or more of illicit opium poppy be subject to annual (March 1st) drug reporting and certification procedures. Current law on International Drug Control Certification Procedures (P.L.107-228, Section 706) requires the President to submit to Congress, not later than September 15 of the preceding fiscal year, a report identifying each country determined to be a major drug transit or drug producing country as defined in section 481(e) of the Foreign Assistance Act of 1961. In the report the President must designate each country that has "failed demonstrably" to meet its counter narcotics obligations. Designated countries are ineligible for foreign assistance unless the President determines that assistance is vital to the U.S. national interest or that the country had made "substantial efforts" to improve its counter narcotics performance.[4] International disaster assistance (such as the food aid received by North Korea) is specifically exempted from all limitations on providing assistance under the act.[5] Previous certification requirements had established a 30- calendar day review process during which the Congress could override the President's determinations and stop U.S. foreign aid from going to specific countries, but this process is no longer extant.[6]

U.S. foreign aid to North Korea is severely restricted because of North Korea's designation by the U.S. Secretary of State as a country that has "repeatedly provided support for acts of international terrorism."[7] Assistance is currently limited to humanitarian assistance (food). In December 2002, the Bush Administration suspended petroleum assistance, i.e., heavy fuel oil shipments to North Korea for electrical generating capabilities as an alternative to nuclear generation of electrical power because North Korea has not lived up to its agreement to suspend its nuclear weapons program. As negotiated in the October 1994 U.S.-DPRK Agreed Framework, the United States committed to provide 500,000 tons

---

[3] U.S. Department of State, *International Narcotics Control Strategy Report* [INCSR], March 2003, p. VIII-45. See also Bach congressional testimony, note 14, below. Note also that experience from the trial by the U.S. of Panamanian leader Manuel Noriega on drug trafficking related charges has heightened concerns in the U.S. criminal justice community that U.S. government released information on drug trafficking activities of foreign leaders may not have the degree of reliability to qualify as evidence in a court of law.

[4] Id., Sec. 614, "Special Authorities."

[5] Id., Sec. 491 (b).

[6] P.L. 87-195 as amended, Sections 481(e)(2), 489, and 490. See CRS Report RL32038, *Drug Certification/ Designation Procedures for Illicit Narcotics Producing and Transit Nations*, by K. Larry Storrs.

of oil annually until completion of two light water nuclear reactors that are less susceptible to proliferation than facilities that North Korea has previously operated, but "frozen" under the agreement. In Fiscal Year 2004, North Korea received 110,000 metric tons of wheat from the United States valued roughly at $52.8 million.[8]

For the year 2003, North Korea's legal exports were estimated by the Korean Trade Promotion Investment Agency (KOTRA) to amount to $1.1 billion in goods — most of which were to its neighbors China, Japan and South Korea.[9] During the same period, imports (mostly from the same three nations) totaled roughly$2 billion, leaving an estimated shortfall of $999 million.[10] North Korea's need for hard currency is exacerbated by ongoing dismal economic conditions — an estimated per capita gross domestic product in the lower range of $750 to $1000 — and an ongoing nuclear program the costs of which may have exceeded $200 million per year in 1998 and which North Korea accelerated from 1999 on.[11]

ALLEGATIONS OF DRUG TRAFFICKING

President George W. Bush, in his Fiscal Year 2007 determination of major illicit drug trafficking and transit countries, raised the issue of heroin and methamphetamine trafficking linked to North Korea, and expressed his demand that North Korean stop its involvement in all criminal activity. In the words of his memorandum for the Secretary of State:

---

[7] See CRS Report RL33600, *International Terrorism: Threat, Policy, and Response*, by Raphael Perl. See also CRS Report RL31696, *North Korea: Economic Sanctions*, by Dianne Rennack.

[8] See CRS Report RS21834, U.S. *Assistance to North Korea*, by Mark Manyin. Prior to October 1998, humanitarian assistance was allocated under Title II of P.L. 480; subsequent food assistance falls under sec. 416 of the Agricultural Act of 1949, P.L. 81-439. Fuel assistance for FY2003 and earlier years is authorized by the corresponding Foreign Operations Appropriations Legislation with some restrictions lifted pursuant to a presidential waiver under Section 614 (a) (1) of the Foreign Assistance Act of 1961. See Presidential Determination 97-21, 62 F.R. 23939.

[9] Contrast this amount with $1.7 billion in exports in 1990 according to South Korea's central bank. According to *Agence France Presse* (October 23, 2003), since the mid-1980s North Korea has exported some 400 SCUD missiles along with missile- related parts to the Middle East valued at approximately $110 million. Estimates by U.S. Military Forces Command in Korea are reportedly substantially higher: $580 million from missile exports to the Middle East for the year 2001 alone. *See Yomiuri Shimbum*, "RiskyBusiness Leading North Korea to Ruin," August 22, 2003; and "New N. Korea Food Aid Pledges Only a Beginning," *Reuters*, March 4, 2003 dispatch from Seoul. Chosen Soren (ethnic North Korean) overseas remittances to the DPRK are estimated at some $200-$600 million annually. See *Yomiuri Shimbum* (file No. 555), May 18, 2003. See generally CRS Report RL32493, *The North Korean Economy: Background and Policy Analysis*, by Dick Nanto and Emma Chanlett-Avery.

[10] Source: KOTRA (Korea Trade Investment Promotion Agency) and Korean Ministry of Unification, 2004. See also, May 20, 2003 congressional testimony by Nicholas Eberstadt of the American Enterprise Institute placed North Korea's overall merchandise trade deficit at about $1,200 million a year. See note 13 for hearing citation details. See also CRS Report RL31785, *U.S. Assistance to North Korea*, by Mark E. Manyin; and "Threats and Responses: The Asian Arena," by James Brooke, *New York Times*, December 30, 2002, p. A8. For a detailed analysis of shortfalls and trends in the DPRK's illicit activity and the importance of such activity for North Korea's economic survival, see the May 20,2003 congressional testimony of Nicholas Eberstadt (hearing citation found in note 13).

[11] The 1998 figure cited on cost of nuclear programs is relatively low because of minimal labor costs. Not included here, but arguably also a motivation for DPRK criminal activity,is the amount of hard currency North Korea needs to support its missile development and production program.

Although there have not been any drug seizures or apprehensions of drug traffickers with a connection to the Democratic People's Republic of Korea (DPRK) since 2004, we remain concerned about DPRK state-directed criminal activity. The United States Government has made clear to the DPRK that an end to all involvement in criminal activity is a necessary prerequisite to entry into the international Community.[12]

President Bush's concern over North Korean drug trafficking activity and other criminal activity is mirrored in earlier testimony before the U.S. Congress on May20, 2003, by William Bach, of the Department of State's Bureau of International Narcotics and Law Enforcement Affairs:

For some 30 years, officials of the DPRK and other North Koreans have been apprehended for trafficking in narcotics and other criminal activity, including passing counterfeit U.S. notes. Since 1976, there have been at least 50 arrests and drug seizures involving North Koreans in more than 20 countries around the world. More recently, there have been very clear indications especially from the series of methamphetamine seizures in Japan that North Koreans traffic in and probably manufacture methamphetamine drugs.[13]

The Department of State's March 2006 International Narcotics Control Strategy Report (INCSR) notes longstanding DPRK links to drug trafficking as well:

For decades, North Koreans have been apprehended trafficking in narcotics and engaging in other criminal behavior and illicit activity, including passing counterfeit U.S. currency and trading in copyrighted products. This year there were no public reports of specific incidents of narcotics trafficking with clear, demonstrable DPRK (Democratic People's Republic of Korea) links. However, given developments during 2005 that linked the DPRK to other forms of state-directed criminality, the Department reaffirms its view that it is likely, but not certain, that the North Korean government sponsors criminal activities, including narcotics production and trafficking, in order to earn foreign currency for the state and its leaders.

Similarly, the Department of State's March 1, 2003 International Narcotics Control Strategy Report (INCSR) states:

For years during the 1970s and 1980s and into the 1990s, citizens of the Democratic People's Republic of (North) Korea (DPRK), many of them diplomatic employees of the government, were apprehended abroad while trafficking in narcotics and breaking other laws. More recently, police investigation of suspects apprehended while making large illicit shipments of heroin and methamphetamine to Taiwan and Japan have revealed a North Korean connection to the drugs. Police interrogation of suspects apprehended while trafficking in illicit drugs developed credible reports of North Korean boats engaged in transporting heroin and uniformed North Korean personnel transferring drugs from North Korean vessels to traffickers' boats. These reports raise the question whether the North Korean government

---

[12] Presidential Determination No. 2006-24, September 15, 2006, *Presidential Determinationon Major Drug Transit or Major Illicit Drug Producing Countries for Fiscal Year 2007*,Federal Register, Vol. 71, No. 189, September 29, 2006.

[13] Testimony of William Bach, Director, Office of Asia, Africa, and Europe, Bureau ofInternational Narcotics and Law Enforcement Affairs, Department of State, before theFinancial Management, Budget, and International Security Subcommittee of the SenateGovernmental Affairs Committee, May 20, 2003.

> cultivates opium illicitly, refines opium into heroin, and manufactures methamphetamine drugs in North Korea as a state-organized and directed activity, with the objective of trafficking in these drugs to earn foreign exchange.[14]

The March 2003 INCSR includes little information on North Korea in its money laundering section, but notes reports that Pyongyong has used Macau to launder counterfeit $100 bills and used Macau's banks as a repository for the proceeds of North Korea's growing trade in illegal drugs.[15] More detail on DPRK criminal activity is included in the 1998 INCSR's money laundering section which reads in part as follows: "The most profitable lines of state-supported illegal businesses remain drug trafficking, gold smuggling, illegal sale and distribution of endangered species, trafficking of counterfeit U.S. currency, and rare earth metals...North Korean officials appear to be increasing their involvement in financial crimes as a means to generate operational funds and support their country's anemic economy."[16]

Concerns over North Korea's role in international drug trafficking were echoed in the December 2000 United States Government International Crime Threat Assessment which states:

> A large share of the methamphetamine consumed in Japan comes from North Korea, according to media reports; more than 40 percent of the methamphetamine seized in Japan in 1999 came from North Korea. There have been regular reports from many official and unofficial sources that impoverished North Korea has engaged in drug trafficking — mostly to Japan, Russia, and China — as a criminal state enterprise to raise badly needed revenue. Over the years, customs and police officials of many countries have apprehended North Korean persons employed as diplomats or in quasi-official capacities at North Korean state trading companies trying to smuggle drugs produced elsewhere.[17]

Concerns over North Korean drug production and trafficking were also expressed in the 1997 Report of the International Narcotics Control Board (INCB). The report, in circumspect language common to such U.N. documents, notes that "The Board has received disquieting reports on the drug control situation in the Democratic People's Republic of Korea. Therefore, the Board expresses its concern that the Government of the Democratic People's Republic of Korea has not yet accepted its proposal, originally made in 1995, to send a mission to that country to study and clarify drug control issues."[18] In June 2002, the Board sent a mission to the DPRK to review the Government's compliance with the international drug control treaties, and reported in its 2002 annual report that the DPRK authorities "have expressed their willingness to cooperate at the regional and international levels in order to address drug control issues in a concerted manner."[19]

---

[14] U.S. Department of State, International *Narcotics Control Strategy Report* [INCSR], March 2003, p. VIII-43.

[15] Id., p. XII-200. Note that one press reports cites the existence of a videotape of Kim Jong Il's son, Kim Jong Nam, using counterfeit supernotes at a Macao casino. See "The Far East Sopranos," by David E. Kaplan, *U.S. News & World Report,* January 27, 2003.

[16] *INCSR,* March 1998, p. 623.

[17] *International Crime Threat Assessment*, December 2000. The assessment is the product of a government interagency working group led by the CIA.

[18] *INCB Report for 1997*, p. 17.

[19] *INCB Report for 2002*, p. 55. U.N. Document E/INCB/2002/1.

In addition, U.S. Drug Enforcement Administration (DEA) data compiled from foreign media services in 1999,[20] Department of Defense analysis[21] dated 2000, and a plethora of domestic and foreign press reports portray an ongoing pattern of drug trafficking, trafficking of counterfeit U.S. currency,[22] and other smuggling-for- profit activities by North Korean diplomats over the past 27 years. Since 1976, North Korea has been linked to over 50 verifiable incidents involving drug seizures in at least 20 countries. A significant number of these cases have involved arrest or detention of North Korean diplomats or officials. All but four of these incidents have transpired since the early 1990s.[23]

Press reports citing North Korean defectors and South Korean intelligence sources as well as U.S. government investigative agency source material, paint a grim picture of an anemic economy in North Korea, held back by disproportionate military spending, dysfunctional economic policies and the consequences of a broad economic and trade

---

[20] See Major Incidents of Drug Trafficking by North Koreans, prepared by the Europe/Asia/Africa Unit Strategic Intelligence Section, DEA, reproduced in *North Korea Advisory Group Report to the Speaker*, U.S. House of Representatives, November 1999, pp. 43-48.

[21] See *North Korean Drug Trafficking*, Department of Defense Joint InteragencyTaskForce West Assessment (unclassified), May 2000. Appendix "A" to the report cites 52 incidents linking the DPRK to drug trafficking activity through the month of February 2000.

[22] For example, the 1998 *INCSR*, p. 623, cites a February 1997 *Izvestia* article on the arrest of a third secretary of the North Korean Embassy who was apprehended attempting to exchange counterfeit U.S. dollars. Russian officials tied him to a smuggling operation designed to sell more than $100,000 in counterfeit U.S. bills which they believe was his main function at the embassy.

[23] For example, May 1976, 400 kg hashish seized from a North Korean (DPRK) diplomat in Egypt; July 1994, Chinese officials arrested a Chinese national on charges of smuggling 6 kg. of North Korean produced heroin through the DPRK Embassy in China; August 1994, a DPRK intelligence agent arrested by Russian authorities for trying to sell heroin to Russian mafia group; January 1995, Chinese officials in Shanghai seize 6 kg. of heroin and arrest two DPRK nationals, one with a diplomatic passport; July, 1998, DPRK. diplomat arrested in Egypt with 500,000 tablets of rohypnol — the so called "date rape" drug; January 1998, Russian officials arrest two DPRK diplomats in Moscow with 35 kg. of cocaine smuggled through Mexico; and October 1998, German officials arrested a DPRK diplomat in Berlin seizing heroin believed made in North Korea. On February 12, 1999, an employee of the DPRK consulate in Shenyang, China, was caught attempting to illicitly sell 9 kilograms of opium. On April 3, 1999, Japanese police caught Yakuza gang members attempting to smuggle 100 kilograms of methamphetamine into Japan on a Chinese ship. In April 1999, authorities at the Prague airport detained a DPRK diplomat stationed in Bulgaria attempting to smuggle 55 kilograms of the "date rape" drug rohypnol from Bulgaria. On May 3, 1999, Taiwanese police apprehended four members of a Taiwanese drug organization attempting to smuggle 157 kilograms of DPRK source methamphetamine. On October 3, 1999, Japanese authorities seized 564 kilograms of DPRK methamphetamine fromthe Taiwanese ship "Xin Sheng Ho"; 250 kilograms of DPRK made methamphetamine were also seized by Japanese authorities on February 5, 2000 leading to arrests of members of a Japanese Crime group and members of a Chosen Soren run trading company. During October through November 2001, Filipino authorities detained a ship twice in their territorial waters which had received first 500 kilograms and then 300 kilograms of methamphetamine from a North Korean ship. On December 22, 2001, Japanese patrol boats, in a skirmish, sank a North Korean vessel believed to be carrying drugs to Japan — the same vessel had been photographed in 1998 smuggling drugs into Japan. On January 6, 2002, Japanese authorities seized 150 kilograms of DPRK source methamphetamine from a Chinese ship in Japanese territorial waters that had earlier rendezvoused with a DPRK vessel for the drug transfer. In July 2002, Taiwanese authorities confiscated 79 kilograms of heroin which a local crime group had received from a North Korean battleship. In November and December 2002, packages containing 500 pounds of methamphetamine believed to be of DPRK origin floated ashore in Japan. On April 20, 2003, Australian police seized the DPRK ship, the "Pong Su", which had attempted to smuggle 125 kilograms of heroin through Singapore into the territorial waters of Australia (note that Pong Su officer crew members were subsequently charged and acquitted of drug trafficking charges). In June 2004, two North Korean diplomats working at the North Korean Embassy in Egypt were detained for smuggling 150,000 tablets of Clonazipam, an anti-anxiety drug. In December 2004, Turkish authorities arrested two North Korean diplomats suspected of smuggling the synthetic drug captagon to Arab markets. The diplomats, assigned to North Korea's Embassy in Bulgaria, were found to be carrying over half a million captagon tablets, with an estimated street value of over $7 million.

embargo led by the United States since the Korean War. Pressed for cash, and perceiving its vital national security at stake, the regime reportedly created an office to bring in foreign currency: "Bureau No. 39," under the ruling North Korean Communist Party which is headed by North Korean Leader Kim Jong Il.[24] This office is reported to be in charge of drug trafficking and according to some reports all crime-for-profit activity including (1) opium production and trafficking; (2) methamphetamine production and trafficking; (3) counterfeiting; and (4) smuggling. Drugs are reportedly exported through China and Russia to Asia and Europe via government trading companies, diplomatic pouches, and concealed in legitimate commercial cargo. Foreign exchange earned by Bureau 39 is reportedly used to: (1) buy loyalty from Party elites and military leaders to Leader Kim Jong Il; (2) fund costs of overseas diplomatic missions; (3) finance national security activity — especially technology and electronic purchases for the intelligence and military services, and (4) procure overseas components for North Korea's weapons of mass destruction programs.[25] Bureau 39 activities, according to interviews conducted by the *Wall Street Journal* with Asian intelligence officials, have generated a cash hoard, of which an amount in the range of $5 billion is believed to be currently stashed away by the Pyongyang regime.[26]

Farmers in certain areas reportedly are ordered to grow opium poppies[27], with cultivation estimates of 4,000 hectares for the early 1990s and 7,000 hectares for 1995. Subsequent production, however, is believed to be below 1995 figures, initially because of heavy rains, but also as part of a broad decline of agricultural output as a consequence of poor policies, and insufficient fertilizer and insecticides. Looking at all available estimates, a cultivation estimate of 3000-4,000 hectares for 1998 would appear reasonable, but nevertheless based on indirect and fragmented information. U.S. government investigative agency sources in 1998 estimated North Korean raw opium production capacity at 50 tons annually, with 40 tons reportedly produced in 1995. The March 2000, INCSR states that estimates of the area under opium cultivation range from 4,200 hectares to 7,000 hectares which would yield from about 30 metric tons to 44 metric tons of opium annually.[28] North Korean government pharmaceutical labs reportedly have the capacity to process 100 tons of raw opium per

---

[24] Note that in April 1998 Russian police reported arresting Kil Chae Kyong [believed to be personal secretary in charge of secret funds for Kim Jong Il] on charges of trying to sell $30,000 in counterfeit U.S. currency.

[25] For a well researched discussion of DPRK crime for profit activity, see "Money Trail," by Jay Solomon, The *Wall Street Journal*, July 14, 2003, p. A1. See also "The Wiseguy Regime," by David E. Kaplan, *U.S. News & World Report*, February 15, 1999, p. 36-39. See also "N. Korea Said To Be in Drug Business," *Washington Times*, February 26, 1995, A-1; "Drug Trafficking by North Korean Service," *Moscow-Interfaks*, June 22, 1997; "Kim Chong-il's Fund Manager Commits Suicide," *Tokyo Sankei Shimbum*, December 29, 1998; "North Korean Business: Drugs, Diplomats and Fake Dollars," AP, May 24, 1998; "Seoul Says N. Korea Increasing Opium Output for Export," *Kyodo*, June 8, 1993; "DPRK Officially Involved in Drugs, Counterfeiting," *Digital Chosun Ilbo* [South Korea], November 12, 1996; "DPRK Defectors Attest to Realities of DPRK System," *Seoul Tong-A Ilbo*, February 14, 1996, p. 5; "N.Korea Accused of Promoting Opium Farms," *Seoul Choson Ilbo*, August 7, 1994, p. 5. Bureau 39 reportedly directs the expenditure of North Korea's foreign exchange resources with two priorities: (1) procurement of luxury products from abroad that Kim Jong-Il distributes to a broad swath of North Korean military, party, and government officials to secure their loyalty — Mercedes Benz automobiles, food, wines, stereos, deluxe beds, Rolex watches, televisions, etc., estimated at $100 million annually by U.S. military officials in Seoul, according to a *Reuters* report of March 4, 2003; and (2) procurement overseas of components and materials for North Korea's WMDs and missiles. See also CRS Report RL33567, *Korea-U.S. Relations: Issues for Congress*, by Larry A. Niksch.

[26] See "Money Trail," by Jay Solomon, *The Wall Street Journal*, July 14, 2003, p.A1.

[27] See North Korea and Narcotics Trafficking: A View from the Inside, by Kim Young Il, *North Korea Review*, Vol 1, Issue 1, Feb. 27, 2005.

[28] *INCSR*, March 2000, p. VIII-39

year.[29] U.S. government production estimates, to the extent that they may be available, would likely be classified, but clearly would not be expected to be below 1998 levels as Pyongyang's need for foreign exchange appears to have grown more pressing to accelerate foreign purchases of components for North Korea's secret uranium enrichment program.

Methamphetamine production in North Korea is reported to have started in 1996 after heavy rains decreased income from poppy production. This coincides with reports that markets for methamphetamine at that time began dramatically expanding in Asia, especially in Thailand, Japan, and the Philippines.[30] For example, in 2002, North Korea was the source of approximately 1/3 of the methamphetamine seized by Japanese authorities.[31] North Korea's maximum methamphetamine production capacity is estimated by some South Korean officials to be 10-15 tons per year of the highest quality product for export. According to the INCB, North Korean legitimate pharmaceutical needs for ephedrine (a traditional precursor for methamphetamine) are 2.5 tons per year, one ton higher than U.S. investigative agency source estimates. INCB officials confirm receipt of reports of North Korean involvement in an alleged diversion of 20 tons of ephedrine.[32] Moreover, U.S. and foreign investigative agency personnel have in the past noted concerns that North Korea may be bypassing the highly regulated market for ephedrine in favor of an alternate technology for a benzine based product, raising speculation that U.S. and allied petroleum assistance to North Korea may be being used to sustain illicit drug production.

Conservative estimates suggest North Korean criminal activity, carefully targeted to meet specific needs, generated about $85 million in 1997: $71 million from drugs and $15 million from counterfeiting.[33] Some recent estimates of Pyongyang's clandestine drug income,

---

29 See "*U.S. says North Korea Sponsors Drug Smuggling,*" *Kyodo News Service* (Japan), December 13, 1998. Total arable land in the DPRK is estimated to exceed 1.3 million hectares.

30 In August 1998, Japanese authorities arrested members of a Japanese criminal organization and seized 200 kg of a 300 kg shipment of methamphetamine believed manufactured in North Korea. Earlier, in April, 58.6 kg of the same drug, thought to have been manufactured in China, was seized by Japanese authorities in the cargo of a North Korean freighter. See "Police Say Seized Drugs Originated in North Korea," *Yomiuri Shimbun* (Japan), January 8, 1999.

31 Between 1999 and 2001, Japanese authorities reportedly seized 1,113 kilograms of methamphetamine en route from North Korea — some 34% of Japanese seizures. For China during the same period the percentage reportedly constitutes 38% (some 1,780 kg). See "Trying a Quick Fix: North Korea Tied to the Drug Trade," by Jay Solomon and Jason Dean, *Asian Wall Street Journal*, April 23, 2003, p. 1.

32 For example, in January 1998, Thai police reportedly seized, but later released, 2.5 tons of ephedrine en route from India to North Korea. This was reportedly part of an 8 ton shipment North Korea had attempted to purchase which the INCB reportedly limited to two 2.5 ton shipments over a two year period. However, INCB officials staunchly deny that such an arrangement transpired. Pyongyang, at the time, reportedly argued for the right to buy 30 tons from India — enough for a 135-year supply of cold tablets (see *Bangkok Times*, June 13, 1999, p. 6).

33 The $71 million for drugs is broken down as $59 million from opium/heroin and $12 million from amphetamines, although one, admittedly speculative, U.S. law enforcement agency source estimate for "world" market price of heroin produced by the DPRK in 1995 was $600 million. For the $15 million figure on counterfeiting, see *Korea Herald*, Nov.16, 1998. See also, "Is Your Money Real?", *Newsweek*, June 10, 1996, p. 10. According to some sources, income from counterfeiting is considerably higher, i.e. $100 million. (See May 20, 2003 congressional testimony of Larry Wortzel of the Heritage Foundation, citation details in note no. 14.) Note also that data on amounts of U.S. dollars counterfeited are not widely publicized (and arguably publicly downplayed) so as not to undermine confidence in the U.S. dollar. North Korean counterfeit U.S. $100 notes have been detected in at least 14 countries including the United States since the 1970s. On June 20, 2004, the BBC aired a "Superdollar" special which traced counterfeit $100 bills from North Korea to an official IRA source in the U.K. Reportedly millions of fake $100 bills were laundered through a bureaux de change in Britain. In July, 1996, a former member of the Japanese Red Army, (Continued ...)

however, are substantially higher with the *Wall Street Journal* citing U.S. military estimates that North Korea's annual drug exports had risen in the year 2003 to at least $500 million from about $100 million a few years ago.[34] Figures widely encountered in the U.S. policy community throughout 2004 are roughly $200 million in profit from the combined illicit methamphetamine and heroin trade and $500 million in profit from additional aggregate criminal activity. Income from counterfeiting of U.S. bills is unclear, with U.S. military sources reportedly estimating such income at $15-20 million for the year 2001.[35]

If credence is to be given to U.N., Department of State reporting, and DEA shared information, as well as press reports citing foreign law enforcement activity, North Korean defectors, and South Korean intelligence sources, a pattern of activity emerges which indicates that (1) in the 1970s, North Korean officials bought and sold foreign source illicit drugs; (2) in the mid-1970s, North Korea began cultivating opium poppy as a matter of state policy; (3) in the mid-1980s, North Korea began refining opium poppy for export and exporting refined opium products; (4) and in the mid-1990s, after heavy rains reduced opium production in 1995 and 1996, North Korea began manufacturing and exporting methamphetamine to expanding markets in Southeast Asia — increasingly enlisting the help of foreign criminal groups in its smuggling operations. If this pattern reflects reality, an important question is the degree to which the government of North Korea may respond to increased financial pressures and expanding methamphetamine markets in Southeast Asia by dramatically increasing already record levels of reported drug trafficking activity.

Some analysts, however, question the reliability of information reported in the press attributed to North Korean defectors and South Korean government sources. They note that in a closed state such as North Korea "hard" data is difficult to obtain, thus what is obtained is fragmentary and indirect at best. North Korea continues to dismiss media reports and speculation on government involvement in drug trafficking activities as anti-North Korean

---

(… Continued) traveling on a DPRK diplomatic passport was arrested in Thailand while trying to pass counterfeit U.S. $100 bills. See "Japanese Fake Bill Suspect Had N. Korean Passport," *Kyodo News*, July 5, 1996. For data on other forms of DPRK criminal/smuggling activity, see *Avoiding the Apocalypse: The Future of the Two Koreas*, by Marcus Noland, Institute for International Economics, Washington, D.C., June 2000, p. 119.

[34] See Money trail, by Jay Solomon, *The Wall Street Journal*, July 14, 2003, p. A1. For another income estimate of "as much as $500 million" see "The Far East Sopranos," by David E. Kaplan, *U.S. News & World Report*, January 27, 2003. Given that drug trafficking is by very nature a clandestine activity and that North Korea is a closed society, any overall estimates of DPRK income from illicit drug sources are based on fragmented data and are speculative at best. However, arguably, what may be more important here than the exact dollar amount generated by such illicit activity, is the strategic significance of the income — whatever the dollar amount be — given speculation that it is being used to underwrite Pyongyang's nuclear weapons program. Clearly such data should be considered a "far cry" from anything that might be remotely considered as evidence in a U.S. court of law. Note also that the dollar amount the DPRK received in profit from drug sales to Japan in 2003 has been roughly and unofficially estimated at $100 million, according to non-U.S. sources.

[35] See "N.K. Exported $580 Million Worth of Missiles to Middle East," Seoul Yonhap (English), May 13, 2003, citing Japanese Yomiuri Shimbum report of May 12, 2003. Media reports suggest that when Assistant Secretary of State, James A. Kelly, visited North Korea in October 2002, he asked that printing of the counterfeit bills be suspended. Some of the bills are reportedly printed on machines stolen by the KGB from the U.S. mint after WWII and provided to North Korea by the USSR in the late 1980s. (See "DPRK Prints Super K Dollar Bills on Machine Provided by Former USSR KGB," Tokyo Forsight (in Japanese) March 15-April 18, 2003.) Others are believed to be printed on equipment purchased by the DPRK in Europe in the 1990s. Quality control is reportedly exercised by use of state of the art equipment designed to detect counterfeiting, reportedly also purchased in Europe. Notethat not only U.S. currency is reportedly counterfeited. DPRK payment for a typicalpurchase of goods or technology from the Middle East, for example, may well include apercentage of top quality Middle Eastern counterfeit bills. See also CRS Report RL33324,North Korean Counterfeiting of U.S. Currency, by Raphael Perl and Dick Nanto.

slander based on politically motivated adversary propaganda sources. North Korean officials are known to stress privately that corruption, drug use, trafficking, and criminal activity in general are maladies to which individuals in all societies may fall prey, and that any involvement by North Korean individuals in such activity is in no way state-connected or state sanctioned. Further, officials have stressed that in instances where such activity has come to the attention of authorities, individuals involved have been duly punished. Finally, North Korean officials maintain that issues such as drug trafficking and production are matters that should be handled, and are best handled, by their government as an internal matter. U.N. officials also point to the politically charged milieu of allegations of drug trafficking by North Korea and point out that drug smuggling by individuals in the diplomatic community is not limited to North Korea.[36]

ISSUES FOR DECISION MAKERS

At least fifty documented drug trafficking incidents coupled with allegations of large scale North Korean state sponsorship of opium poppy cultivation, and heroin and methamphetamine production and trafficking, raise significant issues for the United States and America's allies in combating international drug trafficking. The challenge to policy makers, is how to pursue sound counter-drug policy and comply with U.S. law which may require cutting off aid to North Korea while effectively pursuing other high priority U.S. foreign policy objectives including (1) limiting possession and production of weapons of mass destruction; (2) limiting ballistic missile production and export; (3) curbing terrorism, counterfeiting and international crime, and (4) addressing humanitarian needs.

As of March, 2005, U.S. aid to North Korea is limited to providing food and other humanitarian assistance. Reports that North Korea may be limiting some of its food crop production in favor of drug crop production are particularly disturbing, though the acreage in question is cómparatively small. Another issue of rising concern is the use of profits from any North Korean drug trafficking, counterfeiting, and other crime-for-profit enterprises to underwrite the costs of maintaining or expanding North Korean nuclear and missile programs.[37]

Central to the policy debate over the quantity of DPRK illicit poppy production is the need for hard data such as satellite imagery to confirm the extent of reported opium poppy cultivation in North Korea. If such data have been collected through remote sensing, they have not been publically disclosed.[38]

Enhanced policy focus and law enforcement intelligence cooperation on targeting, reporting, and tracking North Korean opium/heroin and methamphetamine trafficking and production in the late 1990s have made it significantly more difficult for North Korean

[36] Conversations with North Korean and United Nations officials, September 1998.

[37] See generally CRS Report RL33590, *North Korea's Nuclear Weapons Development and Diplomacy*, by Larry Niksch.

[38] Some analysts have compared the alleged poppy cultivation situation in the DPRK with that of Colombia in the mid-1980s. Beginning about 1986, numerous reports were received from informants regarding poppy cultivation in Colombia. However, despite U-2 aircraft broad sweep imagery, it was not until the mid-1990s that such imagery was able to confirm cultivation which at that time approximated the 4,000-5,000 hectare range.

entities to engage in illicit smuggling activities.[39] The apparent result has been a need for North Korean trafficking fronts to enter into joint venture arrangements with criminal organizations in neighboring nations, notably Russian, Chinese, and South Korean and Japanese criminal enterprises. As profits are generally shared (often as much as 50/50) in such ventures, the level of North Korean drugs muggling activity might need to more-or-less double to keep income levels for DPRK illicit drug enterprises constant with levels achieved in 1998.

The case of the "Pong Su," arguably, is demonstrative of such joint venture activity — reportedly Southeast Asian non-DPRK origin heroin carried by a North Korean crew on a North Korean vessel. The April 20, 2003 "Pong Su" case, however, presents an interesting twist of events.[40] Traditionally, it was assumed that any such joint ventures were established to facilitate the smuggling and distribution of DPRK source drugs. In contrast, reported information in the "Pong Su" case can be interpreted as a sign that such joint venture relationships — to the degree they may exist-have become a "two-way street" with North Korean enterprises smuggling drugs for partner groups as well. A growing area of international concern is escalating ties between those in the DPRK who engage in criminal activity and foreign transnational criminal groups.

Notwithstanding, a growing number of analysts attach significance to the fact that there have been few documented instances of DPRK drug trafficking activity being detected recently. They note that the scale of North Korean linked drug trafficking activities that has been detected since 2003 is small relative to seizures linked to the DPRK in previous years. They cite as well the fact that although, in 2004, two incidents were publically reported involving DPRK officials stationed abroad at embassies, these two incidents had been the first to come to light in several years.[41]

In addition, the March 2006 *INCSR* notes that there were no seizures of methamphetamines in Japan in 2005 linked to the DPRK. Traditionally as much as 30% to 40% of methamphetamine seizures in Japan have been linked to the DPRK. However the report speculates that increasingly seizures of DPRK source methamphetamine may be mistakenly identified as "Chinese source" given growing links of Chinese criminal elements to North Korea's drug production/trafficking activities. Supporting the theory of a decline in DPRK drug production/trafficking activity, the March 2005 *INCSR* notes that the origin of

---

[39] See, for example, "U.S. to Send Signal to North Koreans in Naval Exercise," by Steven R. Weisman, *New York Times*, August 18, 2003, p. 1., which refers to the existence of a program known as the "D.P.R.K. Illicit Activities Initiative," characterized as a quiet crackdown by many nations against North Korea's narcotics trade, counterfeiting, moneylaundering, and other illicit smuggling activity.

[40] See text at end of note number 23. The DPRK government maintains that the "Pong Su" is a civilian trading ship and that its owner had no knowledge of the heroin and subsequent acquittal of the crew in Australia on drug trafficking charges arising out of the incident arguably supports such an assertion. Heroin seized may have been of Burmese origin (and picked up in Myanmar or Thailand), raising speculation of a budding relationship between the DPRK and criminal enterprises in either Myanmar or Thailand. See "Dangerous Bedfellows," by Bertil Lintner and Shawn W. Crispin, *Far Eastern Economic Review*, November 20, 2003. Myanmar (reportedly the world's largest opium cultivator in 2002) is often characterized as one of the most isolated nations in the world as well as a nation where rampant corruption prevails. See "N. Korea's Growing Drug Trade Seen in Botched Heroin Delivery," by Richard Paddock and Barbara Demick, *Washington Post*, May 21, 2003; and Myanmar's Problems Are Thailand's Dilemma by Sorapong Buaroy, *Bankok Post*, January 28, 2003.

[41] For details on the two incidents involving DPRK diplomats stationed in Bulgaria and Egypt, see the Department of State's March 2005, *INCSR* which states: "It is impossible to say with certainty that such individuals were acting under the instructions of their government...."

heroin and methamphetamine seized in Taiwan during 2004 was generally ascribed to domestic manufacture; whereas in past years, DPRK origin illicit drugs have been among those seized. Moreover, Japanese press reports cite government officials in that nation as stating that as of early 2006, there had been no seizures of DPRK source stimulants for the third consecutive year.[42] However, a December 2006 Japanese TV documentary stated that 14 kilograms of narcotics believed to be of DPRK origin were seized on December 1, 2006 in Yokohama from a ship that arrived from Dalian, China. In the same report, what appears to be a Chinese mafia figure states in fluent Japanese that Japanese yakuza members are now buying DPRK source methamphetamine directly in China and that since 2002, drug trafficking between China and the DPRK has increased by several to ten times, both in number [of transactions?] and volume.[43]

Notwithstanding lack of hard evidence of any recent seizures involving illicit drugs of confirmed DPRK origin or drugs being trafficked by DPRK nationals with confirmed or likely links to DPRK officials, press reports in early 2007 cite earlier arrests in China of North Korean nationals involved with Chinese criminals in the trafficking of methamphetamine.[44] For example, in November 2006, Chinese police in Shenyang reportedly arrested a North Korean and others connected to an international drug ring which had trafficked large quantities of methamphetamine into China. Earlier, in July 2006, the media reported arrests by Chinese police in two other cities, Dalian and Dandong, where Chinese police arrested other North Koreans and Japanese apparently trying to bring methamphetamine purchased near the North Korean/Chinese border to Japan.[45] These were the first cases of involvement of DPRK (Democratic People's Republic of Korea) nationals in drug trafficking to become public in two years.

Arguably however, fewer seizures may simply be the result of changes in patterns of shipments designed to conceal any direct DPRK role in the process — countermeasures spurred by increased international scrutiny of North Korean trading activities. Consistent with this line of reasoning would be the conclusion that since levels of enforcement success against DPRK linked trafficking in illicit drugs often vary dramatically, it is not possible at this time to reach a definitive consensus about any changes in trends underlying such enterprise. An alternative explanation would be that North Korea has cut back on, if not dramatically curbed, its drug trafficking activity and is compensating from the loss of income in this arena by beefing up its production and trafficking of counterfeit brand cigarettes.

In contrast, the aggregate portfolio of North Korean criminal activity over the past decade paints a different picture. Information available points to an expansion in both the scale and scope of North Korean cash generating criminal activity.[46] In addition to production and trafficking in heroin and methamphetamines, major sources of revenue from criminal activity for the DPRK now include (1) counterfeit cigarettes; (2) counterfeit pharmaceuticals (for example "USA" manufactured Viagra; (3) counterfeit currency (e.g. U.S. $100 bill

---

[42] See "Japan's illegal drug seizures down 50% in 2005: MOF," report by *Kyodo News*, February 23, 2006.

[43] See Tokyo TBS Television "News 23" program of December 27, 2006, of 14:26 GMT available in video from the Open Source Center [GSG_VSD@rccb.ossis.gov].

[44] See footnote below. Note, however, that it is not clear from the reports whether the drugs were of DPRK origin or whether the North Koreans arrested had linkswith DPRKofficials.

[45] See China Busts Huge N. Korean Drug Ring, *Bankok Post*, Jan. 11, 2007[DPA report].

[46] For a discussion of U.S. response options reportedly under discussion see "U.S. is Shaping Plan to Pressure North Korea," by David E. Sanger, *New York Times*, February 14, 2005, A-1.

"supernotes"); and (4) indiscriminate sales of small arms, i.e. "gun running."[47] The result is a situation in which criminal activity is seen as playing an increasingly pivotal role in supporting North Korea's fragile economy.

Best U.S. available source estimates suggest that the DPRK earns at least $500 million per year in profit from combined criminal activity, and gross revenues are suggested by some to total $1 billion or more. Regardless, however, of the current dollar amount such ventures generate, it appears that the scale and scope of North Korean criminal activities are on the rise. Increasingly, analysts view this as a global and not just as a regional concern.

Another question, yet unresolved, is the degree to which Pyongyang will be able to maintain control over drug smuggling — and other foreign currency generating — activities if they become more decentralized with more foreign criminal organizations and gangs participating. Deteriorating economic conditions and rising corruption among mid-level DPRK party functionaries threatened with declining lifestyles gives rise to speculation in the intelligence community that rogue operations constitute an increasing proportion of any current DPRK drug smuggling activity.[48]

A final and daunting challenge facing policymakers both in the DPRK and beyond, is the degree to which the North Korea regime would be able to curtail any remaining illicit drug activity — and other foreign currency generating criminal enterprises — should it desire to do

[47] In July 2004, for example, the U.S. Secret Service reportedly uncovered a network selling counterfeit North Korean made cigarettes, pharmaceuticals, and $100 bills. See "Fakes," by Frederik Balfour, et al., *Business Week*, February 7, 2005. See also CRS Report RL33324, *North Korean Counterfeiting of U.S. Currency*, by Raphael Perl and Dick Nanto.

[48] DPRK defectors maintain that North Korea's underground economy is controlled by some 1000 "big dealers" who regularly give bribes in U.S. dollars and valuable gifts to Kim Jong-il and party, administration and military elites, See "DPRK Defectors Say Underground Economy Spawning Influential 'Big Dealers,' *Seoul Chugan Chosen* (in Korean), June 19, 2003. Mr. Kim's personal assets in foreign countries havebeen estimated to be in $130 billion range, with as much as $4.3 billion reportedly in Swiss bank accounts. See "Kim Jong Ils Huge Secret Assets," *Tokyo Shukan Posuto*, June 16, 2003, citing Chuck Downs, a former Pentagon official in the Bush I and Clinton Administrations. Press reports citing U.S. military sources in Seoul state that Pyongyang spends about $100 million a year on imported luxury cars and liquor for its elite, see "New N. Korea Food Aid Pledges Only a Beginning," *Reuters*, March 4, 2003 dispatch from Seoul.

so.[49] Policy analysts in the past have suggested that North Korean drug trafficking activity has been carefully controlled and limited to fill specific foreign exchange shortfalls. However, increasingly concern exists that North Korean crime-for-profit activity may become a "runaway train," gaining momentum, but out of control. Experience suggests that those engaged in the drug trade and other continuing criminal enterprises often find themselves "addicted" to the income generated and are unlikely to cease such activity, absent draconian disincentives. Moreover, over time, such illicit activity is often seen as becoming "institutionalized" — taking on a life on its own, a phenomenon which does not bode well for those who would seek to curb drug trafficking and other revenue generating international criminal activity based in North Korea.

---

[49] See the "Narcotics Economy in the Making in North Korea" which featured an interview with Kansai University's Professor (Young Hwa?) Lee carried by Japan's TBS-TVon January 16, 2007, 17:30-18:30 local time. In the interview, Lee suggests that a local narcotics economy is emerging in North Korea due to what he refers to as Pyongyang's softening of its position against the use of indigenously produced drugs to compensate for revenue lost due to its decreasing narcotics trade abroad. He characterizes this phenomenon as the "privatization" of the DPRK drug trade. Lee also suggests that as a result, drug use in the DPRK is on the rise, especially among party elites and other affluent people.

In: The War on Drugs: Winning, Losing or Treading Water ISBN 978-1-59454-235-0
Editor: Arcos, Nelson V

Chapter 8

COLOMBIA: ISSUES FOR CONGRESS *

Colleen W. Cook and Clare Ribando Seelke

SUMMARY

In the last decade, Colombia — a key U.S. ally in South America — has made significant progress in reasserting government control over much of its territory, combating drug trafficking and terrorist activities by illegally armed groups, and reducing poverty. Since the development of Plan Colombia in 1999, the Colombian government, with substantial U.S. support, has stepped up its counter narcotics and security efforts. Congress has provided more than $6 billion to support Plan Colombia from FY2000 through FY2008. Since 2002, Congress has granted the State Department expanded authority to use counter narcotics funds for a unified campaign to fight both drug trafficking and terrorist organizations in Colombia. Proponents of the current U.S. policy towards Colombia point to the inroads that have been made in improving security conditions in Colombia and in weakening the Revolutionary Armed Forces of Colombia (FARC) guerrillas. Critics argue that, despite these security improvements, U.S. policy has not rigorously promoted human rights, provided for sustainable economic alternatives for drug crop farmers, or reduced the amount of drugs available in the United States.

President Alvaro Uribe, re-elected in May 2006, has made headway in addressing Colombia's 40-year plus conflict with the country's leftist guerrillas, as well as the rightist paramilitary groups that have been active since the 1980s. Uribe enjoys strong popular support, which has not been significantly affected by an ongoing scandal concerning past government ties to illegal paramilitary groups. Uribe's popularity soared after Colombia's March 2008 raid of a FARC camp in Ecuador resulted in the killing of a top guerrilla commander and the seizure of his computer files. It spiked again following the Colombian military's successful July 2, 2008 rescue of 15 hostages long held by the FARC. Those hostages included three

---

* Excerpted from CRS Report RL32250, dated September 12, 2008

U.S. defense contractors and a former Colombian presidential candidate. Many Colombians are calling for President Uribe to seek a third presidential term, a move that would require a constitutional amendment.

Concerns in the 110th Congress regarding Colombia have focused on funding levels and U.S. policy regarding Plan Colombia, U.S. hostages, trade, and human rights. The FY2008 Consolidated Appropriations Act (P.L. 110-161) attempted to raise the level of U.S. funding provided for economic and social aid closer to that provided for security-related programs. In 2007, the Senate passed a resolution. (S.Con.Res. 53) demanding that the FARC release the 3 U.S. contractors that were being held in Colombia. In July 2008, both the House and Senate passed resolutions expressing gratitude to the Colombian government for successfully rescuing the U.S. hostages (H.Con.Res. 389/S.Res. 627). The House also passed an amendment (H.Amdt. 112 to H.R. 5959) expressing the importance of continuing to provide U.S. assistance to Colombia. While acknowledging the progress that the Uribe government has made in improving security conditions in Colombia, some Members of Congress have expressed concerns about labor activist killings and the parapolitical scandal. These issues came to the fore during consideration of the U.S.Colombia Free Trade Agreement (CFTA). For more information on CFTA, see CRS Report RL34470, *The U.S.-Colombia Free Trade Agreement: Economic and Political Implications*, by M. Angeles Villarreal. This report will be updated.

RECENT DEVELOPMENTS

On September 10, 2008, the U.S. Office of National Drug Control Policy (ONDCP) reported that while the area under coca cultivation in Colombia increased slightly in 2007, the productivity of that area fell sharply due to aerial spraying and manual eradication efforts.

On August 19, 2008, the Colombian Prosecutor General's office ordered the release of Mario Uribe, a second cousin and ally of President Alvaro Uribe, stating that the evidence against him did not merit his imprisonment while he awaits his trial. Mario Uribe was arrested a few months ago on charges of suspected collusion with paramilitary groups. Some 69 Colombian legislators, many from pro-Uribe parties, are under investigation for possible paramilitary ties.

On July 28, 2008, Secretary of State Condoleezza Rice issued a certification to Congress asserting that the Colombian government and armed forces are meeting the statutory requirements with regard to human rights.

On July 2, 2008, the Colombian military carried out a successful operation to rescue 15 hostages long held by the Revolutionary Armed Forces of Colombia (FARC) guerrillas. Those hostages included three U.S. citizens — Marc Gonsalves, Thomas Howes, and Keith Stansell — held since February 2003 and former Colombian presidential candidate Ingrid Betancourt held since February 2002.

On May 25, 2008, the FARC confirmed that its leader, Manuel Marulanda, had died of a heart attack in March.

In mid-May 2008, President Uribe extradited 15 top paramilitary leaders, including Salvador Mancuso and Carlos Mario Jiménez, to the United States to stand trial on drug trafficking charges.

On May 15, 2008, Interpol released a report confirming that Colombian officials did not tamper with computer files seized during a raid of a FARC camp in Ecuador.

On April 10, 2008, the House voted 224-195 in favor of changing the rules that had allowed the President to "fast-track" trade agreements through Congress, effectively putting congressional consideration of the U.S.-Colombia Free Trade Agreement (CFTA) on hold.

On March 18, 2008, after extended debate, the OAS adopted a resolution rejecting, but not condemning, Colombia's bombing raid of a FARC camp in Ecuador and calling for the restoration of diplomatic ties between Ecuador and Colombia. Those ties have still not fully been restored.

On March 11, 2008, the State Department released its annual human rights report, which stated that "although serious problems remained, the [Colombian] government's respect for human rights continued to improve, which was particularly evident by progress in implementing the Justice and Peace Law." (See the full report at [http://www.state.gov/g/drl/rls/hrrpt/2007/].)

On March 5, 2008, a second member of the FARC's secretariat, Ivan Rios, was murdered by his own security agent.

On March 1, 2008, the Colombian military bombed a FARC camp in Ecuador, killing at least 25 people, among them, Raúl Reyes, the terrorist groups' second highest commander. Computer files found on laptops seized during the raid allege that the government of Hugo Chávez of Venezuela was planning to provide millions of dollars in assistance to the FARC for weapons purchases.

INTRODUCTION

Colombia is a South American nation of roughly 44 million people, the third most populous country in Latin America. It is an ethnically diverse nation — 58% of the population is mestizo, 20% white, 18% black, 3% black-Amerindian, and 1% Amerindian.[1] Colombia has one of the oldest democracies in Latin America, yet it has been plagued by violence and a conflict that has been ongoing for over 40 years. The country's rugged terrain historically made it difficult to establish state control over large swaths of the nation's territory. High rates of poverty have also contributed to social upheaval in the country. In 2006, 45% of Colombians lived in poverty, down from close to 60% in 2000.[2] Colombia's ability to reduce poverty in recent years is at least partly due to increases in the country's economic growth rates, which reached 7.5% in 2007.[3] Security improvements and a more stable economy have likely led to the recent increase in foreign direct investment (FDI). FDI grew from roughly $6.5 billion in 2006 to some $9 billion in 2007, with the bulk of new

---

[1] U.S. Department of State, "Background Note: Colombia," March 2008.

[2] These statistics are taken from the Colombia National PlanningDepartment as cited by the U.S. Department of State. See U.S. Department of State, "Charting Colombia's Progress," March 2008. The United Nations Economic Commission for Latin America and the Caribbean's (ECLAC) *Social Panorama 2006* data also showed a decline in both poverty and indigence rates since 1999. ECLAC reported that 55% of Colombians lived in poverty in 1999, with 27% living in indigence. By 2005 those poverty and indigence rates fell to 47% and 20%, respectively. No new data on poverty rates in Colombia were included in ECLAC's *Social Panorama 2007.*

[3] "Country Report - Colombia," *Economist Intelligence Unit*, August 2008.

investments occurring in the oil, manufacturing, and mining sectors. Despite the Colombian government's success in reducing poverty levels, income inequality and land concentration are still significant problems.[4]

Drug trafficking has helped to perpetuate Colombia's conflict by providing earnings to both left- and right-wing armed groups. The two main leftist guerrilla groups are the FARC and the National Liberation Army (ELN), both of which have kidnapped individuals for ransoms, committed serious human rights violations, and carried out terrorist activities. Most of the rightist paramilitary groups were coordinated by the United Self-Defense Forces of Colombia (AUC), which disbanded in 2006 after more than 30,000 of its members demobilized. Members of the AUC have been accused of gross human rights abuses and collusion with the Colombian Armed Forces in their fight against the FARC and ELN.

Colombia is a democratic nation with a bicameral legislature. The Liberal and Conservative parties, which dominated Colombian politics from the 19th century through much of the 20th century, have been weakened by their perceived inability to resolve the roots of violence in Colombia. In 2002, Colombians elected an independent, Alvaro Uribe, as President, largely because of his aggressive plan to reduce violence in Colombia. The major political parties currently represented in the Colombian Congress include the Liberal, Conservative, Alternative Democratic Pole, National Unity, and Radical Change parties, as well as several smaller political movements. The legitimacy of the Colombian Congress has been seriously called into question as roughly a fifth of its members, many from pro-Uribe parties, have either been jailed or placed under investigation for allegedly having ties to illegal paramilitary groups.[5]

POLITICAL SITUATION

The First Uribe Administration

During his first term (2002-2006), President Uribe took steps to fulfill his campaign promises to address the paramilitary problem, defeat leftist guerrilla insurgents, and combat narcotics trafficking.[6] President Uribe took a hard-line approach to negotiations with illegally armed groups, declaring that the government would only negotiate with those groups who are willing to give up terrorism and agree to a cease-fire, including paramilitary groups with which former President Pastrana had refused to negotiate. Negotiations with the AUC paramilitaries resulted in a July 15, 2003 agreement in which the AUC agreed to demobilize its members by the end of 2005. President Uribe endorsed a controversial Justice and Peace Law that was designed to provide a framework for those demobilizations. At the same time, Uribe sought to build up the size and strength of the Colombian military and police, whose

[4] ECLAC reports that Colombia is now the fourth most unequal society in Latin America and the Caribbean, after Bolivia, Brazil, and Honduras. Colombia also has one of the most unequal land tenure patterns in Latin America, with 0.4% of land holders owning 61% of registered rural property. See ECLAC, Social Panorama 2006; J.D. Jaramillo, *El Recurso Suelo y la Competividad del Sector Agrario Colombiano*, 2004.

[5] Frank Bajak, "Head of Colombian Governing Party Arrested for Alleged Paramilitary Ties," *Associated Press*, July 25, 2008.

[6] See CRS Report RS21242, *Colombia: The Uribe Administration and Congressional Concerns*, by Nina M. Serafino.

forces stepped up their counter narcotics operations and activities against the FARC. High public approval ratings, likely due to reductions in violence that had occurred largely as a result of his security policies, prompted Colombia to amend its constitution in 2005 to permit Uribe to run for re-election.

The Second Uribe Administration

On August 7, 2006, Alvaro Uribe was sworn into his second term as president. Pro-Uribe parties won a majority of both houses of congress in elections held in March 2006, giving President Uribe a strong mandate as he started his second term. The domination of pro-Uribe parties, most of them new, appears to have further weakened the traditionally dominant Liberal and Conservative parties. Nevertheless, there is not a high level of unity among the pro-Uribe parties.

Two years into his second presidential term, President Uribe retains widespread support in Colombia. His popularity derives from the progress his government has made in improving security situation in Colombia, demobilizing the AUC, and defeating the FARC and ELN. According to U.S. State Department figures, kidnappings in Colombia have declined by 83%, homicides by 40%, and terrorist attacks by 76% since Uribe first took office in 2002. Police are now present in all of Colombia's 1,099 municipalities, including areas from which they had been previously ousted by guerrilla groups.[7] President Uribe has also overseen the demobilization and disarmament of more than 31,000 AUC paramilitaries, although the demobilization process has been criticized for failing to provide adequate punishments for perpetrators and reparations to victims of paramilitary violence.[8] On March 1, 2008, the Colombian military successfully carried out a raid of a FARC camp in Ecuador that resulted in the killing of a top FARC leader and the capture of his computer files. This was followed by a successful operation on July 2 that resulted in the rescue of 15 hostages long held by the FARC, including three U.S. defense contractors and a former Colombian presidential candidate.

Despite this progress, Colombia continues to face serious challenges. While its numbers have been dramatically reduced in the last year or so, the FARC still has thousands of fighters capable of carrying out terrorist attacks, kidnappings, and other illicit activities. Not all paramilitaries demobilized, and still others have returned to paramilitary activities since demobilizing. Moreover, there are credible reports that a new generation of paramilitaries is forming that is much more criminal than political in nature.[9] Further concern has focused on the ability of the government to re-incorporate ex-fighters into law-abiding civilian life and to provide some type of restitution to their victims.[10] Although President Uribe has not been

---

[7] U.S. Department of State, "Charting Colombia's Progress," March 2008.

[8] Latin American Working Group, "The Other Half of the Truth," June 2008.

[9] Those concerns are cited in the U.S. Department of State, *Country Reports on Human Rights Practices* 2007, March 2008. See also: International Crisis Group (ICG), "Colombia's New Armed Groups," May 2007; Chris Kraul, "In Colombia, ParamilitaryGangs Control Much of Guajira State," *Los Angeles Times*, August 31, 2008.

[10] Washington Office on Latin America (WOLA), "Post-Election Colombia: Careful Monitoring of the Paramilitary Demobilization Process Should be Top Priority of Congress," May 30, 2006; ICG,"Colombia: Towards Peace and Justice?," March 14, 2006.

personally implicated, the Colombian Supreme Court is pursuing ongoing investigations into possible links between Colombian politicians, many from pro-Uribe parties, and paramilitary groups. Ongoing peace talks with the ELN have yet to yield any tangible results. Since the 2006 elections, there have several scandals involving some Colombian military officials and lingering concerns exist about extrajudicial killings committed by Colombian security forces.[11] Drug production and trafficking continue to generate millions of dollars annually for illicit groups. While ONDCP recently reported large declines in Colombia's coca production potential, a June 2008 U.N. Office on Drugs and Crime (UNODC) report found that, although yields were down, the coca acreage planted in Colombia increased by 27% in 2007. Additionally, as a result of the ongoing conflict and drug-related violence, Colombia now has one of the largest populations of internally displaced persons in the world, with some 250,000 people displaced in 2007.

President Uribe's high approval ratings have led many of his supporters to urge him to seek a third presidential term. In order for Uribe to be re-elected, the Colombian constitution would have to be amended (as it was in 2005) to allow him to seek a second term. Uribe's supporters have delivered a petition with five million signatures to Colombian election authorities urging them to convoke a referendum on whether to reform the constitution to allow a third Uribe term. The petition must now be debated in the Colombian legislature and reviewed by the country's Constitutional Court. President Uribe has yet to publicly comment on whether or not he wishes to run again. Many Colombian and international observers have urged Uribe not to seek another term out of respect for the integrity of Colombian democracy. Some have expressed concerns about his past conflicts with Colombian democratic institutions and his authoritarian tendencies.[12]

Progress in Addressing Colombia's Internal Conflict

Roots of the Conflict

Colombia has a long tradition of civilian, democratic rule, yet has been plagued by violence throughout its history. This violence has its roots in a lack of state control over much of Colombian territory, and a long history of poverty and inequality. Conflicts between the Conservative and Liberal parties led to two bloody civil wars — The War of a Thousand Days (1899-1903) and The Violence (1946 to 1957) — that killed hundreds of thousands of Colombians. While a power sharing agreement (the so-called National Front pact) between the Liberal and Conservative parties ended the civil war in 1957, it did not address the root causes of the violence. Numerous leftist guerrilla groups inspired by the Cuban Revolution formed in the 1960s as a response to state neglect and poverty. Right-wing paramilitaries were formed in the 1980s to defend landowners, many of them drug traffickers, against guerrillas. The shift of cocaine production from Peru and Bolivia to Colombia in the 1980s increased drug violence, and provided a new source of revenue for both guerrillas and paramilitaries. The main paramilitary organization, the AUC, began demobilization in 2003

---

[11] "Amnesty Says all Sides in Colombia Have Bloody Hands," EFE, May 28, 2008; Chris Kraul, "Colombia Military Atrocities Alleged," Los Angeles Times, August 20, 2008.

[12] Patricia Markey, "Colombia's Uribe Mulls Re-election, but Will he run?" *Reuters*, August 22, 2008; "Editorial: Mr Uribe's Choice," *New York Times*, August 22, 2008.

and disbanded in 2006. Major armed groups today are the FARC, the National Liberation Army (ELN), and the new generation of paramilitary groups.

Revolutionary Armed Forces of Colombia (FARC)

The FARC can trace its roots to armed peasant self-defense groups that had emerged during "the Violence" of the 1940-50s. By the 1960s, those groups, located in the remote, mountainous regions between Bogotá and Cali, had developed into a regional guerrilla movement. In 1966, the guerrillas announced the formation of the FARC.[13] The FARC is the oldest, largest, and best-equipped and financed guerrilla organization in Latin America. It mainly operates in rural areas, but has shown its ability to strike in urban areas, including Bogotá. It conducts bombings, murders, mortar attacks, kidnappings, extortion, and hijackings mainly against Colombian targets. The FARC is fully engaged in the drug trade, including cultivation, taxation of drug crops, and distribution, from which it reaps significant profits. In recent years, the FARC has increased it activities along Colombia's borders with Ecuador and Venezuela.

During the Pastrana Administration, the FARC entered into peace negotiations under which it was granted control of a Switzerland-size territorial refuge while the peace process was underway. With continued FARC military activity, including the kidnapping of a Colombian senator, President Pastrana halted the negotiations and ordered the military to retake control of the designated territory. During the inauguration of President Uribe on August 7, 2002, the FARC launched a mortar attack on the Presidential Palace that killed 21 residents of a nearby neighborhood.

In mid-2003, the Colombian military's *Plan Patriota*, a campaign to recapture FARC-held territory, began operations in what was largely seen as a successful effort to secure the capital and environs of Bogotá. In 2004, military operations, conducted by up to 17,000 troops, turned to regaining FARC territory in the southern and eastern regions of the country. The FARC initially responded with a tactical withdrawal of forces, but launched a new counter-offensive in February 2005. The conflict with the FARC has, however, largely remained in the countryside and the FARC was unable to disrupt President Uribe's August 7, 2006, inauguration. In 2006 the FARC controlled an estimated 30% of Colombian territory.[14] The Colombian government maintains that *Plan Patriota* enabled it to reduce FARC ranks, recapture land held by the FARC, and confiscate large amounts of materials used to process cocaine. Despite these advances, critics pointed out that large numbers of civilians were displaced during the campaign.

Colombia's Raid of a FARC Camp in Ecuador

On March 1, 2008, the Colombian military bombed a FARC camp in Ecuador, killing at least 25 people, among them, Raúl Reyes, the terrorist groups' second highest commander whose real name is reportedly Luis Edgar Devia Silva, four Mexican students visiting the camp, and one Ecuadorian citizen reportedly tied to the FARC.[15] This mission marked the

---

[13] See Mark Chernick, "FARC-EP: From Liberal to Marxist to Post-Cold War Guerrillas," in *Terror, Insurgency, and the State*, edited by Marianne Heiberg, et al., Philadelphia: University of Pennsylvania Press, 2007.

[14] "Colombia: Executive Summary," *Jane's Sentinel Security Assessment*, August 24, 2006.

[15] Simon Romero, "Files Released by Colombia Point to Venezuelan Bid to Arm Rebels," *New York Times*, March 30, 2008.

first time in the Colombian military's 44-year struggle against the leftist FARC insurgency that it has be enable to kill a member of the FARC's seven-member ruling secretariat. A few days later, Ivan Rios, another member of the FARC's secretariat, was murdered by his own security agent. Many assert that these high-level killings dealt a significant blow to the FARC, particularly following a FARC announcement in May 2008 that its top commander, Manuel Marulanda, had died in March of a heart attack.

During the raid, the Colombian military captured three laptop computers that allegedly belonged to Reyes. Computer files on those laptops allege that the government of Hugo Chávez of Venezuela was planning to provide millions of dollars in assistance to the FARC for weapons purchases. As a result, some Members of Congress called for the Bush Administration to include Venezuela on the U.S. state sponsors of terrorism list; the Administration began an inquiry into the matter in March. The files also allege that President Raphael Correa of Ecuador received campaign donations from the FARC in 2006. Both Chávez and Correa vigorously reject these claims. Venezuelan officials have dismissed the data as having been fabricated even though Interpol verified in May 2008 that the files had not been tampered with since they were seized. In a welcome turn of events on June 8, 2008, President Chávez called for the FARC to release all hostages unconditionally and to cease military operations, maintaining that guerrilla warfare "has passed into history," signaling a major change in his public stance.[16]

Hostage Releases, Escapes, and the July 2nd 2008 Hostage Rescue

Since 2007, prisoner escapes, hostage deaths, and later hostage releases have focused international attention on the plight of hundreds of hostages held by the FARC. In April 2007, Colombian police office Jhon Frank Pinchao escaped after eight years in FARC custody. In June 2007, eleven departmental deputies who had held since 2002 were reportedly executed by the FARC.[17] In August 2007, President Uribe authorized leftist Senator Piedad Córdoba and Venezuelan President Hugo Chávez to conduct dialogue with the FARC to secure the release of some 45 high-profile hostages, including the three American contractors held since 2003. Negotiations stalled in November due to the FARC's failure to provide proof of life of the hostages and allegations that President Chávez inappropriately contacted the head of the Colombian Army. However, the Colombian government did find over a dozen proof of life videos, including videos of the three American contractors, in a November 2007 raid on the FARC. In December 2007, Fernando Araujo, a former Minister of Development, escaped from the FARC after being held as a hostage for more than six years. From February through July 2008, Araujo served as Colombia's Foreign Minister.

Six hostage releases occurred during early 2008. In January 2008, two hostages were released to a delegation led by President Chávez and the Colombian government was able to successfully reunite one of the hostages with a son born to her in captivity that the FARC had turned over to the Colombian foster care system more than two years ago. A day after the two hostages' release, Chávez's called for the international community to no longer label the FARC and the ELN as terrorist groups prompted widespread condemnation. Nevertheless,

---

[16] "Analysis: Chávez Reverses FARC Stance, Domestic Moves Ahead of Elections," *Open Source Center*, June 19, 2008.

[17] U.S. Department of State, *Country Report on Human Rights Practices 2007*, March 11, 2008.

his role in the release of hostages continued. On February 27, 2008, the FARC released four former members of the Colombian Congress to Venezuelan officials in Colombian territory.

On July 2, 2008, after months of planning and tracking the FARC, the Colombian military successfully tricked the FARC into releasing 15 of their prized hostages. Those hostages included three U.S. defense contractors — Marc Gonsalves, Thomas Howes, and Keith Stansell — held since February 2003 and former Colombian presidential candidate Ingrid Betancourt held since February 2002. The success of the bloodless hostage rescue has been widely cited as an example of the Colombian military's increasing professionalism and intelligence capabilities, which has occurred largely as a result of years of the U.S. training and security assistance programs provided through Plan Colombia.[18] Some press reports indicate that the United States provided millions of dollars to help Colombia find and rescue the hostages, including tactical support and training provided by the U.S. military and technical assistance supplied by a unit of planners, intelligence analysts, and hostage negotiators based in Bogotá.[19]

Many analysts have hailed the recent hostage rescue as evidence that the FARC is disintegrating, but others think it may be too premature to draw that conclusion. This year the FARC has lost three of its top commanders and suffered a series of humiliating defeats at the hands of the Colombian military. Their communications systems have been infiltrated, their leadership is in disarray, and reports indicate that many guerrilla units are running short on supplies.[20] By mid-June 2008, more than 1,506 FARC guerrillas had voluntarily demobilized. Many rebels reportedly hoped to take advantage of the Colombian government's offer to allow the Justice and Peace Law's provisions to apply to those who surrender.[21] Although the FARC, now led by Alfonso Cano, is still unwilling to negotiate with the Uribe government, their position is much weaker than it was just months ago.

National Liberation Army (ELN)

The smaller ELN was formed in 1965, inspired by the ideas of Fidel Castro and Che Guevara. With a membership of about 3,000, it is less active than the FARC, but has still been able to carry out a number of high profile kidnappings and bombings. In addition to the rural civilian population, the ELN has also targeted the country's infrastructure, especially its oil and electricity sectors. Its operations are mainly located in the rural areas of the north, northeast, the Middle Magdalena Valley, and along the Venezuelan border. The ELN earns funds from the taxation of illegal crops, extortion, attacks on the Caño-Limón pipeline, and kidnapping for ransom. Its size and military strength have been dramatically reduced since the late 1990s.[22]

In recent years, the ELN has shown more of a willingness to attempt peace negotiations with the government. In December 2003, President Uribe revealed that he had met with an ELN leader to discuss possible peace initiatives, but a subsequent ELN statement ruled out any possibility of demobilization. However, in 2004, the ELN and the Colombian

---

[18] Colombian Officials Recount Rescue Plan; Commandos Took Acting Classes to Prepare," *Washington Post*, July 6, 2008.

[19] "U.S. aid was a key to the Hostage Rescue," *New York Times*, July 13, 2008.

[20] Patrick McDonnell and Chris Kraul, "Colombian Rebels Splintering," *Los Angeles Times*, July 5, 2008; "After the War in Colombia," *El Pais*, July 10, 2008.

[21] Closing the net on the FARC, Striking at the ELN," *Latin American Security and Strategy Review*, July 2008.

[22] International Crisis Group, "Colombia: Moving Forward with the ELN?" October 11, 2007.

government accepted an offer from Mexican President Vicente Fox to facilitate peace negotiations. In June 2004, Mexico named Andres Valencia, a former Mexican ambassador to Israel, as its facilitator. Meetings with Valencia and the ELN occurred, but the rebel group rejected Uribe's offer of a cease-fire.[23] In April 2005, the ELN rejected further Mexican facilitation after Mexico voted to condemn Cuba at the U.N. Human Rights Commission. The Colombian government and the ELN held several rounds of exploratory talks in Havana, Cuba between December 2005 and August 2007, but those talks resulted in no concrete agreements. In June 2008, the ELN announced that it would not continue negotiating with the Uribe government for the time being. President Uribe responded by ordering the Colombian military to step up its operations against the ELN.[24]

Paramilitaries

Paramilitary groups trace their origins to the 1980s when wealthy ranchers and farmers, including drug traffickers, organized armed groups to protect them from kidnappings and extortion plots by the FARC and ELN. The largest paramilitary organization, the AUC, was formed in 1997 as an umbrella organization for a number of local and regional paramilitary groups operating in the country. As discussed in more detail below, the AUC disbanded in 2006. Not all paramilitary groups joined the AUC umbrella. The AUC conducted massacres and assassinations of suspected insurgent supporters and directly engaged the FARC and ELN in military battles. The Armed Forces of Colombia have long been accused of turning a blind eye to these activities. The AUC, like the FARC, earned most of its funding from drug trafficking. *Jane's World Insurgency and Terrorism* estimated that in 2006 paramilitaries handled 40% of Colombian cocaine exports.[25]

On July 15, 2003, the AUC reached an agreement with the Colombian government to demobilize its troops by the end of 2005. At that time, the State Department estimated that there were between 8,000 and 11,000 members of the AUC, although press reports used numbers ranging up to 20,000. The demobilization process begun in 2004 officially ended in April 2006. As of that time, over 30,000 AUC members had demobilized and turned in over 17,000 weapons.[26] AUC leaders remained at large, however, until August 2006 when President Uribe ordered them to surrender to the government to benefit from the provisions of the Peace and Justice Law.[27] It remains to be seen how Uribe's May 2008 decision to extradite 15 paramilitary leaders to the United States to stand trial for drug trafficking charges will affect ongoing investigations into the "parapolitical" scandal, as well as efforts to ensure that victims of paramilitary violence receive compensation for their suffering.

Not all paramilitaries demobilized, and still others have returned to paramilitary activities since demobilizing. Moreover, there are credible reports that a new generation of paramilitaries has formed and may be recruiting demobilized paramilitaries. Membership in

---

[23] Kate Joynes, "ELN Rebels Rebut Colombian Government's Peace Pledge," *WMRC Daily Analysis*, July 12, 2004.

[24] Closing the net on the FARC, Striking at the ELN,"Latin American Security and Strategy Review, July 2008.

[25] U.S. Department of State, *Country Reports on Terrorism 2005*, and, "Autodefensas Unidas de Colombia," *Jane's World Insurgency and Terrorism,* August 10, 2006.

[26] "Only 2% of 30,150 Demobilized Paramilitaries to Stand Trial," *Associated Press*, April 18, 2006.

[27] Vicente Castaño, brother of AUC founder Carlos Castaño, remains at large. Vicente Castaño is under investigation by Colombian authorities for ordering the 2004 murder of his brother who reportedly planned to turn paramilitary leaders over for extradition to the United States as part of peace negotiations.

the new paramilitary organizations is estimated at 3,000 to 9,000. Some former AUC members continue to be active in the drug trade.[28] There are reports that the AUC continues to take part in drug trafficking, in spite of the demobilization process. *Jane's World Insurgency and Terrorism* reports that since demobilization the AUC's purpose has shifted from combating the FARC and ELN to protecting drug trafficking networks and preventing the extradition of leaders wanted on drug trafficking charges in the United States. The State Department and U.N. both note that the new illegal groups do not share the political ideology of the AUC, which sought to defeat leftist guerrillas. Despite their ad-hoc nature, the new illegal groups pose a threat to Colombian civilians and the Uribe government is taking steps to combat them.[29]

Remaining Political Challenges

Parapolitical Scandal

A scandal involving alleged paramilitary ties to politicians, including current members of the Colombian Congress, erupted in November 2006. Paramilitary leaders claimed to control 35% of the congress in 2005. On November 9, 2006, the Colombian Supreme Court ordered the arrest of three congressmen for their alleged role in establishing paramilitary groups in the Caribbean state of Sucre. Since the scandal broke, several Colombian politicians, including several past and current members of the Colombian Congress, have been charged with ties to paramilitary groups. Former Foreign Minister Maria Consuelo Araujo was forced to resign due to the investigation into her brother's and father's connections to the paramilitaries and their involvement in the kidnapping of Alvaro Araujo's opponent in a Senate election. In December 2007, Congressman Erik Morris was sentenced to six years in prison for his ties to the paramilitaries, making him the first Member of Congress to be sentenced in the ongoing scandal. In February 2008, the former head of Colombia's Department of Administrative Security (DAS), Jorge Noguera, was formally charged with collaborating with paramilitaries, including giving paramilitaries the names of union activists, some of whom were subsequently murdered by the paramilitaries. In April 2008, Mario Uribe, a former senator, second cousin, and close ally of President Alvaro Uribe, was arrested for colluding with the paramilitaries. As of early August 2008, some 70 legislators were under investigation for possible ties with the paramilitaries.[30]

The parapolitical scandal has increased tensions between President Uribe and the Supreme Court, which is charged with investigating the politicians accused of having paramilitary ties, many of whom are from pro-Uribe parties. In July 2008, representatives from the two branches met in a series of meeting to discuss President Uribe's concern that the paramilitary investigations were advancing too quickly. Despite those meetings, the Supreme Court ordered the arrest of Senator Carlos Garcia, head of Uribe's main coalition party, in late

---

[28] International Crisis Group, *Colombia's New Armed Groups*, May 10, 2007; WOLA, *Captive States: Organized Crime and Human Rights in Latin America*, October 2007.

[29] United Nations General Assembly -Human Rights Council, "Report of the United Nations High Commissioner for Human Rights on the Situation of Human Rights in Colombia," February 29, 2008; U.S. Department of State, "Memorandumof Understanding Concerning Human Rights Conditions with Respect to Assistance for the Colombian Armed Forces,"July 28, 2008, available at [http://justf.org/files/primarydocs/080728cert.pdf].

[30] "Saving Congress at a Cost to the Courts," *Latin American Andean Group Report*, August7, 2008.

July. Tensions escalated again in August when press reports announced that two of President Uribe's advisers had met with representatives of Don Berna, the top paramilitary leader, at the presidential palace in April.[31] Government critics have questioned whether President Uribe's decision in May 2008 to extradite key paramilitary figures to the United States may have been done, at least partially, in order to thwart ongoing investigations into government-paramilitary ties. They have also questioned the motives behind a judicial reform package recently submitted by Uribe to the Congress that would remove the Supreme Court's power to investigate legislators.[32]

The Justice and Peace Law and Demobilization

As part of the paramilitary demobilization process, President Uribe introduced a Justice and Peace Law granting conditional amnesties to illegal combatants, which would mean that the law could also apply to FARC and ELN fighters if they decide to enter into negotiations with the government. Colombia's congress approved the legislation in 2005. The Justice and Peace Law called on demobilized fighters to provide a voluntary account of their crime and to forfeit illegally acquired assets in exchange for an alternative penalty of up to eight years' imprisonment. If the accused was subsequently found to have intentionally failed to admit to a crime, the alternative penalty could be revoked and the full sentence imposed. Critics contended that the penalties provided for in the law were too lenient and amount to impunity. The Uribe Administration argued that without the inducement of the new law, paramilitary leaders and fighters would be unwilling to demobilize and a spiral of violence would continue in Colombia.

In July 2006, Colombia's Constitutional Court upheld the constitutionality of the law. In the same ruling, however, the Constitutional Court limited the scope under which demobilizing paramilitaries can benefit from the reduced sentences. Paramilitaries who commit crimes or fail to fully comply with the law will have to serve full sentences. The ruling also stipulates that paramilitaries must confess all crimes and make reparations to victims using both their legally and illegally obtained assets. Paramilitary leaders reacted by stating that they would not comply with the law. In response, President Uribe ordered paramilitary leaders to turn themselves in. By October 2006 all but 11 paramilitary leaders had complied with this order.[33]

The merits of the Justice and Peace Law have been fiercely debated both in Colombia and the United States. Supporters believe it is an effective means to end paramilitary activities. The Bush Administration has expressed support for the law, noting that it has facilitated the demobilization of more than 31,000 paramilitary members. Supporters of the law maintain that paramilitaries must act in good faith and avoid further participation in illegal activities in order to benefit from the peace process. The Uribe administration has removed some demobilized paramilitaries, including Carlos Mario "Macaco" Jiménez, from the Justice and Peace process due to their continued participation in illegal activities. In May

---

[31] "Uribe Squares up to Supreme Court and Liberals as Parapolitical Scandal Deepens,"Latin American Weekly Report, August 28, 2008.

[32] Juan Forero, "U.S. Extraditions Raise Concerns in Colombia," *Washington Post*, August 19, 2008; Human Rights Watch, "Colombia: Proposal Threatens 'Parapolitical'Investigations," August 4, 2008.

[33] "Country Report - Colombia," *Economist Intelligence Unit*, October 2006; Human RightsWatch, "Colombia: Court's Demobilization Ruling Thwarts Future Abuses," July 19, 2006;"Gobierno colombiano abrirá debate público sobre decretos reglamentarios de ley deJusticia y Paz," *El Tiempo*, August 29, 2006.

2008, Uribe extradited Jiménez, Salvatore Mancuso, and 13 other paramilitary leaders who had violated the terms of the law to the United States where to stand trial on drug trafficking charges.

Despite these results, the OAS Mission to Support the Peace Process in Colombia and other observers have expressed concern about the institutional frailty of the Justice and Peace process. Human rights groups are also concerned that the paramilitaries have not been held accountable for their illegal activities and, that by under reporting illegally obtained assets, have failed to provide adequate reparation to their victims.[34] Other observers have expressed concerns that many paramilitaries have elected not to participate in the Justice and Peace process. Of the more than 31,000 paramilitary members that had demobilized as of June 2008, just 3,297 had been found eligible to receive benefits under the Justice and Peace Law's framework. In response to concerns that the Justice and Peace Unit tasked with investigating and prosecuting the paramilitaries was severely understaffed, the Uribe government issued a decree this spring that authorizes tripling the size of its staff.[35] The International Criminal Court is monitoring the investigations and prosecutions of former paramilitaries to ensure that those who guilty of human rights abuses are held accountable for their crimes.[36]

Human Rights Violations by Colombian Security Forces

In its 2008 State of the World's Human Rights report, Amnesty International asserted that, between June 2006 and June 2007, at least 280 civilians were extrajudicially killed by Colombian security forces and that many of them were subsequently presented by those forces as guerrillas killed in conflict. The State Department's *Country Reports on Human Rights Practices* for Columbia covering 2007 stated that "while the government's overall respect for human rights continued to improve...there were periodic reports that members of the security forces committed extrajudicial killings." In a February 2008 report, the U.N. High Commissioner for Human Rights acknowledged that, although it continued to receive complaints of extra judicial killings by security officers, Colombian military and civilian officials have developed new directives to deal with allegations of abuses by security officials. However, this year human rights groups have continued to document extrajudicial killings by some Colombian military forces.[37]

Internally Displaced Persons (IDPs)

Colombia has one of the largest internally-displaced populations in the world, with indigenous and Afro-Colombians disproportionately represented among those displaced. There is some discrepancy over the current rate of displacement. The Colombian government registered over 250,000 IDPs in 2007, a decline of about 8,000 from 2006. Some IDPs do not register with the Colombian government out of fear and procedural barriers. As such, estimates of new displacements put forth by NGOs tend to be higher than government figures. For example, the Consultancy for Human Rights and Displacement (CODHES), a Colombian

[34] Latin America Working Group Education Fund, *The Other Half of the Truth*, June 2008.

[35] U.S. Department of State, "Memorandum of Understanding Concerning Human Rights Conditions with Respect to Assistance for the Colombian Armed Forces," July 28, 2008.

[36] "International Criminal Court not to Allow Colombian Paramilitary Members Impunity," *Noticias Financieras*, August 31, 2008.

[37] "Amnesty Says all Sides in Colombia Have Bloody Hands," EFE, May 28, 2008; "Activists say Army Killing Civilians to Gain Points," *Irish Times*, March 25, 2008.

NGO, estimated that some 305,000 people were displaced in 2007, about 27% higher than the number CODHES recorded in 2006. Although still concerned by the overall numbers of individuals displaced, international NGOs found that the rate of mass displacements decreased in 2007. Colombian government assistance to IDPs increased by 10% in 2007, with total assistance provided estimated at $500 million.[38] This year the U.N. High Commissioner for Refugees (UNHCR) has expressed particular concern about new displacements occurring along southern Colombia's Pacific Coast.[39]

Landmines

Landmines appear to be an ongoing problem in Colombia. The International Committee to Ban Landmines reports that Colombia had the highest number of landmine casualties in the world in 2006, with 1,106 in 2006, down from 1,112 in 2005. Landmine casualties increased nearly 25% in 2005. Afghanistan and Cambodia continue to have higher rates of landmine casualties than Colombia. Both Human Rights Watch and the International Committee to Ban Landmines report that the vast majority of landmines are laid by the FARC and ELN.[40]

Colombia and Global Drug Trends

Colombia's prominence in the production of cocaine and heroin is cited as justification for the U.S. focus on anti-narcotics efforts in the Andean region. According to various sources, Colombia produces 60% of the world's cocaine.[41] It is the source of over 90% of cocaine consumed in the United States. Even though Colombia produces only a small fraction of global heroin production, it is the leading supplier of heroin in the eastern United States, according to the State Department's 2008 *International Narcotics Control Strategy Report.*

The world's supply of cocaine is produced by just three countries: Peru, Bolivia, and Colombia. Until the mid-1990s, Peru and Bolivia were the two major producers. Colombia eclipsed Bolivia in 1995 and Peru in 1997, the result of increased eradication programs in those two countries and the displacement of coca cultivation to Colombia. Cocaine production in Colombia increased fivefold between 1993 and 1999. UNODC recently reported a 27% increase in coca cultivation in Colombia in 2007, with smaller increases of 5% and 4% reported in Bolivia and Peru respectively.[42]

Global production of the opium poppy, from which heroin is produced, increased 17% in 2007, largely due to production increases in Afghanistan and Burma (Myanmar). Its principal source countries are Afghanistan (82%) and Burma (Myanmar) (11%). Most heroin consumed in the United States, however, comes from Mexico and Colombia. In 2007, the U.N. found that opium poppy cultivation in Colombia fell to about 714 hectares, whereas cultivation in Mexico increased to 19,147 hectares.[43]

---

[38] U.S. Department of State, *Country Reports on Human Rights Practices 2007*, March 2008

[39] U.N. High Commissioner for Refugees (UNHCR), "Thousands Displaced in Southern Colombia," August 22, 2008.

[40] International Committee to Ban Landmines, *Landmine Monitor 2007* and Human Rights Watch, *Maiming the People*, July 2007.

[41] United Nations Office on Drugs and Crime (UNODC), *Coca Cultivation in the AndeanRegion*, June 2008.

[42] Ibid.

[43] UNODC, *World Drug Report* 2008.

In recent years, the Colombian government, with significant U.S. assistance, has stepped up its eradication efforts, with manual eradication accounting for an increasing percentage of total eradication efforts. In 2007, the Colombian government eradicated over 219, 529 hectares of elicit coca crops, up from 215,421 hectares eradicated the previous year. Aerial eradication accounted for 70% of the coca crops destroyed in 2007.[44] ONDCP has credited ongoing aerial spraying and manual eradication programs with recent declines in the cocaine productivity of the coca currently cultivated in Colombia.[45] The Colombian Ministry of Defense has recently asserted that, due to recent declines in U.S. security assistance, its forces will probably only be able to spray about 100,000 hectares this year (as compared to the roughly 153,000 hectares they eradicated through aerial spraying in 2007).[46]

After a long period of stable prices, purity, and availability of illegal drugs in the United States, evidence indicated that the price of cocaine rose in the first nine months of 2007. On November 8, 2007, the U.S. Office of National Drug Control Policy announced that cocaine prices rose 44% in the first nine months of 2007 and purity was down 15% during the same period. The supply of drugs is often judged by changes in price, with higher prices signifying decreased supply. Declining purity is also used as a measure indicated decreased availability. ONDCP Director John Walters attributed this increase to regional counter narcotics efforts, including U.S. funded programs in Colombia. However, information contained in the *National Drug Threat Assessment 2008* released in early November cast doubt on the likelihood that this trend will continue. The report, published by the Department of Justice's National Drug Intelligence Center (NDIC) stated that cocaine shortages are unlikely to continue because "cocaine production in South America appears to be stable or increasing."[47]

Some observers have expressed caution in interpreting the ONDCP figures on price, purity, and availability. They maintain that short-term fluctuations are not uncommon and may not be sustainable.[48] Still others express caution because cocaine production levels have not fallen. Another possible explanation for the declining cocaine supply in the United States is that cocaine is being diverted to Europe where drug traffickers can earn more money, presumably because of the strong euro.[49]

Colombia and Regional Security

Another justification of current U.S. policy in the Andean region is that drug trafficking and armed insurgencies in Colombia have a destabilizing effect on regional security. With porous borders amid rugged territory and an inconsistent state presence, border regions are seen as particularly problematic. Colombia shares a 1,367 mile border with Venezuela,

---

44 U.S. Department of State, *International Narcotics Control and Strategy Report* (INCSR)2008.

45 U.S. Office of National Drug Control Policy, "Official U.S. Colombia Survey Reveals Sharp Decline in Cocaine Production," September 10, 2008.

46 Republic of Colombia, Ministry of National Defense (MOD), "Colombian MOD Observations to U.S. Security Assistance for 2009," July 2008.

47 U.S. Department of Justice, National Drug Intelligence Center, *National Drug Threat Assessment 2008*, October 2007.

48 "U.S. Drug Czar Claims Cocaine Prices Fall," Associated Press, November 8, 2007.

49 Ibid and Chris Kraul, "U.S. Says War on Narcotics is Working," *Los Angeles Times*, November 9, 2007; "Editorial: Not Winning the War on Drugs," *New York Times*, July 2, 2008.

approximately 1,000 miles each with Peru and Brazil, and much smaller borders with Ecuador and Panama. The conflict in Colombia and its associated drug trafficking have led to spillover effects in Colombia's neighboring countries.

Cross-Border Incursions and Safe Havens

Colombia's relations with its neighbors have been strained by the spillover from Colombia's civil war, including cross-border military activity. Colombia has asked both Venezuela and Ecuador for assistance in patrolling border areas where the FARC is strong. Press accounts in 2006 and 2007 reported numerous FARC attacks in Colombia along its border with Venezuela. The State Department's *2007 Country Reports on Terrorism* report states that Venezuelan President Hugo Chávez's "ideological sympathy for the FARC and ELN limited Venezuelan cooperation with Colombia in combating terrorism." The FARC and ELN use Venezuelan territory as safe havens, and to transship arms and drugs, secure logistical supplies, and commit kidnappings and extortion. Splinter groups of the FARC also operate in Venezuela where they participate in drug trafficking.

Opponents of President Chávez regularly accuse him of harboring FARC guerrillas. While the FARC uses Venezuelan territory as a safe haven, the State Department notes, "it remained unclear to what extent the Venezuelan Government provided material support to Colombian terrorist organizations. However, limited amounts of weapons and ammunition, some from official Venezuelan stocks and facilities, have turned up in the hands of Colombian terrorist organizations"[50] President Chávez's comments that the FARC and ELN should be considered belligerent groups, not terrorist organizations, following the January 2008 release of two hostages held by the FARC increased tension between Colombia and Venezuela.

Tensions with Ecuador have also increased, with accusations of incursions by Colombian troops chasing FARC units across the border. Colombia is concerned that the FARC are using Ecuadorean territory to launch attacks. Leftist Ecuadorian President Rafael Correa opposes U.S. involvement in Colombia and has indicated that he will not renew the United States' lease on the Manta airbase when it is up for renewal in 2009. Ecuador is also concerned that aerial spraying of coca crops in southern Colombia is reaching into Ecuador potentially damaging licit Ecuadorian crops. *Jane's Intelligence Digest* reports that the FARC are producing cocaine in laboratories based in Ecuador. Other concerns between the countries relate to refugees from Colombia's conflict.[51]

Crisis in the Andes and Efforts at Resolution

In March 2008, Colombia's unauthorized raid on a FARC camp in Ecuador prompted one of the most serious diplomatic crises that the Andean region has faced in recent years. President Correa responded to the raid by breaking diplomatic ties with Colombia and sending additional troops to the Ecuador-Colombia border. In a show of solidarity with Ecuador, President Chávez broke diplomatic and trade ties with Colombia and sent 10 battalions of troops to Venezuela's border with Colombia.

---

[50] Department of State, Office of the Coordinator for Counterterrorism, *Country Reports on Terrorism 2006.*

[51] "Border Clashes Boost Crime in Colombia," *Jane's Intelligence Digest*, May 29, 2007 and "Ecuador Moves Colombians from Border," *LatinNews Daily*, August 28, 2007.

While some feared that the diplomatic crisis might escalate into a military conflict, those concerns were allayed after a Rio Group summit held in the Dominican Republic on March 7. At the Rio summit, Uribe, Chávez, and Correa each had a chance to voice his concerns, which resulted in heated exchanges that lasted some six hours. President Uribe publicly apologized for the incursion and vowed that it would never happen again. President Chávez appeared to accept the apology and called for an end to the crisis, but President Correa remained angered by the affair. The Rio Group issued a resolution that rejected Colombia's incursion of Ecuadorian territory, but acknowledged Uribe's apology.[52]

The Rio Group summit was followed by a March 17-18 OAS Meeting of Consultation of Ministers of Foreign Affairs held at the organization's headquarters in Washington D.C. On March 18, after extended debate, the OAS adopted a resolution rejecting, but not condemning, the bombing raid and calling for the restoration of diplomatic ties between Ecuador and Colombia.[53] While Colombia and the United States reportedly view the raid as justified within the context of Colombia's longstanding battle against terrorist groups, most countries reject it as a violation of Ecuador's national sovereignty per Article 21 of the OAS Charter.[54]

Tensions between Colombia, Ecuador, and Venezuela continued throughout the spring of 2008, particularly after Interpol published a report in May confirming that Colombian officials did not tamper with computer files seized at the FARC camp in Ecuador. Those files allege that the government of Hugo Chávez of Venezuela was planning to provide millions of dollars in assistance to the FARC for weapons purchases and that the Correa government received campaign contributions from the FARC. Venezuelan and Ecuadorian officials have dismissed the data as having been fabricated. Whereas Venezuela has restored diplomatic relations with Colombia, Ecuador has yet to do so.

Issues for Congress

Recent debate on U.S. policy toward Colombia has taken place in a context of concern over the sheer volume of illegal drugs available in the United States and elsewhere in the world. The United States approved increased assistance to Colombia as part of a six-year plan called Plan Colombia in June 2000, and has provided over $6 billion in assistance from FY2000 to FY2008. The United States now provides assistance to Colombia on an annual basis through the Andean Counterdrug Program (ACP) account, formerly known as the Andean Counterdrug Initiative (ACI), and other aid accounts.

In addition to the larger debate over what role the United States should play in supporting Colombia's ongoing struggle against drug trafficking and illegally armed groups, Congress has repeatedly expressed concern with a number of specific policy issues. These include

52 "How Diplomacy Silenced the Drums of War in Less Than a Week," *Latin American Security and Strategic Review*, March 2008; Francis Robles, "Ecuador Rages, Colombia and Venezuela Make Up," *Latinnews Daily*, March 14, 2008; "Leaders Defuse South American Crisis," *Miami Herald*, March 8, 2008.

53 Report of the Organization of American States (OAS) Commission That Visited Ecuador and Colombia, Washington D.C., March 17, 2008; Resolution of the Twenty-Fifth Meeting of Consultation of Ministers of Foreign Affairs, Washington D.C., March 17, 2008.

54 "OAS Resolution Stops Short of Condemning Colombia," *Latin America Weekly Report*, March 19, 2008; "Latin America: Insecurity Raises Sovereignty Fears," *Oxford Analytica*, March 25, 2008.

continuing allegations of human rights abuses; the health and environmental consequences of aerial eradication for drug control; the progress of alternative development to replace drug crops with non-drug crops; judicial reform and rule of law programs; and the level of risk to U.S. personnel working in Colombia. Prior to the release of the three U.S. hostages held by the FARC in early July 2008, securing the release of those hostages was also a key issue of congressional concern.

Proponents of the current U.S. policy towards Colombia point to the progress that has been made in improving security conditions in Colombia and in weakening the FARC guerrillas. They favor maintaining the current level of security assistance to Colombia in order to help Colombian security forces continue to combat the FARC and ELN, solidify their control throughout rural areas, and eradicate illicit narcotics. They also believe that guerrilla forces regularly cross borders using neighboring countries' territory for refuge and supplies, and that this has a potentially destabilizing effect in the region.

Opponents of current U.S. policy in Colombia respond that the counterdrug program uses a repressive approach to curbing drug production which could provoke a negative popular reaction in rural areas. They argue for halting aerial fumigation of drug crops, limiting aid to the Colombian military, and stressing interdiction rather than eradication so that the direct costs to peasant producers is less. Some critics of U.S. policy would support a policy that focuses largely on economic and social aid to combat what they consider to be the conflict's root causes, curbs human rights abuses by paramilitary groups and security forces, provides vigorous support for a negotiated end to the fighting, and emphasizes illicit drug demand reduction in the United States.[55]

Plan Colombia and the Andean Counterdrug Program (ACP)

Plan Colombia was developed by former President Pastrana (1998-2002) as a plan to end the country's 40-year old armed conflict, eliminate drug trafficking, and promote development. The initial plan was a $7.5 billion three-year plan, with Colombia providing $4 billion of the funding and requesting $3.5 billion from the international community. The U.S. Congress approved legislation in support of Plan Colombia in 2000, as part of the Military Construction Appropriations Act of 2001 (P.L.106-246) providing $1.3 billion for counter narcotics and related efforts in Colombia and neighboring countries. Plan Colombia was never authorized by Congress and subsequent funding has been approved annually. President Bush has continued support for the plan under the ACP aid account. The ACP account also fund counter narcotics programs in Bolivia, Brazil, Ecuador, Panama, Peru, and, until recently, Venezuela. Because narcotics trafficking and the guerrilla insurgency have become intertwined problems, in 2002 Congress granted the Administration flexibility to use U.S. counterdrug funds for a unified campaign to fight drug trafficking and terrorist organizations.[56]

---

55 Julia E. Sweig, Andes 2020: *A New Strategy for the Challenges of Colombia and the Region,* Council on Foreign Relations Center for Preventive Action, January 2004.

56 The State Department and the Department of Defense explain expanded authority as providing them with flexibility in situations where there is no clear line between drug and terrorist activity.

Through the ACP and Foreign Military Financing (FMF) accounts, the United States supports the eradication of coca and opium poppy crops, the interdiction of narcotics shipments, and the protection of infrastructure through training and material support for Colombia's security forces. U.S. assistance also supports alternative crop development and infrastructure development to give coca and opium poppy farmers alternative sources of income, and institution building programs to strengthen democracy. Alternative development (AD) programs were shifted from the ACP account to the Economic Support Fund (ESF) account in FY2008. U.S. assistance includes human rights training programs for security personnel in response to Congressional concerns about human rights abuses committed by Colombian security forces. Congress has prohibited U.S. personnel from directly participating in combat missions and has capped the number of U.S. military and civilian contractor personnel that can be stationed in Colombia in support of Plan Colombia at 800 and 600 respectively.[57]

The United States also supports the interdiction of drug shipments through the Air Bridge Denial (ABD) Program. The Air Bridge Denial program began as a joint interdiction effort between the United States, Peru, and Colombia that sought to identify possible drug flights and to interdict them by forcing them to land, and if necessary to shoot down the aircraft. The program was suspended in 2001 after a flight carrying American missionaries was shot down over Peru. Following the establishment of new safeguards against accidental shoot downs, the program was renewed in Colombia in 2003. The State Department credits the ABD program with reducing the number of illegal flights over Colombia by some 73% since 2003.[58] This year the U.S. government has begun to transfer control of the ABD program to the Colombian government.

Aerial Eradication and Alternative Development.[59]

Upon taking office, President Uribe announced that aerial eradication, along with alternative crop development, would form a significant basis of the government's efforts. The Plan Colombia eradication spraying program began in December 2000 with operations by the U.S.-funded counter narcotics brigade in Putumayo. It should be noted, however, that spraying does not prevent, although it may discourage, the replanting of illicit crops. During 2007, the Colombian government sprayed 153,000 hectares of coca and poppy and manually eradicated 66,000 hectares of coca and poppy.[60]

The United Nations and United States use different methodologies to estimate annual coca cultivation levels in Colombia. The different methodologies yield results that not only show different levels of cultivation, but different trends as well. **Table 1** and **Table 2** include United Nations and United States data on coca cultivation in Colombia since 2000. The area of cultivation is measured in hectares. For 2007, the United Nations reported a 27% increase

---

[57] The FY2005 National Defense Authorization Act (H.R. 4200; P.L. 108-375) raised the military cap from 400 to 800 and the civilian cap from 400 to 600. The cap does not apply to personnel conducting search and rescue operations, or to U.S. personnel assigned as part of their regular duties to the U.S. embassy. According to the State Department, military personnel levels in 2007 varied from 194 to 563, while civilian personnel levels varied between 257 and 440.

[58] U.S. Department of State, *INCSR 2008.*

[59] Also see CRS Report RL33163, *Drug Crop Eradication and Alternative Development in the Andes*, by Connie Veillette and Carolina Navarette-Frias.

[60] U.S. Department of State, *INCSR 2008.*

in coca cultivation to 99,000 hectares.[61] U.S. data from the ONDCP showed a % increase in coca cultivation in 2007. Some of the 9% increase in cultivation that ONDCP reported for 2006 may be attributed to the fact that the area surveyed increased significantly from the previous year.

Table 1. UNODC Coca Cultivation in Colombia

Year	2000	2001	2002	2003	2004	2005	2006	2007
Area	163,000	145,000	102,000	86,000	80,000	86,000	78,000	99,000
% change	—	**-11%**	**-30%**	**-16%**	**-7%**	**8%**	**-9%**	**27%**

Table 2. U.S. ONDCP Coca Cultivation in Colombia

Year	2000	2001	2002	2003	2004	2005	2006	2007
Area	136,200	169,800	144,450	113,850	114,100	144,000	157,200	167,000
% change	—	**25%**	**-15%**	**-21%**	**0.2%**	**26%**	**9%**	**6.2%**

Aerial eradication has been controversial both in Colombia and the United States. Critics charge that it has unknown environmental and health effects, and that it deprives farmers of their livelihood, particularly in light of a lack of coordination with alternative development programs.[62] With regard to environmental and health consequences, the Secretary of State, as required by Congress, has reported that the herbicide, glyphosate, does not pose unreasonable health or safety risks to humans or the environment. In consultation for the certification, the U.S. Environmental Protection Agency confirmed that application rates of the aerial spray program in Colombia are within the parameters listed on U.S. glyphosate labels. However, press reports indicate that many Colombians believe the health consequences of aerial fumigation are grave, and many international non-governmental organizations criticize the certification for being analytically inadequate.

The U.S. Agency for International Development (USAID) funds alternative development programs to assist illicit crop farmers in the switch from illicit to licit crops, and provides assistance with infrastructure and marketing. Through 2007, the United States has supported the cultivation of 158,000 hectares of licit crops and completed 1, 179 social and productive infrastructure projects. These programs have benefited more than 135,000 families in 17 departments.[63]

The success of alternative development in Colombia has been limited both by security concerns and the limited scope of the program. Security concerns were blamed for the

---

[61] U.N. Office on Drugs and Crime (UNODC), *World Drug Report* 2008; and "Coca Cultivation in the Andean Region," June 2008.

[62] "Chemical Reactions: Spreading Coca and Threatening Colombia's Ecological and Cultural Diversity," *Washington Office on Latin America*, February 2008.

[63] U.S. Department of State, *INCSR 2008.*

planned withdrawal of USAID assistance to five departments where coca production was increasing, according to a USAID memo leaked to the press in October 2006. UNODC reported in June 2006 that alternative development programs have been successful, but only reach 9% of Colombian coca growers and called for a tenfold increase in international donor support for alternative development programs. In 2007, UNODC reported a disparity in spending on alternative development programs. The departments of Norte de Santander, Antioquia, and Santander received 65% of ongoing alternative development project funding, yet coca cultivation in these three departments is about 10% of the national total. In contrast, 40% of current coca cultivation is in the departments of Meta, Caqueta, Guaviare, and Vichada, which receive just 10% of ongoing alternative development project funding. Proponents of U.S. policy argue that both eradication and alternative development programs need time to work. USAID has argued that alternative development programs do not achieve drug crop reduction on their own, and that the Colombia program was designed to support the aerial eradication program and to build "the political support needed for aerial eradication efforts to take place."[64]

Funding for Plan Colombia

From FY2000 through FY2008, U.S. funding for Plan Colombia and its follow-on, the Strategy for Strengthening Democracy and Promoting Social Development, totaled over $6 billion in State Department and Defense Department programs. Most U.S. assistance is provided through the ACP account. In FY2008 Congress funded eradication and interdiction programs through the ACP account, and funded alternative development and institution building programs through the Economic Support Fund (ESF) account. In previous years, alternative development and institution building were funded through the ACP account. In addition, support for aerial eradication programs is provided from the State Department's Air Wing account. The Defense Department requests a lump sum for all counter narcotics programs worldwide under Sections 1004 and 1033, and under Section 124, of the National Defense Authorization Act. DOD can reallocate these funds throughout the year in accordance with changing needs. While not considered a formal component of the ACP Program, the Defense Department has provided Colombia with additional funding for training and equipment for a number of years, as well as the deployment of personnel in support of Plan Colombia.

Recently there has been significant debate in Congress over the proper level and components of U.S. assistance to Colombia. While some Members support the Bush Administration's emphasis on security-related assistance to Colombia, others have expressed concerns that the Administration has put too much of an emphasis on so-called "hard-side" security assistance, rather than traditional development and rule of law programs. Many Members have expressed a desire to see a more rapid transfer of responsibility for the military operations associated with Plan Colombia from the United States to Colombia. The FY2008 Consolidated Appropriations Act (P.L. 110161) reduced interdiction,

---

[64] Ibid, Joshua Goodman, "U.S. Pulling Economic Aid from Colombia's Coca Infested South," Associated Press, October 12, 2006; United Nations Office on Drugs and Crime (UNODC), "Coca Cultivation in Andes Stabilizes in 2005," June 20, 2006; UNODC, *Coca Cultivation in the Andean Region*, June 2006; and, UNODC, *Colombia Coca Cultivation Survey*, June 2007.

eradication, and military aid to Colombia by roughly $104 million to about $305 million and increased funds for alternative development, human rights, and institution building programs by some $84 million to $236 million.[65] **Table 3** details how U.S. aid to Colombia shifted from FY2007 through the FY2009 request. **Table 4** at the conclusion of this report provides a more detailed breakdown of U.S. assistance to Colombia from FY2000 through the FY2009 request. The FY2008 changes reflected an attempt to raise the level of U.S. funding provided for economic and social aid closer to that provided for security-related programs. These changes were criticized by Bush Administration officials.

The Colombian Ministry of Defense has asked Congress to consider restoring a higher level of security assistance in the FY2009 budget at levels that are similar to the Bush Administration's FY2009 request. Although Congress has yet to complete action on the FY2009 foreign operations legislation, the Senate Appropriations Committee report (S. 3288, S.Rept. 110-425) would, as in FY2008, cut security-related assistance to Colombia from the levels requested by the Administration.

Table 3. U.S. Assistance to Colombia: FY2007-FY2009 (in millions $)

Program	FY2007	FY2008 Estimate	FY2008 Est. Compared to FY2007	FY2009 Request
Andean Counterdrug Program (ACP)-Interdiction/Eradication	325.10	244.62	. 80.40	329.56
ACP-Alternative Development	139.90	0.00		
Economic Support Funds	0.00	194.41	54.51b	142.37
International Narcotics and Law Enforcement	0.00	41.91	41.91	0.00
Non-Proliferation, Antiterrorism, Demining, and Related Programs	4.09	3.72	. 0.37	3.15
Foreign Military Financing	85.50	55.05	. 30.0	66.39
International Military Education and Training	1.65	1.43	. 0.22	1.40
P.L. 480 (Food Aid)	4.86	0.00	. 4.86	0.00
Total DOS	561.10	541.14	. 19.96	542.87
Defense Department Counternarcotics Aid (Section 1004/1033)		na		na

Source: U.S. Department of State *Foreign Operations Congressional Budget Justifications*, FY2008-FY2009; DOD "Counterdrug Activity" Reports to Congress for FY2005-FY2007. a. In FY2008, the Andean Counterdrug Initiative (ACI) was renamed the Andean Counterdrug Program (ACP). Until FY2008, ACI funds were divided between programs that supported drug eradication and interdiction efforts and those focused on alternative development and democratic institution building. In FY2008 funding for alternative development programs and institution building were requested from the Economic Support Fund (ESF) rather than the ACP account. b. This column compares Alternative Development figures from FY2008 and FY2007.

---

65 For FY2007, security assistance is calculated by adding relevant portions of the Andean Counterdrug Program (ACP) account, Foreign Military Financing (FMF), International Military Education and Training (IMET), and Non-proliferation, Terrorism, Demining and Related Programs aid totals. Economic and social aid in FY2007 is calculated by adding the alternative development and rule of law portions of ACP to the P.L. 480 food aid total. For FY2008, security assistance is calculated by adding ACP, FMF, IMET, and NADR. Economic social aid includes Economic Support Fund (ESF) aid and International Narcotics and Law Enforcement (INCLE) aid provided to support the Colombian justice sector, primarily the Attorney General's Office.

Paramilitary Demobilization

The 110th Congress will likely want to monitor the developing scandal involving paramilitary ties to Colombian politicians. Some Members of Congress have expressed concern about both the AUC demobilization process and the overall demobilization framework under the Justice and Peace Law approved by the Colombian Congress in 2005. The FY2006 Foreign Operations Act (P.L. 109-102) provided $20 million to assist in the demobilization of former members of foreign terrorist organizations, provided that the Secretary of State certified that the assistance only went to individuals who had verifiably renounced and terminated membership in the FTO; that the Colombian government was cooperating with the United States on extradition; that the Colombian government was working to dismantle FTO structures; and that the funds would not be used to make cash payments to individuals. A foreign operations appropriations measure was not enacted for FY2007 and funding remained at FY2006 levels under a continuing resolution (P.L. 110-5). The FY2008 Consolidated Appropriations Act (P.L. 110161) provided just over $11 million to assist the demobilization of former members of foreign terrorist organizations (FTOs), pending a certification from the Secretary of State that was issued on August 28, 2008. In that certification, she certified the following to Congress:

- that assistance will be provided only for individuals who have verifiably renounced and terminated any affiliation or involvement with FTOs, and are meeting all the requirements of the Colombia Demobilization program, including disclosure of past crimes; the location of kidnap victims and bodies of the disappeared; and, knowledge of FTO structure, financing, and assets.
- that the Colombian government is fully cooperating with the United States in extraditing FTO leaders and members who have been indicted in the United States for murder, kidnapping, narcotics trafficking, and other violations of U.S. law; and is extraditing former paramilitary leaders who have been indicted in the United States and have breached the terms of the demobilization process;
- that the Colombian government is not knowingly taking steps to legalize titles of land or other assets illegally obtained by FTOs, their associates, or their successors; and that the Colombian government has established effective procedures to identify such land and assets;
- that the Colombian government is implementing a concrete and workable framework for dismantling the organizational structures of FTOs; and
- that funds will not be used to make cash payments to individuals, and funds will only be available for any of the following activities: verification, reintegration (including training and education), vetting, recovery of assets for reparations for victims, and investigations and prosecutions.

Human Rights

Debate in Congress has continued to focus on allegations of human rights abuses by the FARC and ELN, paramilitary groups, and the Colombian Armed Forces. In its 2008 State of the World's Human Rights report, Amnesty International asserted that, between June 2006 and June 2007, at least 280 civilians were extra judicially killed by Colombian security forces and that many of them were subsequently presented by those forces as guerrillas killed in conflict. The State Department's *Country Reports on Human Rights Practices* for Columbia covering 2007 stated that "while the government's overall respect for human rights continued to improve...there were periodic reports that members of the security forces committed extrajudicial killings." In a February 2008 report, the U.N. High Commissioner for Human Rights acknowledged that, although it continued to receive complaints of extrajudicial killings by security officers, Colombian military and civilian officials have developed new directives to deal with allegations of abuses by security officials. However, this year human rights groups have continued to document extrajudicial killings by some Colombian military forces.[66] In February 2008, Senators Dodd and Feingold reportedly sent a letter to Secretary of State Condoleezza Rice expressing their concern over reports that civilian killings by Colombian army forces appear to have increased in recent years.

Congress has annually required that the Secretary of State certify to Congress that the Colombian military and police forces are severing their links to the paramilitaries, investigating complaints of abuses, and prosecuting those who have had credible charges made against them. Congress has made funding to the Colombian military contingent on these certifications. In the latest certification, issued on July 28, 2008, the Secretary of State asserted that the Colombian government and armed forces are meeting the statutory requirements with regard to human rights. The Secretary noted that "while the Government of Colombia needs to do more to address serious human rights problems that persist, we see encouraging signs, including concrete examples of progress: the suspension, arrest, or conviction of military violators of human rights, including several general officers; greater civilian access and handling of human rights cases involving the military; and credible investigations of dozens of politicians who allegedly collaborated with the paramilitaries."[67]

Congress has also regularly included the so-called Leahy amendment in foreign operations appropriations legislation that denies funds to any security force unit for which the Secretary of State has credible evidence of gross human rights violations. The Secretary may continue funding if she determines and reports to Congress that the foreign government is taking effective measures to bring the responsible members of these security forces to justice. According to a State Department official, Congress just released its last hold on FY2006 funds in mid-August 2008, but $52.5 million in FY2007 funds and $16.5 million in FY2008 funds for the Colombian military remain on hold.[68] Despite these actions, human rights organizations claim that the U.S. government often turns a blind eye to questionable activities of Colombian security forces.

66 "Amnesty Says all Sides in Colombia Have Bloody Hands," EFE, May 28, 2008; "Activists say Army Killing Civilians to Gain Points," *Irish Times*, March 25, 2008.

67 U.S. Department of State, "Memorandum of Understanding Concerning Human Rights Conditions with Respect to Assistance for the Colombian Armed Forces," July 28, 2008, available at [http://justf.org/files/primarydocs/080728cert.pdf].

68 Information provided by State Department official, August 18, 2008.

Internal Displacement and Refugee Flows to the United States

In addition to the more than three million internally-displaced persons in Colombia, there are nearly 500,000 Colombian refugees and asylum seekers outside the country. The vast majority of Colombian refugees and asylum seekers are in Ecuador (over 200,000) and Venezuela (over 200,000). UNHCR has also reported that there are also 20,000 indigenous Colombians living in refugee-like conditions in the Amazon region of Brazil.[69]

The United States began resettling Colombian refugees in 2002. Admissions peaked at 577 in FY2004, but declined to 323 in FY2005 due to provisions of the REAL ID Act which bar the admission of persons who have provided material support to terrorist groups.[70] In 2005, the UNHCR stopped referring as many Colombians as before for resettlement to the United States, partially because of this issue. The State Department reports that 54 Colombian refugees were admitted to the United States in FY2007. H.R. 5918, introduced in the House on July 27, 2006, would amend the Immigration and Nationality Act so that persons who have provided material support to a terrorist organization under duress or coercion can be admitted to the United States. On September 6, 2007, the Department of Homeland Security issued a memorandum to U.S. Citizenship and Immigration Services (USCIS) to permit USCIS to exempt certain individuals who provided material support to the FARC under duress from the material support bar to admission. In December 2007, a similar directive was issued concerning individuals who provided material support to the ELN under duress. This exemption applies to all applications for admission (including refugees), permanent residence, and asylum, but does not apply to naturalization applications. It is not clear how this discrepancy will affect adjudication of naturalization applications submitted by individuals who have benefited from the exemption.[71]

U.S.-Colombia Free Trade Agreement[72]

In 2003, the Bush Administration announced its intentions to begin negotiating an Andean region free trade agreement (FTA) with Colombia, Peru, Ecuador, and Bolivia. In its announcement, the Administration asserted that an FTA would reduce and eliminate foreign barriers to trade and investment, support democracy, and fight drug activity. After regional talks broke down, the United States pursued bilateral trade agreements with Colombia and Peru. The United States and Colombia signed the U.S.-Colombia Trade Promotion Agreement on November 22, 2006, now called the U.S.-Colombia Free Trade Agreement

---

69 United Nations High Commissioner for Refugees, "UNHCR Global Appeal 2008-2009: Colombia Situation," December 1, 2007; U.S. Committee for Refugees, *World Refugee Survey 2007*; Agencia Presidencial para la Acción Social y la Cooperación Internacional, "Tabulados Generales de la Población Desplazada," December 31, 2007; and, Agencia Presidencial para la Acción Social y la Cooperación Internacional, "Gerencia de Sistemas de Información de Población Desplazada," July 31, 2006.

70 Department of State Bureau of Population, Refugees, and Migration, "Refugee Admissions Program for Latin America and the Caribbean," May 9, 2006.

71 U.S. Citizenship and Immigration Services, "Question and Answer: USCIS National Stakeholder Meeting," January 29, 2008; and U.S. Citizenship and Immigration Services, "Fact Sheet: USCIS Implements Authority to Exempt Certain Persons who Provided Material Support under Duress to the Revolutionary Armed Forces of Colombia (FARC)," September 26, 2007.

72 See CRS Report RL34470, *The U.S.-Colombia Free Trade Agreement: Economic and Political Implications*, by M. Angeles Villarreal.

(CFTA); the agreement must now be ratified by both nations' congresses. Colombia, Bolivia, Ecuador, and Peru currently benefit from the Andean Trade Preference Act (ATPA).[73] On February 14, 2008 the House Committee on Ways and Means voted to extend ATPA preferences (H.R. 5264) until December 31, 2008. The ATPA authorizes the President to grant duty-free treatment to certain products, with more than half of all U.S. imports in 2004 from the Andean countries entering under these preferences.

Critics of the free trade agreement are concerned about the status of labor rights in Colombia, as well as the ongoing parapolitical scandal. An issue of contention is the level of violence against labor activists in Colombia. Killings of labor activists declined under President Uribe, but increased in 2006. Data on the number of labor leaders murdered in any given year vary widely. In 2002, the Colombian government estimated that 99 labor activists were killed, while the National Labor School (ENS, a Colombian NGO) estimated that 178 labor activists were killed. In 2006, the Colombian government estimated that 60 labor activists were killed, while ENS estimated that 72 labor activists were killed. One reason for the discrepancy is that the Colombian government counts deaths of unionized teachers separately from other labor union deaths.

Another point of contention is whether or not labor activists were killed because of their union activity. Very few investigations have been completed — of the 470 union murders that have occurred since President Uribe first took office in 2002, 97% remain unsolved. More than 2,000 killings between 1991 and 2006 remain unsolved. In January 2007, the Colombian attorney general's office set up a unit of 13 prosecutors and 78 investigators to investigate 200 priority cases. In 2007, 36 people were convicted on charges related to the murder of union members, more than were convicted from 2004 through 2006.[74]

On April 8, 2008, President Bush submitted implementing legislation to Congress for the (CFTA). The 2002 Trade Promotion Authority procedures stipulated that Congress must vote on that implementing legislation within 90 legislative days of its introduction. But on April 10, 2008, the House voted 224-195 in favor of changing those procedures, effectively putting congressional consideration of the U.S.-Colombia Free Trade Agreement (CFTA) on hold.

[73] See CRS Report RS22548, *ATPA Renewal: Background and Issues*, by M. Angeles Villarreal.

[74] Frank Bajak, "U.S. Unionists Alarmed by Colombia Woes," *Miami Herald*, February 13, 2008; and "Trade, Death and Drugs," *The Economist*, May 19, 2007.

Table 4. U.S. Assistance For Plan Colombia, FY2000-FY2009
(in millions $)

	ACI	ESF	FMF	IMET	INCLE	NADR	Air Wing	DOD	Total
FY2000	60.1	—	—	—	—	—	38.0	128.5	**226.6**
P.L.106-246	832.0	—	—	—	—	—	—	100.7	**932.7**
FY2001	48.0	—	—	—	—	—	38.0	190.2	**276.2**
FY2002	379.9a	—	—	—	—	25.0	38.2	119.1	**562.2**
FY2003	580.2b	—	17.1	1.2	—	3.3	41.5	165.0	**808.3**
FY2004	473.9	—	98.5	1.7	—	.2	45.0	122.0	**741.3**
FY2005	462.8	—	99.2	1.7	—	5.1	45.0	200.0	**813.8**
FY2006	464.8	—	89.1	1.7	—	—	45.0	112.0	**712.6**
FY2007	465.0	—	85.5	1.6	—	4.1	na	na	**556.2**
FY2008 (est)	244.6	194.4	55.1	1.4	41.9	3.7	na	na	**541.1**
FY2009 (req)	329.6	142.4	66.4	1.4	—	3.2	na	na	**543.0**
Total	**4,340.9**	**336.8**	**510.9**	**10.7**	**41.9**	**44.6**	**290.7**	**1,137.5**	**6,714.0**

Sources: Figures are drawn from the annual State Department Foreign Operations Congressional Budget Justifications for fiscal years 2002 through 2009; the State Department's Washington File, "U.S. Support for Plan Colombia, FY2000 Emergency Supplemental Appropriations," July 5, 2000; the FY2006 Foreign Operations Appropriations Act, P.L. 109-102, and conference report, H. Rept. 109-265; and the FY2008 Consolidated Appropriations Act (P.L. 110-161) and Division J Joint Explanatory Statement.

Notes: For FY2000 and thereafter, Plan Colombia funds are assigned to the State Department's International Narcotics and Law Enforcement Bureau (INL) or the Andean Counterdrug Initiative (ACI). The State Department transfers funds to other agencies carrying out programs in Colombia, of which USAID has received the largest portion. Defense Department funding is from is Counter Narcotics account. DOD requests one sum for programs around the world and adjusts its regional allocations as needed.

a. Includes $6 million appropriated to FMF but transferred to the ACI account.

b. Includes $93 million in FMF regular appropriations and $20 million in FMF supplemental funds that were transferred to the ACI account.

Source: Map Resources. Adapted by CRS. (K.Yancey 2/6/04)

Figure 1. Map of Colombia

In: The War on Drugs: Winning, Losing or Treading Water ISBN 978-1-59454-235-0
Editor: Arcos, Nelson V.

Chapter 9

DRUG CERTIFICATION/DESIGNATION PROCEDURES FOR ILLICIT NARCOTICS PRODUCING AND TRANSIT COUNTRIES *

K. Larry Storrs

SUMMARY

This report summarizes the congressionally mandated presidential designation procedures on major illicit narcotics producing and transit countries in Section 706 of the Foreign Relations Authorization Act for FY2003 (H.R. 1646/P.L. 107-228) enacted in September 2002. To put the new procedures in perspective, the report also provides information on the past procedures, the congressional modifications, and recent presidential designations under the revised procedures.

From the mid-1980s to 2001, Congress required the President to certify in early March that specified drug producing and drug transit countries were ``cooperating fully" with the United States in counter narcotics efforts in order to avoid a series of sanctions, including suspension of U.S. foreign assistance, and opposition to loans in the multilateral development banks. The sanctions would also apply if the Congress, within 30 calendar days, passed a joint resolution of disapproval to overturn the presidential certification. Spokesmen from many countries complained about the unilateral and non-cooperative nature of the drug certification requirements, and a movement to modify the process developed in Congress in 2000-2002.

In 2001 (on a temporary, one year basis) and in 2002 (on a permanent but initially transitional basis), a law with new procedures was enacted. This law requires the President to make a report in mid-September of each year that identifies the major drug producing or transit countries. At the same time, the President is required to designate and to withhold assistance from any of the named countries that has ``failed demonstrably," during the previous 12 months, to adhere to international counter narcotics agreements. Under the

* Excerpted from CRS Report RL32038, dated September 20, 2005

legislation, the President may waive the withholding of assistance if he determines this to be in the national interest.

Acting under this legislation, President Bush made designations on a transitional basis for FY2002 and FY2003 and then made determinations on the designated date for FY2004, FY2005, and FY2006.

- On February23, 2002, the President designated Afghanistan, Burma and Haiti as having ``failed demonstrably'' but granted national interest waivers to Haiti and Afghanistan under the new government.
- On January 31, 2003, the President designated Burma, Guatemala, and Haiti, but granted national interest waivers to Guatemala and Haiti.
- On September 15, 2003, the President designated Burma and Haiti, but granted a national interest waiver to Haiti.
- On September 15, 2004, the President designated Burma as having ``failed demonstrably'' in counter narcotics efforts.
- On September 15, 2005, the President designated Burma and Venezuela but granted a national interest waiver to Venezuela to permit a continuation of U.S. assistance.

DRUG CERTIFICATION REQUIREMENTS FOR FY1987-FY2001

Congress Sets Certification Requirements

In the mid-1980s, Congress became increasingly concerned that the Executive was giving inadequate attention and effort to blocking and controlling foreign drug trafficking. As a result, beginning with the Drug Abuse Act of 1986, Congress required the President to certify that certain countries were cooperating fully with the United States in counter narcotics efforts in order to avoid the suspension of U.S. foreign assistance. Sections 489-490 of the Foreign Assistance Act of 1961, as amended, required the President to designate the major illicit drug producing and drug transit countries by November 1 of each year. These sections further required the President to withhold 50% of U.S. assistance for the designated countries for that fiscal year until he certified by March 1 of each year that the countries had cooperated fully with the United States in drug control efforts, or had taken adequate steps on their own to achieve the goals and objectives of the 1988 United Nations Drug Convention. [1]

In the event the President was unable to certify that a country was fully cooperative, or to determine that a less-than-fully-cooperative country should be given a certification in the national interest, certain sanctions applied to the countries denied certification. Among the

[1] For more detail, see U.S. Department of State, Bureau for International Narcotics and Law Enforcement Affairs, Fact Sheet: Majors List and the Certification Process, March 1, 2001; and CRS Report 98-159, Narcotics Certification of Drug Producing and Trafficking Nations: Questions and Answers, by Raphael F. Perl. There were some slight modifications in the procedures in the 1986-2001 period. Earlier, Congress required reports on drug producing and transit countries in 1981, and it gave the President the authority to suspend assistance to non-cooperative countries in 1984.

sanctions applied to decertified countries were the following: (1) most foreign assistance and financing of military sales for the decertified country were to be suspended, with the exception of counter narcotics and humanitarian aid; (2) U.S. representatives were required to vote against loans for the country in the multilateral development banks; and (3) certain trade sanctions, including increased tariffs and denial of preferential trade benefits, could be applied at the President's discretion. The imposed sanctions were to remain in force until the country was subsequently certified.

The sanctions would also apply if Congress, within 30 calendar days, passed a joint resolution of disapproval to overturn the presidential certification, thereby decertifying a country. However, any such congressional resolution would-be subject to a presidential veto, and would require a two thirds vote of both houses to override. Moreover, Section 614 of the Foreign Assistance Act of 1961, as amended, gives the President the authority to provide assistance to a country, notwithstanding other provisions in the act, if he determines and notifies Congress, that to do so is important to the security interests of the United States.

Presidential Certifications

Acting under the congressionally imposed requirements, U.S. Presidents regularly certified the vast majority of illicit drug producing and transit countries, especially countries that were friendly to the United States and that were trading and diplomatic partners. In a smaller portion of cases, where there were serious doubts about the counter narcotics efforts of trade and diplomatic partners, these countries were given ``national interest" waivers that freed them from sanctions on the grounds that continued aid would facilitate better relations and encourage greater counter- narcotics efforts. [2] In general, the remaining countries that were denied certification (or decertified) were pariah states, or states with which the United States had little or no contact.

Presidents Ronald Reagan and George H.W.Bush decertified Iran, Syria, Burma and Afghanistan, and gave ``national interest" waivers to Lebanon. President Bush decertified Panama in 1988 and 1989, just before and after the United States intervened militarily to remove military ruler General Manuel Noriega from power in part because of his involvement in drug trafficking activities. President William Clinton, decertified Nigeria in 1994, while Bolivia and Peru were given waivers; Colombia, Paraguay, and Pakistan were given waivers in 1995; and Colombia was decertified in 1996 and 1997 on grounds that Colombia's President had received campaign contributions from drug traffickers. This determination caused considerable consternation in Bogota, and some disagreement in Congress. In 1997-1999, there was criticism in Congress when the Administration removed Iran, Syria, and Lebanon from the list of major drug producing and transit countries, and when North Korea was not included in the Majors List.

In action relating to Mexico, which was often the center of attention despite being fully certified each year, congressional resolutions to disapprove Mexico's certification were

[2] See Passing Judgement: The U.S. Drug Certification Process, Annenberg School for Communication, University of Southern California, 1998, pp. 1-2.

introduced in 1987, 1988, 1997, 1998, and 1999. [3] Resolutions of disapproval failed to reach floor action in most years, but both houses passed separate versions of weakened resolutions of disapproval in 1997, and a Senate resolution of disapproval reached the floor but was defeated in 1998. Responding to domestic and international criticisms, measures to modify the drug certification requirements were introduced but not enacted in 1997.

On March 1, 2001, in the last presidential certifications under the old provisions, President George W. Bush certified 20 of the 24 designated drug producing or transit countries as fully cooperative in counter narcotics efforts, and he granted national interest certifications to Cambodia and Haiti. Only two countries --- Afghanistan and Burma --- were decertified and subject to the sanctions. President Bush's determinations were very similar to the determinations of President Clinton in the previous year, except that Nigeria and Paraguay were elevated from national interest waiver status to fully cooperative status. By the end of the 30-day period for congressional review of presidential drug certifications, no resolutions of disapproval had been introduced to disapprove President Bush's 2001 certification of Mexico or any other country.

Drug Designation Requirements for FY2002

Congressional Reform Efforts Lead to One Year Waiver and New Requirements in Foreign Operations Appropriations

After more than a year of efforts to modify the drug certification requirements, in December 2001 and January 2002, Congress passed and the President signed the Foreign Operations Appropriations Act for FY2002 (P.L. 107-115) that contained a temporary, one year suspension of the drug certification procedures, along with new requirements.

Following the July 2000 election of opposition candidate Vicente Fox as President of Mexico, bills were introduced but not enacted to exempt Mexico from the drug certification requirement in FY2001. However, the Senate did pass S. Res. 366 in October 2000, expressing the sense of the Senate that a one-year waiver was warranted for Mexico so that the new presidents in Mexico and the United States could develop more effective and cooperative counter-narcotics programs.

In late January 2001, Senator Dodd introduced S. 219 to suspend the existing drug certification process for all countries for two years and encourage a high-level conference to develop an effective multilateral strategy. In mid-February 2001, Senator Kay Bailey Hutchison introduced S. 353 to exempt Mexico from the drug certification requirement in FY2001 but require enhanced bilateral counter-narcotics cooperation. About the same time, Senator Grassley and Senator DeWine introduced S. 376 to modify the certification process for FY2002-FY2004 to require the President to identify only those countries that are failing to cooperate fully with the United States in drug control efforts.

In mid-February 2001, on the eve of President Bush's visit with President Fox in Mexico, the Senate passed S. Con. Res. 13 expressing the sense of the Congress that the President

[3] For details on the certification process and an illustration of the possible consequences of decertification of Mexico, see CRS Report RL30080, *Mexico and Drug Certification in 1999: Consequences of Decertification*, March 4, 1999, by K. Larry Storrs.

should work with the President of Mexico to advance bilateral cooperation. The measure urged the President to seek, among other things, ``to review the current illicit drug certification process, and should seek to be open to consideration of other evaluation mechanisms that would promote increased cooperation and effectiveness in combating the illicit drug trade." During the joint press conference following the meeting in Mexico, President Bush indicated that there was a movement in Congress to review the drug certification requirements, and he expressed confidence in President Fox's efforts to combat drug trafficking.

In late February and early March, additional measures were introduced to modify the existing drug certification procedures. On February 27, 2001, Representative Kolbe introduced H.R. 753 to exempt Mexico from the drug certification requirements in FY2001. On March 1, 2001, Senators Boxer and Gramm introduced S. 435 to provide that the drug certification procedures would not apply to countries with which the United States has bilateral counter-narcotics agreements; and Representative Reyes introduced H.R. 841 to suspend the certification procedures for two years and encourage development of an effective multilateral strategy.

On March 1, 2001, the same day that President Bush certified that Mexico was cooperating fully with the United States in counter-narcotics areas, the Senate Foreign Relations Committee held a hearing in which several of the proposed modifications to the drug certification requirements were discussed. Then Assistant Secretary of State for International Law Enforcement Affairs Rand Beers testified that the certification process had been ``an effective, if blunt, policy instrument," but he recognized a growing sense in Congress that there may be more effective approaches. He added: ``Any regime that might modify or replace certification should have an enforcement mechanism to ensure continued international counter- narcotics cooperation. If there were efforts to suspend the certification procedure, we believe the President must retain in the interim the power to decertify or sanction individual countries using the standards of the current process. We do not believe that there should be exemptions for individual countries or regions at this time. Future carve outs maybe appropriate, however, for regions where there is a mutually acceptable and credible multilateral evaluative mechanism in place." [4]

On April 3, 2001, the Senate Foreign Relations Committee reported out S. 219 with an amendment in the nature of a substitute, with elements from the various proposals, that would suspend the existing drug certification procedures for three years, require the President to designate only the worst offenders subject to sanctions, and encourage a high-level conference to develop effective multilateral drug reduction and prevention strategies. On

---

4 This was a reference to the Multilateral Evaluation Mechanism (MEM) developed by the Inter-AmericanDrugAbuseControl Commission (CICAD)of the Organization of American States (OAS). Following up on the Hemispheric Anti-Drug Strategy of 1996 and the Plan of Action of Summit of the Americas II (1998) in Santiago, Chile, the CICAD agreed upon the Multilateral Evaluation Mechanism (MEM) in 1999, and a CICAD working group developed a questionnaire with 61 indicators to which governments responded for the first time in 2000. A Governmental Experts Group, made up of one representative from each country, assessed achievements in 1999-2000 for all countries except their own country. The resulting overview Hemispheric Report and the individual National Reports make assessments and recommendations for future action. Critics argue that the reports are preliminary, bland, and without any sanctions. Proponents argue that the reports make important recommendations, that the MEM process will advance beyond the early efforts, and that countries care about their performance under the agreed upon criteria. For more detail on the CICAD and the MEM process, see the CICAD's internet site at [http://www.cicad.oas.org/MEM/ENG/About.asp].

August 1, 2001, the Senate Foreign Relations Committee approved S. 1401, the Foreign Relations Authorizations Act for FY2002-FY2003, with the provisions of the previously reported S. 219 incorporated as Sections 741-745 in Title VII, Subtitle D, Reform of Certification Procedures Applicable to Certain Drug Producing or Trafficking Countries. The Committee reported out S. 1401 (S. Rept. 107-60) on September 4, 2001, and the measure was placed on the Senate Legislative Calendar, but not acted upon in 2001.

During President Fox's official state visit to the United States on September 5-7, 2001, the Mexican President, in addressing a joint session of the U.S. Congress, called upon Congress to pass legislation to suspend the drug certification requirements as a gesture of trust and faith in the new government, arguing that ``trust requires that one partner not be judged unilaterally by the other." Following the Bush-Fox talks, the joint communiqué praised the growing law enforcement cooperation between the countries, expressed support for the OAS' multilateral evaluation of counter narcotics efforts, and noted President Bush's commitment ``to work with the U.S. Congress, on a priority basis, to replace the annual counter- narcotics certification regime with new measures designed to enhance international cooperation in this area."

In December 2001 and January 2002, Congress passed and the President signed the Foreign Operations Appropriations Act for FY2002 (H.R. 2506/P.L. 107-115) that contained a temporary, one-year waiver of the drug certification procedures on a global basis for all major drug transit and drug producing countries. In place of the old requirements, the legislation required the President to designate and withhold assistance from the worst offending countries, namely the countries among the major illicit drug producing and trafficking countries that have ``failed demonstrably," during the previous 12 months, to make substantial efforts to adhere to obligations under international counter-narcotics agreements. It provided, however, that notwithstanding poor counter-narcotics performance, the President could waive the sanctions and continue to provide assistance to the designated countries if he determined and reported to Congress that the assistance to the countries was vital to the national interests of the United States.

President Bush's Designations under the Appropriations Act

Acting under the provisions of the Foreign Operations Appropriations Act for FY2002, President Bush designated the countries with the worst counter-narcotics records on February 23, 2002, having previously identified the major illicit drug producing and drug transit countries in November 2001. He designated three countries --- Afghanistan, Burma, and Haiti --- as having failed demonstrably within the last 12 months to make substantial counter narcotics efforts, but he granted national interest waivers to Haiti and Afghanistan under the new regime. [5] Shortly thereafter, on March 1, 2002, the State Department issued the annual International Narcotics Control Strategy Report, in accordance with a requirement that was

[5] See State Department Fact Sheet, Overview of Annual Presidential Determinations on Major Illicit Drug Producing and Drug-Transit Countries, February 25, 2002, available on line at [http://www.state.gov/p/inl/ris/fs/8480.htm] for information on the procedures and the presidential action.

not changed, with descriptions of the counter narcotics activities of illicit drug producing and trafficking countries. [6]

Drug Designation Requirements for FY2003 and Thereafter

Congress Establishes Permanent New Requirements in Foreign Relations Authorization, with Transitional Provisions for FY2003

Continuing the reform efforts of the previous years, in September 2002, Congress passed and the President signed the Foreign Relations Authorization for FY2003 (H.R. 1646/P.L. 107-228), with permanent new requirements in Section 706 of the act dealing with International Drug Control Certification Procedures.

Drawing from S. 1401, mentioned above, the new procedures require the President to make a report, not later than September 15 of each year (15 days before the start of the fiscal year), identifying the major drug transit or major illicit drug producing countries. At the same time, the President is required to designate any of the named countries that has ``failed demonstrably," during the previous 12 months, to make substantial efforts to adhere to international counter narcotics agreements (defined in the legislation) and to take other counter narcotics measures. [7] U.S. assistance would be withheld from any designated countries unless the President determines that the provision of assistance to that country is vital to the national interest of the United States, or that the designated country subsequently made substantial counter narcotics efforts. Notwithstanding the general suspension of the previous drug certification and sanctions procedures, subsection 706(5)(B) of the act provides that the President may apply those procedures at his discretion.

Given the lateness of passage, a transition rule in the legislation provided that for FY2003, the required report had to be submitted at least 15 days before foreign assistance funds could be obligated or expended.

President Bush's Designations for FY2003 under the Transition Rule

Acting under the transition rule in Section 706 of the Foreign Relations Authorization Act (P.L. 107-228), President Bush identified 23 countries as major drug producing or transit countries [8] on January 31, 2003, four months into the fiscal year, rather than the established

---

6 See the International Narcotics Control Strategy Report covering 2001, available online at [http://www.state.gov/p/inl/rls/nrcrpt/2001/].

7 According to statements in the floor debate, September 15 was picked as a time just before the start of the new fiscal year when the Congress could exercise oversight and take some action if it was dissatisfied with the identifications and designations.

8 The countries identified as major illicit drug producing or transit countries were: Afghanistan, Bahamas, Bolivia, Brazil, Burma, China, Colombia, Dominican Republic, Ecuador, Guatemala, Haiti, India, Jamaica, Laos, Mexico, Nigeria, Pakistan, Panama, Paraguay, Peru, Thailand, Venezuela, and Vietnam. In general, nations are identified as major drug producing countries when a thousand hectares of illicit opium poppy or illicit coca, or five thousand hectares of illicit cannabis are harvested or cultivated during a year. Nations are identified as major drug transit countries when they are a significant direct source of illicit drugs affecting the United States, or such drugs are transported through the nation's territory.

date of September 15, before the start of the fiscal year. As he identified the countries, he designated three countries --- Burma, Guatemala, and Haiti --- as having ``failed demonstrably" within the last 12 months to make substantial counter-narcotics efforts, but he granted national interest waivers to Guatemala and Haiti on grounds that continued U.S. assistance to those countries serves U.S. national interests. At the same time, the President expressed concern about the amount of illegal synthetic drugs (particularly ecstasy) entering the United States from Europe (particularly the Netherlands), and the amount of pseudoephedrine and high potency marijuana entering the United States from Canada.[9]

By making the identifications and the designations at the time and the way that he did, the President made clear, and it was so stated in a fact sheet on the FY2003 narcotics certification process, that he was not exercising his option to utilize the procedures and standards of the old certification system.

Several months later, on March 1, 2003, the State Department issued the annual International Narcotics Control Strategy Report, in accordance with a requirement that was not changed by the legislation, with descriptions of the counter-narcotics activities of illicit drug producing and trafficking countries.[10]

President Bush's Designations for FY2004

Acting under Section 706 of the Foreign Relations Authorization Act for FY2003 (P.L. 107-228), President Bush identified 23 countries as major drug producing or transit countries[11] on the established date of September 15, 2003 --- 15 days before the start of the new fiscal year as intended by Congress. The countries named on the ``majors list" were the same countries identified in the previous determination.

In keeping with the new procedures, among the countries on the majors list, the President designated two countries --- Burma and Haiti --- as having ``failed demonstrably" within the last 12 months to make substantial counter-narcotics efforts. However, Haiti was exempted from sanctions byapresidential determination that continued U.S. assistance to Haiti advances U.S. national interests.

In the text of the presidential determination, the President expressed concern about the flow of illegal synthetic drugs (particularly ecstasy) to the United States from the Netherlands, the amounts of precursor chemicals for producing methamphetamine as well as the amounts of high potency marijuana entering the United States from Canada, and the involvement of North Korea in heroin and methamphetamine traffic in East Asian countries. He indicated that the government of Guatemala had more adequately met international counter-narcotics obligations in the eight months since the last determination when it was

---

[9] See the text of the presidential determination, the factsheet on the procedures, and the briefing and explanation on the FY2003 narcotics certifications available online at the State Department's website at [http://www.state.gov/p/inl/narc/c8342.htm].

[10] See the International Narcotics Control Strategy Report covering 2002 at [http://www.state.gov/p/inl/rls/nrcrpt/2002/].

[11] The countries identified as major illicit drug producing or transit countries were Afghanistan, Bahamas, Bolivia, Brazil, Burma, China, Colombia, Dominican Republic, Ecuador, Guatemala, Haiti, India, Jamaica, Laos, Mexico, Nigeria, Pakistan, Panama, Paraguay, Peru, Thailand, Venezuela, and Vietnam.

listed as having failed demonstrably, but he explicitly stated that further progress was expected in the coming year. [12]

More than five months later, on March 1, 2004, the State Department issued the annual International Narcotics Control Strategy Report, in accordance with a requirement that was not changed by the legislation, with descriptions of the counter- narcotics activities of illicit drug producing and trafficking countries. [13]

President Bush's Designations for FY2005

Acting under Section 706 of the Foreign Relations Authorization Act for FY2003 (P.L. 107-228), on September 15, 2004, about two weeks before the start of the new fiscal year, as intended by Congress, President Bush made the annual presidential determinations regarding major illicit drug producing and drug transit countries, and he authorized the Secretary of State to submit the determinations to Congress.

The President identified 22 countries as major drug producing or transit countries. [14] The countries named on the ``majors list" were the same countries identified in the previous determination, except that Thailand was removed from the list because the country's opium poppy cultivation is well below the levels specified in the legislation, no heroin processing labs have been discovered for several years, and the country is no longer a significant source or country of transit of illicit narcotic products affecting the United States.

The President designated only one country, Burma, among the countries on the majors list, as having ``failed demonstrably" within the last 12 months to make substantial counter-narcotics efforts. Since the President did not exercise his option to make a national interest waiver with regard to Burma, the specified sanctions would be fully in effect against Burma. For the last four years Burma has been the only country subject to sanctions for counter-narcotics deficiencies.

While Haiti had been included with Burma in the President's designations in 2003 as a country that had failed demonstrably to meet counter-narcotics obligations, the President explained that Haiti was not included in the 2004 determinations because ``the new interim Government of Haiti, headed by Prime Minister Latortue, has taken substantive --- if limited --- counter-narcotics actions in the few months it has been in office." Even so, the President explained that the U.S. government was deeply concerned about the ability of law enforcement agencies of Haiti ``to reorganize and restructure sufficiently to carry out sustained counter-narcotics efforts."

In addition, in the text of the presidential determination, the President expressed concern about the efforts of a number of other countries. He expressed concern about the flow of illegal synthetic drugs to the United States from the Netherlands, the amounts of high potency marijuana entering the United States from Canada, the increase in opium crop production in

[12] See the text of the presidential determination and the briefing on the FY2004 narcotics certification determinations available online at the State Department's website at [http://www.state.gov/p/inl/narc/].

[13] See the International Narcotics Control Strategy Report covering 2003, available online at [http://www.state.gov/p/inl/rls/nrcrpt/2003/].

[14] The countries identified as major illicit drug producing or transit countries were: Afghanistan, Bahamas, Bolivia, Brazil, Burma, China, Colombia, Dominican Republic, Ecuador, Guatemala, Haiti, India, Jamaica, Laos, Mexico, Nigeria, Pakistan, Panama, Paraguay, Peru, Venezuela, and Vietnam.

Afghanistan, the pervasive political corruption in Nigeria, and the involvement of North Korea in heroin and methamphetamine traffic in East Asian countries. He called upon each of the named countries to cooperate more effectively with the United States in counter-narcotics efforts. At the same time, he expressed appreciation for the efforts of China, Hong Kong, Taiwan, and others in the region to stop the diversion of pseudoephedrine and ephedrine used to manufacture methamphetamine, and called for additional collaborative efforts. [15]

More than five months later, on March 4, 2005, the State Department issued the annual International Narcotics Control Strategy Report, in accordance with a continuing requirement, with descriptions of the counter-narcotics activities of illicit drug producing and trafficking countries. [16]

President Bush's Designations for FY2006

Acting under Section 706 of the Foreign Relations Authorization Act for FY2003 (P.L. 107-228), on September 15, 2005, several weeks before the start of the fiscal year, President Bush made the annual presidential determinations regarding major illicit drug producing and drug transit countries, and he authorized the Secretary of State to submit the determinations to Congress. [17]

The President identified 20 countries as major drug producing or transit countries. The countries named [18] on the ``majors list'' were the same countries identified in the previous determination, except that China and Vietnam were removed from the list. According to the Presidential Determination, China was removed because there is insufficient evidence to suggest that China is a major source or transit country for illicit narcotics that significantly affect the United States. Vietnam was removed because there are no indications of a significant Vietnam- based drug threat to the United States, and Vietnamese claims that opium poppy cultivation has been virtually eliminated could not be refuted.

The President designated two of the countries, Burma and Venezuela, as having ``failed demonstrably'' within the last 12 months to adhere to international counter- narcotics obligations, but he waived the sanctions against Venezuela by determining that U.S. programs to aid Venezuela's democratic institutions were vital to the national interests of the United States.

---

[15] See the text of the presidential determination and other information on the FY2005 narcotics certification determinations on the State Department's websites at [http://usinfo.state.gov/gi/Archive/2004/Sep/17-404122.htm] and [http://www.state.gov/ p/inl/rls/rm/36249.htm].

[16] See the International Narcotics Control Strategy Report issued in March 2005, but covering 2004 at [http://www.state.gov/p/inl/rls/nrcrpt/2005/].

[17] See the text of the presidential determination and other information on the FY2006 narcotics certification determinations on the State Department's websites at [http://www.state.gov/p/inl/c15808.htm].

[18] The countries identified as major illicit drug producing or transit countries were: Afghanistan, Bahamas, Bolivia, Brazil, Burma, Colombia, Dominican Republic, Ecuador, Guatemala, Haiti, India, Jamaica, Laos, Mexico,Nigeria, Pakistan, Panama,Paraguay, Peru, and Venezuela.

Table 1. Comparison of Features of Sections 489-490 of FAAct (Old Provisions) and Section 706 of Foreign Relations Authorization (New Provisions)

Features	Sections 489-490 of FAAct of 1961	Section 706 of Foreign Relations Authorization
Legal status of the legislation	Sections 489-490 are permanent law	Section 706 is permanent law with new requirements; old provisions available to President as an option
Naming of major illicit drug producing and drug transit countries	Known as Majors List, required by November 1, four months before certification	Required by Sept. 15, same time as designation of worst offenders.
International Narcotics Control Strategy Report (INCSR) describing country performance and U.S. programs	Required by March 1	Still required by March 1
Certification/Designation Procedures: a. Responsibility for certification or designation	President	President
b. Congressional review/reversal	Congressional review and disapproval of certification	No congressional review of determination, but oversight available
c. Date of certification or designation	By March 1	By Sept. 15, at same time as designation of Majors List
d. Country coverage of certification or designation	All "major" countries must be certified as fully cooperative to avoid sanctions	President to designate worst offenders only.
e. Period for evaluation	Previous Jan.-Dec. calendar year	During the previous 12 months
f. Standards for certification or designation	Country has fully cooperated with U.S., taken steps to comply with U.N. Convention objectives, and engaged in other cooperative measures	Designation of worst offenders which have failed demonstrably to meet defined international counter-narcotics obligations
g. Effect of non-certification, or designation as worst offender	Withholding of U.S. assistance and sales financing, voting against country loans in MDBs, and possible trade sanctions	Withholding of U.S. assistance
h. Presidential waiver	President may waive sanctions if in vital national interest of United States	President may waive sanctions if in vital national interest of United States
International counter-narcotics cooperation	Defined as compliance with U.N. drug convention, and bilateral and multilateral agreements	Defined as compliance with U.N. drug convention, and bilateral and multilateral agreements, with key features specified.

Table 1 compiled by K. Larry Storrs, Congressional Research Service.

Table 2. Majors List, FY1987-FY2003, Countries Determined To Be Major Illicit Narcotics Producing and/or Transit Countries

Country	1987	1988	1989	1990	1991	1992	1993	1994	1995	1996	1997	1998	1999	2000	2001	2002	2003
Afghanistan	X	X	X	X	X	X	X	X	X	X	X	X	X	X	X	X	X
Aruba											X	X	X				
Bahamas	X	X	X	X	X	X	X	X	X	X	X	X	X	X	X	X	X
Belize	X	X	X	X	X	X	X	X		X	X	X	X				
Bolivia	X	X	X	X	X	X	X	X	X	X	X	X	X	X	X	X	X
Brazil	X	X	X	X	X	X	X	X	X	X	X	X	X	X	X	X	X
Burma	X	X	X	X	X	X	X	X	X	X	X	X	X	X	X	X	X
Cambodia										X	X	X	X	X			
China						X	X	X	X	X	X	X	X	X	X	X	X
Colombia	X	X	X	X	X	X	X	X	X	X	X	X	X	X	X	X	X
Dom Rep									X	X	X	X	X	X	X	X	X
Ecuador	X	X	X	X	X	X	X	X	X	X	X	X	X	X	X	X	X
Guatemala					X	X	X	X	X	X	X	X	X	X	X	X	X
Haiti									X	X	X	X	X	X	X	X	X
Hong Kong	X	X	X	X	X	X	X	X	X	X	X	X	X	X			
India	X	X	X	X	X	X	X	X	X	X	X	X	X	X	X	X	X
Iran	X	X	X	X	X	X	X	X	X	X	X	X					
Jamaica	X	X	X	X	X	X	X	X	X	X	X	X	X	X	X	X	X

Table 2. (Continued)

Country	1987	1988	1989	1990	1991	1992	1993	1994	1995	1996	1997	1998	1999	2000	2001	2002	2003
Laos	X	X	X	X	X	X	X	X	X	X	X	X	X	X	X	X	X
Lebanon	X	X	X	X	X	X	X	X	X	X	X						
Malaysia	X	X	X	X	X	X	X	X	X	X	X	X	X				
Mexico	X	X	X	X	X	X	X	X	X	X	X	X	X	X	X	X	X
Morocco	X	X	X	X	X	X	X										
Nigeria	X	X	X	X	X	X	X	X	X	X	X	X	X	X	X	X	X
Pakistan	X	X	X	X	X	X	X	X	X	X	X	X	X	X	X	X	X
Panama	X	X	X	X	X	X	X	X	X	X	X	X	X	X	X	X	X
Paraguay	X	X	X	X	X	X	X	X	X	X	X	X	X	X	X	X	X
Peru	X	X	X	X	X	X	X	X	X	X	X	X	X	X	X	X	X
Syria	X	X	X	X	X	X	X	X	X	X	X						
Taiwan									X	X	X	X	X	X			
Thailand	X	X	X	X	X	X	X	X	X	X	X	X	X	X	X	X	X
Venezuela					X	X	X	X	X	X	X	X	X	X	X	X	X
Vietnam									X	X	X	X	X	X	X	X	X

Table 3. Countries on Majors List, FY1987-FY2001, That Failed to "Cooperate Fully," and Were Decertified or Given National Interest Certification

Country	1987	1988	1989	1990	1991	1992	1993	1994	1995	1996	1997	1998	1999	2000	2001
Afghanistan	Decert.	Decert.	Decert.	Decert.	Decert.	Decert.	NIC	NIC	Decert.	Decert.	Decert.	Decert.	Decert.	Decert.	Decert.
Iran	Decert.	Decert.	Decert.	Decert.	Decert.	Decert.	Decert.	Decert.	Decert.	Decert.	Decert.	Decert.			
Syria	Decert.	Decert.	Decert.	Decert.	Decert.	Decert.	Decert.	Decert.	Decert.	Decert.	Decert.				
Panama		Decert.	Decert.					NIC							
Laos	NIC	NIC	Decert.					NIC							
Lebanon	NIC	NIC	NIC	NIC	NIC	NIC	NIC	NIC	NIC	NIC	NIC				
Burma			Decert.	Decert.	Decert.	Decert.	Decert.	Decert.	Decert.	Decert.	Decert.	Decert.	Decert.	Decert.	Decert.
Bolivia							NIC	NIC							
Nigeria								Decert.	Decert.	Decert.	Decert.	Decert.	NIC	NIC	
Peru								NIC	NIC						
Colombia									NIC	Decert.	Decert.	NIC			
Pakistan									NIC	NIC	NIC	NIC			
Paraguay									NIC	NIC		NIC	NIC	NIC	
Belize											NIC				
Cambodia												NIC	NIC	NIC	NIC
Haiti													NIC	NIC	NIC

Legend:

Decert. = Decertified.

NIC =National interest certification.

Note: Prepared by K. Larry Storrs, with technical support by T. Lisbeth, from *International Narcotics Control Summary* provided by the Department of State. In nearly all cases, certifications were made on March 1 of each year.

Table 4. Countries on Majors List, FY2002-FY2006, That "Failed Demonstrably" and Were Subject to Sanctions or Given Waivers in National Interest

Country	2002	2003	2004	2005	2006
Afghanistan	NIW				
Burma	SS	SS	SS	SS	SS
Haiti	NIW	NIW	NIW		
Guatemala		NIW			
Venezuela					NIW

Legend:
SS = Subject to sanctions.
NIW = National interest waiver.

Note: Prepared by K. Larry Storrs, with technical assistance from Nancy Shaffer and Sarah Mitchell, from *International Narcotics Control Summary* provided by the Department of State, and the FY2004, FY2005, and FY2006 presidential determinations.

Determinations for FY2002 were made on February 23, 2002; for FY2003 were made on January 31, 2003; for FY2004 were made on September 15, 2003; for FY2005 were made on September 15, 2004; and for FY2006 were made on September 15, 2005.

Burma has been decertified every year since 1988, and for the last five years, it has been the only country subject to sanctions for counter-narcotics deficiencies. According to the Presidential Determination and the Statement of Justification, Burma, despite continued reduction in poppy cultivation, remains the second largest producer in the world of illicit opium and is among the largest producers and traffickers in the world of amphetamine-type stimulants, with traffickers of methamphetamine operating with apparent impunity.

Venezuela was designated as having failed demonstrably to meet international counter-narcotics obligations for the first time. Venezuela is a major transit country, with increasing quantities of cocaine and heroin moving through the country to the United States and Europe. According to the Administration's Statement of Justification, Venezuela has not adequately addressed this increasing traffic, it has failed to eradicate coca and opium poppy fields found near the border with Colombia, and it has dramatically reduced counter-narcotics cooperation with the United States, including ending cooperation with the Drug Enforcement Administration (DEA).

Apart from the designated countries, the Presidential Determination expressed concern about the apparent increase of opium poppy cultivation in Afghanistan, the continuing flow of Ecstasy from Canada and the Netherlands, the weaknesses in the law enforcement and criminal justice systems in Haiti, the corruption and criminal activity in Nigeria, and the continued involvement of the North Korean government in criminal and drug trafficking activities.

Table 5. Majors List, FY2004-FY2006, Countries Determined on September 15th before Fiscal Year to be Major Illicit Narcotics Producing and/or Transit Countries

Country	2004	2005	2006
Afghanistan	X	X	X
Bahamas	X	X	X
Bolivia	X	X	X
Brazil	X	X	X
Burma	X	X	X
China	X	X	
Colombia	X	X	X
Dominican Republic	X	X	X
Ecuador	X	X	X
Guatemala	X	X	X
Haiti	X	X	X
India	X	X	X
Jamaica	X	X	X
Laos	X	X	X
Mexico	X	X	X
Nigeria	X	X	X
Pakistan	X	X	X
Panama	X	X	X
Paraguay	X	X	X
Peru	X	X	X
Thailand	X		
Venezuela	X	X	X
Vietnam	X	X	

INDEX

A

G

H

I

J

K

L

S

T

U

V

W

Y